Rethinking Early Christian Identity

Rethinking Early Christian Identity

Affect, Violence, and Belonging

Maia Kotrosits

Fortress Press
Minneapolis

RETHINKING EARLY CHRISTIAN IDENTITY

Affect, Violence, and Belonging

Copyright © 2015 Fortress Press. All rights reserved. Except for brief quotations in critical articles or reviews, no part of this book may be reproduced in any manner without prior written permission from the publisher. Visit http://www.augsburgfortress.org/copyrights/ or write to Permissions, Augsburg Fortress, Box 1209, Minneapolis, MN 55440.

Unless otherwise noted, English translations of the New Testament texts will be taken from the New Revised Standard Version of the Bible, © 1989 by the Division of Christian Education of the National Council of the Churches of Christ in the U.S.A.; English translations of the Septuagint will be taken from Albert Pietersma and Benjamin G. Wright, eds., *A New English Translation of the Septuagint* (Oxford: Oxford University Press, 2007).

Cover design: Alisha Lofgren

Cover image © HIP/Art Resource, NY

Library of Congress Cataloging-in-Publication Data

Print ISBN: 978-1-4514-9265-1

eBook ISBN: 978-1-4514-9426-6

The paper used in this publication meets the minimum requirements of American National Standard for Information Sciences — Permanence of Paper for Printed Library Materials, ANSI Z329.48-1984.

Manufactured in the U.S.

This book was produced using PressBooks.com, and PDF rendering was done by PrinceXML.

Contents

	Acknowledgements	vii
	Abbreviations	xi
	Introduction: Making Sense of Ourselves	1
1.	The Force of History	21
2.	On the Historical Queerness of Christianity	47
3.	Reading Acts in Diaspora	85
4.	Expanding the Diasporic Imagination: The Secret Revelation of John	117
5.	Above It All: The Affective Life of Transcendence	147
6.	Pleasure, Pain, and Forgetting in the Gospel of Truth	173
7.	Returning to Rome	201
	Conclusion	227
	Bibliography	233
	Index	259

Acknowledgements

In a project that theorizes complex emotional involvements and diffuse corporealities, how does one do justice to the intricacies of the forces, moments, and relationships that make one's writing possible? As it was originally the culminating work of my formal graduate education, this book is of course marked by the general pressures attending that form of institutional life. But it is also inflected with the atmosphere of the specific institution in which I wrote it, one that has been vibrant, but not consistently so, and crowded with people I have simply enjoyed knowing. This project is also full of New York City in ways that I can't quite put my finger on—perhaps New York City's plump sense of miscellany has something to do with my desire for more chaos in our accounts of social life, and more textural variation and richness in our renderings of ancient texts and history. Union Theological Seminary and New York City were, incidentally, both frustrating and endearing places in which to live, sometimes lending a creeping specificity to my descriptions of the pushes and pulls of social life.

In terms of people, a good portion of whatever humor and artfulness this project exhibits is possible because of my wildly creative and wonderfully hilarious friends, who have given me many occasions to tone down my academic self-seriousness while still listening to me talk about my work with care and vested interest. Likewise my son Rocco, who was six weeks old when I began writing this book, and my husband John, gave me relief and a distinct sense of an outside—saving graces for any immersive endeavor. John's ideas are also likely peppered in here (though I can't recall which suggested re-phrasings or conceptualities were his), and he deserves credit for enduring hundreds of "no, sweetheart, it's more like *this*" explanations of my work while we walked in the park. I've been lucky to have the emotional support of both John's and my family, plus the very material gift of regular childcare help, which meant the dissertation and its revisions got done much more quickly than they would have otherwise. Of my academic relationships (and in a somewhat random order): Celene Lillie's companionship over the course of my program, our shared politics, heroes, and interests, and, perhaps just as critical, the different expressions of our work, made every inch of the doctoral program less frustrating and lonely. The warmth and respect of my students and other New Testament department colleagues at Union were heartening, and the friendships and banter of Jenny Barry and John Penniman simultaneously grounded me and kept me on my toes. Brigitte Kahl has been an important teacher throughout my masters and doctoral programs. Her commitment to staying in conversation with me and her real investment in my work despite our theoretical differences (which are neither small nor unbridgeable) are recorded in some form here. I hope that I have, as her student, honored and reflected her sense of relevance and her attachment to close reading. Jennifer Wright Knust and Erin Runions have been energetic, sharp, and thoughtful writers and conversation partners about affect theory, and Erin deserves the credit or blame for feeding that interest in its early stages. Dennis Smith and Richard Ascough helped me think through some of the more nitty-gritty socio-historical issues I tackle here, and managed to

ACKNOWLEDGEMENTS

be both affable and rigorous while doing so. Neil Elliott, my editor at Fortress, immediately understood this somewhat unusual project, and had such confidence in and enthusiasm for this book that he deserves especially hearty thanks. The sheer volume and the plush and precise language of Stephen Moore's work regularly humbled me and provoked my writing. His interest and involvement in this project was hugely gratifying, and I'm not ashamed to say there are snippets of our emails cut and pasted in these chapters. Karen King lives in this book in many explicit ways, but she fostered much thinking behind the scenes, as well. If this project has muses, one of them is certainly Karen, but at no point did that perhaps ambivalent position prevent her from genuine, thick, and wholehearted interaction with it. Aside from being one of the most generous and enthusiastic readers of this book (in its many draft versions), Alexis Waller was my most constant conversation partner on affect theory in all its riveting particulars and the ways it might be read with "early Christian" literature. So many chunks of what I surface in these close readings were worked out within the space of our interactions. I'm also happy for any slivers of our ruminations on art, psychoanalysis, gender, relationships, and academic life that have settled into this book. Finally, Hal Taussig was my primary mentor and teacher for the decade leading up to and including the writing of this book. He saw the pieces of this project appear unevenly over the course of our work together, finally guiding it to completion. He provided the safety for all its daring, carving out countless tender little spaces for what were often only initial meanderings—ones sometimes shrouded in self-doubt—making it possible for them to thrive into fuller expression. He read every word of the project probably a dozen times, often seemed far more clear than I on what exactly I was doing, and enabled me to feel what, based on anecdotal evidence, so few graduating doctoral students feel about their work: that it is thoroughly mine. It is to him that this book is dedicated.

Abbreviations

AThR	*Anglican Theological Review*
CBQ	Catholic Biblical Quarterly Monograph Series
CBQMS	Catholic Biblical Quarterly Monograph Series
HTR	*Harvard Theological Review*
JAAR	*Journal of the American Academy of Religion*
JBL	*Journal of Biblical Literature*
JECS	*Journal of Early Christian Studies*
JHC	*Journal of Higher Criticism*
JSJ	*Journal for the Study of Judaism*
JSNT	*Journal for the Study of the New Testament*
JSNTSup	Journal for the Study of the New Testament: Supplement Series
JST	*Journal of Theological Studies*
MTSR	*Method and Theory in the Study of Religion*
NovT	*Novum Testamentum*
NovTSup	Novum Testamentum Supplements
NTS	*New Testament Studies*
PTMS	Princeton Theological Monograph Series
R&T	*Religion and Theology*
RevExp	*Review and Expositor*

SBLSS	Society of Biblical Literature Semeia Studies
SBLSymS	Society of Biblical Literature Symposium Series
SHR	Studies in the History of Religions (Supplement to *Numen*)
SR	*Studies in Religion*
SwJT	*Southwestern Journal of Theology*
USQR	*Union Seminary Quarterly Review*
VC	*Vigiliae Christianae*
WW	*World and World*
ZAC	*Zeitschrift für Antikes Christentum*

Introduction: Making Sense of Ourselves

What follows is a re-examination of the centrality of the designation "Christian" in the doing of what we call early Christian history, and a set of proposals for how to understand New Testament and affiliated literature without it. The story of Christian identity is usually told as one of a private and provisional identity that is shaped and made public in confrontation with empire, or of a movement that finds its legs (and maybe loses its soul) in the larger Greco-Roman culture, or a new constituency that must reckon with its multiplying size and differences. In contrast, this book contends that the texts under discussion, which scholarship has largely assumed are fully ensconced in a Christian construction of belonging or identity, are not particularly invested in or reflective of any kind of distinct Christian self-understanding or sociality.

Re-reading a cluster of texts from the late first and early second centuries (the letters of Ignatius, 1 Peter, the Acts of the Apostles, the Secret Revelation of John, the Letter to the Hebrews, the Gospel of John, and the Gospel of Truth) through affect and diaspora theoretical lenses, I suggest that rather than negotiating or generating a distinctly Christian self-understanding, belief system, or set of practices, these texts are thick with the dynamics of national haunting and ongoing and transgenerational trauma; they mark the strange and unpredictable turns of social life.[1] These re-readings of ancient texts come, however, in the context of a set of proposals about the mutual involvements and unexpected collusions between ancient texts and contemporary readers, and, more broadly, the ways our historical narrations speak our collective emotional lives. What does

1. I present these ancient texts as roughly contemporaneous. Although I do not propose a particular decade or locale for any of the texts under discussion, scholarship before me warrants placing these texts in some basic temporal proximity to one another (i.e., after the Roman-Jewish war, before the mid-second century). I use the close-enough temporal relationship of these texts, supported by what I find to be strong thematic, imagistic, and gestural similarities between them, to propose these texts as significant moments of diasporic responsiveness, and to suggest connective tissue between them that is not some kind of Christian phenomenon, identity, or theology. The precursors, inspirations, and list of enabling models for this project are many. First among them is Karen King's deconstruction of the category of "Gnosticism," in which she finds Gnosticism to be a modern fascination with no apparent historical referents, as well as her efforts at re-writing a history of Christianity with canonical and non-canonical materials side by side. Karen L. King, *What is Gnosticism?* (Cambridge: Harvard University Press, 2003). The particular publications by King that have made a significant impact on this project include: "Christianity Without Canon," lecture given at the Jesus Seminar (New Orleans, La., November, 1996); *The Gospel of Mary of Magdala: Jesus and the First Woman Apostle* (Santa Rosa: Polebridge Press, 2003); and "Which Early Christianity?" in *The Oxford Handbook of Early Christian Studies*, ed. Susan Ashbrook Harvey and David Hunter (Oxford: Oxford University Press, 2010), 66-84. Closely related to King's work is the work of Daniel Boyarin and Virginia Burrus with their respective creativities in historical readings of early Christian literature, and Judith Lieu who catalyzed widespread interest in the term "Christian identity"—interest that perhaps contradicted her original and provisional uses of it. While the respective work of Boyarin, Lieu, and Burrus is rather extensive and covers a range of ancient texts, themes, and subject matter, in this project I am especially interested in and influenced by the dimensions of their work that deal with heresiology, early Christian identity production, self-understanding, and subjectivity, as well as the affective and affected aspects of their writing and theorization. This primarily means the following: Daniel Boyarin, *Border Lines: The Partition of Judaeo-Christianity* (Philadelphia: University of Pennsylvania Press, 2004). As I will discuss in more detail over the course of the book, I assume much of Boyarin's argument in *Border Lines*, even while I feel it could be pushed further. I also respect (and find theoretically compelling) his moves towards self-disclosure. Virginia Burrus, "Heretical Woman as Symbol in Alexander, Athanasius, Epiphanius, and Jerome," *HTR* 84:3 (1993): 229-248; *The Sex Lives of Saints: An Erotics of Ancient Hagiography* (Philadelphia: University of Pennsylvania Press, 2004); and *Saving Shame: Martyrs, Saints and Other Abject Subjects* (Philadelphia: University of Pennsylvania Press, 2008). I am generally inspired by Burrus's sharp theorizing and writing, not to mention her sometimes subtle, sometimes explicit, pressing of the matter of affect in ancient literature.Judith Lieu, *Christian Identity in the Jewish and Graeco-Roman World* (Oxford: Oxford University Press, 2004); and *Neither Jew Nor Greek? Constructing Early Christianity* (London: T & T Clark International, 2002). The sheer variety and number of ancient texts addressed in Lieu's texts is humbling—not to mention her distinct scholarly cautions and reservations about how those texts might be said to relate to one another.

the sudden popularity of Christian identity as an optic, and the historical imaginations that attend it, tell us about what those of us interpreting these texts (professionally or otherwise) need and want out of history? Thus the curiosities guiding this project are not just about history per se, but also about how the set of ancient texts associated with what we call early Christianity figure in the way we make sense of ourselves in the present.

Asking how these ancient texts figure in the way we make sense of ourselves involves a number of suppositions.[2] I assume, very much in the tradition of postmodern historiography, that the work of sense-making in the present is not subsidiary or tangential to presumably less subjective historical description. Consequently, I do not wish to make sharp or qualitative distinctions between the interpretive work of scholars and lay people, academic intelligentsia and popular culture. I assume that whatever the register in which one speaks about early Christian literature or its history, one is no more or less engaged in the work of contemporary significance. Most crucially, however, this question of contemporary sense-making makes an important epistemological assumption: thinking and feeling are hopelessly interwoven experiences. I hint at this in my choice of the word "sense," a term which simultaneously implies both cognition and emotion. This dual implication flies in the face of a long history—strongly Cartesian but also pre-Cartesian—of emphatic differentiations between cognition and emotion as categories of experience. It is also a term that cues one into the primary generative force of this book: theories of affect.

---

2. Aside from those I list above, there is also a set of unspoken suppositions usually implied in terms like "we" and "the present." The temporality and set of circumstances that seem to comprise "the present," as well as who, exactly, is imagined in and among this "we," are open and debatable issues. I don't mean to suggest any kind of natural content to either of these terms. Indeed, part of the work of this book is to offer one kind of re-examination of how "early Christian history" and its concomitant literature is engaged to give content to and naturalize certain subjectivities and temporalities.

As a set of cross-disciplinary reflections on the bodily, social, and linguistic entanglements of that which is often more colloquially understood as "emotion,"[3] much recent theorizing around affect has thoroughly frustrated any hope to preserve thinking or knowing from the rather slippery, indistinct, oceanic, and, frankly, feminized realm of emotive experience. To say we "make sense" of something, for instance, is to accord an intuitive, bodily, and non- or beyond-conscious force to knowing. Knowledge arrives as an "impression." As Sara Ahmed writes, "*We need to remember the 'press' in 'impression.'*"[4]

In other words, "affect" means being *affected*; it suggests being touched, moved. It implies less some kind of internal, personal experience than relationality, physicality, and susceptibility. Embedded in this epistemology is a reminder about the vagueness of knowing, suggested in the terms sense and impression. We cannot fully know how we know what we know. Even the baldest of facts can be undone by a notion that it just "doesn't feel right," and we may or may not be able to say what exactly about it doesn't quite feel right. In those moments we are forced to encounter the contingencies of our knowing, and it is no coincidence that what *feels* right or wrong is often the kind of knowing most vigorously defended.

This impressionistic basis of knowing also suggests that the subjects and objects of knowing cannot be responsibly or reliably distinguished. What is produced as an object of knowledge is the trace of a moment of contact, one that is already freighted with affective social histories and one's subjective disposition.[5] The knowledge we acquire is beyond our knowing, though not in the

---

3. Though as I will describe in more detail below, not everyone theorizing on affect would agree that emotion and affect are so easily equated.
4. Sara Ahmed, *The Cultural Politics of Emotion* (New York: Routledge, 2004), 6. Emphasis in original.
5. Ibid., 1–19.

sense that the knowledge itself is outside of us. It is rather that we are dispossessed of fully naming how it is we are so sure of something. Knowing, as embroiled in affect, is both fully subjective and deeply "impersonal."[6] That which we know and how we know are open to momentary contingencies, shifting relationships, and even material minutia. As Jane Bennett recounts: "The sentences of this book also emerged from the confederate agency of many striving macro- and microactants: from 'my' memories, intentions, contentions, intestinal bacteria, eyeglasses, and blood sugar, as well as from the plastic computer keyboard, the bird song from the open window, or the air or particles in the room, to name only a few of the participants."[7]

Eve Sedgwick's approach to affect theory, for instance, directs one's attention to the affective forces and bases of certain kinds of intellectual analysis. In a generous but frank essay on the state of current academic theorizing, Sedgwick writes about the near-total collapse of theories into simply "Theory," now almost synonymous with the hermeneutics of suspicion. The hermeneutics of suspicion, in its insistence on fanatically uncovering hidden violences, is, for Sedgwick, closely tied to the paranoid worldview.[8] Sedgwick writes that the problem with the ascendency and prestige around the hermeneutics of suspicion and the paranoid worldview that attends it is that there is "a great loss when paranoid inquiry comes to seem entirely coextensive with critical theoretical inquiry rather than being viewed as one kind of cognitive/affective theoretical practice among other, alternative kinds."[9] The hermeneutics of suspicion not only

---

6. That is, affect is not a matter of self-containment, and operates on an always-already social level. Those who view affect as non- or impersonal include Brian Massumi, *Parables for the Virtual: Movement, Affect, Sensation* (Durham: Duke University Press, 2002), and Teresa Brennan, *The Transmission of Affect* (Ithaca: Cornell University Press, 2004).
7. Jane Bennett, *Vibrant Matter: A Political Ecology of Things* (Durham: Duke University Press, 2010), 23.
8. Sedgwick is careful, however, not to suggest "paranoid" as a mental illness or pathologizing diagnosis.

contains an almost ironically naïve faith in the tactics of exposure, Sedgwick observes, but paranoid knowing also has a nasty habit of "disavowing its affective motive and force and masquerading as the very stuff of truth."[10] Importantly, she does not suggest abandoning paranoid knowing entirely, but since it "knows some things well and others poorly," she suggests engaging reparative, accretive, and pleasure-seeking impulses and practices alongside of it.[11]

Sedgwick's scrutiny of the affectivity of certain kinds of knowing initiated this project in many ways, not only because of her critique of the hermeneutics of suspicion,[12] but also because biblical and early Christian studies as disciplines have a distinct habit of exactly "disavowing [their] affective motive and force," usually through the highly technical and seemingly impartial apparatus of "exegesis" and the myriad criticisms and historical categories indebted to scientific methods. The collective disposition of biblical and early Christian studies, not unlike many other academic disciplines, has been to invest itself in a kind of apparently *un-affected* practice and self-presentation. This investment has a history with roots more specific to the discipline than any modernist valorization of rationalism, though. The discipline emerged unevenly from early modern moral criticism of the Bible, criticism that found itself initially less at odds with the historicity of the text than the dubious actions of its central characters, including—and especially—its god.[13] But, as Yvonne Sherwood and Stephen Moore opine, an immoral biblical god was perhaps too thorny a theological issue:

---

9. Sedgwick, *Touching Feeling: Affect, Pedagogy, Performativity* (Durham: Duke University Press, 2003), 126.
10. Ibid., 138.
11. Ibid., 130.
12. In chapter 7, for example, I suggest that the hermeneutics of suspicion has been over-identified with political readings, particularly within scholarly reflections on empire.
13. Stephen D. Moore and Yvonne Sherwood, *The Invention of the Biblical Scholar: A Critical Manifesto* (Minneapolis: Fortress Press, 2011), 58-59.

> [Q]uestions of historical possibility were easier to deal with than questions of moral possibility. Even the 'Deists' seemed to recoil from the audacity of charging the biblical god of immorality and declaring Holy Writ antecedently unfit, impossible, or incredible on moral grounds. It is hardly surprising, therefore, that the more orthodox form of emergent biblical criticism entailed taking up the programmatic question 'Could it have happened?' in its historical sense while closing the question down in its moral or philosophical sense. . . . Thus the category of the historical in biblical scholarship became a surrogate not only for the ethical but also for the theological, and did not disturb either category directly . . . The historical now served as a place marker for the theological, but also, paradoxically, as a license to do biblical scholarship in a thoroughly de-theologized mode . . . one that shattered every biblical-scholarly mold that has been handed down since antiquity.[14]

This sublimation of ethical and theological questions into historical ones has certain affective consequences for the way business is now done in biblical studies. For one, the move described by Sherwood and Moore is acutely de-personalizing in its filtration (or avoidance) of theological crises through the dispassionate language of historical inquiry. This depersonalization has trailed the discipline ever since, primarily through the continuing predominance of scientific methods. Even more subjective interventions into the presumptions of historical-criticism tend to use the safe distance and/or cold language of social positions and identity categories.[15]

Very few have critically engaged the affective stakes of early Christian history and biblical interpretation. And yet one need not do more than lightly scratch the surface of off-the-record, collegial conversation to find that the affective stakes are indeed quite high

---

14. Ibid.
15. This self-revelation on a primarily categorical level is what Stephen Moore has dubbed "impersonal criticism," or positional criticism, work in the vein of autobiographical criticism that seeks to be "located" but also seems to avoid confessional or personal reflection. "True Confessions and Weird Obsessions: Autobiographical Interventions in Literary and Biblical Studies," in *The Bible in Theory: Critical and Postcritical Essays* (Atlanta: Society of Biblical Literature, 2010).

for most people studying the Bible or early Christian history professionally. Studying this literature is not simply a strategic cultural or political intervention or an antiquarian fascination, though it certainly can be all of these things as well. It is work fraught with deep affective entanglements, threaded as the Bible is into so many other attachments and burned injuriously into so many folks' skin. In fact it seems that just as the historical serves as a place marker for the theological, often the political and ideological can do their own place-marking and substitutive work if their affective and experiential motivations aren't carefully cross-examined. Especially in the first two chapters of this book, I press (gently, I hope) on recent scholarship to ask about its various affects. This pressing is, I emphasize, not a psychological reading of individual scholars, or a set of indictments of scholars failing to be self-reflective. It is a reading of the social circuits of emotion that course through the field, and an inquiry into what collective reckonings with the felt present surface in contemporary attempts at describing ancient Christians. I suggest over the course of this book, for instance, that as scholarship tries to pinpoint the relationship of texts to imperium and Israel, it simultaneously works out its own confusing relations to and haunted histories of American and European imperialism and Christian violence.

Again, this affectivity is not a failure of scholarship to do good or proper history (although it might seem so by traditional definitions of history), but it does have implications for historical claims. So while I offer my own historical conclusions, it is not a supposedly less subjective correction to scholarship. In keeping with affect theory's emphasis on the impressionist basis of knowing, I claim the felt present, as it is expressed in and between the lines of contemporary scholarship, as one important if roundabout resource for reading and understanding ancient texts and history. The "sense" we get from texts is not only a historical resource, but also an inevitable aspect of both their materiality and our involvement with them. Our distancing techniques (techniques, by the way, that I do not wholly disavow) only testify to the overwhelming nature of our affective involvement in texts. I theorize on this explicitly in my final chapter, turning to New Testament scholarship on the Roman Empire to make some constructive suggestions about how to understand the political and affective work of reading ancient texts.

In general, there have been only limited and quirky engagements with the affectivity of "early Christian" texts. As a case in point, much of the secondary literature on Revelation reads (only) a kind of anger or aggression bubbling up through the text, but doesn't go much further than this observation.[16] Such readings of Revelation write almost as if affectivity is a quality specific to Revelation—not something that animates or gives rise to all texts in complicated ways. Similarly, Paul's very impassioned and turbulent tone often gets read as a side effect of his beliefs/values, a frustration with his client communities for missing the point, rather than an issue for critical consideration in and of itself.[17]

Theories of affect suggest that what we know is shaped by the contingencies of social-emotional forces. But it also suggests that *we* are, as subjects and collectives, shaped and reshaped by diffuse and motile forces—forces working sometimes in concert and sometimes at cross-purposes with one another. Affect offers a considerable contrast, then, to the prevailing understanding of the subject as definitively formed by Foucaultian Power with a capital "P."

---

16. See my discussion in chapter 7.
17. By this I do not mean a reading that "psychologizes" Paul (or anyone else), but rather a reading that foregrounds the social life of emotion as it shapes the rhetoric and relationships in/represented by texts. I have done this affective reading of the Corinthian correspondence in "The Rhetoric of Intimate Spaces: Affect and Performance in the Corinthian Correspondence," *USQR* 62: 3-4 (2011): 134-51.

Reframing the decades-long obsession with the subject and identity that had seized most theorizing circles—an obsession of which I have heartily partaken—affect takes the concept of the constructedness of the subject and identity performance seriously, but reimagines it with a new degree of rigor. It strips the term *identity performance* of its implications of individuality, ontology, and coherence (identity), and of its appeal to an act and an actor (performance), implications that are inimical to the very impulse for such theories in the first place. Analytics making use of identity categories, and even the term identity itself, assume a formed subject and relatively stable belonging. They are product-based analytics, bent as they are on the apparently static "effects" of power or discourse. Affect theory, on the other hand, re-orients one towards process, queer or surprising affiliations, and futurity.

It is through affect theory's more fluid assumptions about subjectivity and belonging, as well as scholarship on ancient associations and meals, that I begin to question the usefulness of "Christian identity" as a historical category for understanding the social gestures, assumptions, and constructions of the texts under discussion. But it is also in these reflections on the confusions and hairpin turns of social life that affect theory and diaspora theory coincide to engender attentiveness to the affective depths of colonized, displaced, and otherwise violated social contexts.[18] Diaspora, in the context of diaspora theory, means not simply an exilic existence—removal from one's place of birth—but rather the

---

18. Questions of affect and diaspora come together in a significant number of recent projects within cultural studies. Cf. Brian Keith Axel, "The Diasporic Imaginary," *Public Culture* 14, no. 2 (2002): 411-28; Ann Cvetkovich *An Archive of Feelings: Trauma, Sexuality, and Lesbian Public Cultures* (Durham: Duke University Press, 2003); Jasbir Puar, *Terrorist Assemblages: Homonationalism in Queer Times* (Durham: Duke University Press, 2007); and Grace Cho, "Voices from the *Teum*: Synesthetic Trauma and Ghosts of the Korean Diaspora" in *The Affective Turn: Theorizing the Social*, ed. Patricia Ticineto Clough and Jean Halley (Durham: Duke University Press, 2007).

many and often subtle effects and circumstances of migratory movement, colonization, and resettlement.[19] Overlapping with postcolonial criticism, diaspora theories in the vein of Stuart Hall, Brian Keith Axel, Rey Chow, and others have moved away from a foundational focus on origin and place in diaspora and towards the analysis of diasporic relational dynamics, imperial and colonial violence, national boundary production, negotiations of belonging, and cultural interimplication. Diaspora theory at large might be described as a thematic interest in the social and discursive dilemmas and creativities of displaced populations, an interest that, not unlike affect, has engaged a huge number of fields and disciplines. It accommodates not only analyses of what politics beget the condition of diaspora, or of the violent effects of geographical and cultural dispersion, but also the ways diaspora as a condition *enables* a sense of belonging. It addresses the *production* of place and shared origins. But as much as the focus of something like diaspora would seem to be wholly collective, the theorizing around diaspora that I have found most generative also provocatively treats the intricacies of personal experience as an index and instance of social traumas.[20]

My reconstruction is thus a reconstruction of a social-affective landscape. By "social-affective landscape" I mean to say that I both depend on a broad context with affective implications, and lean strongly into the subjectivity of texts as a resource rather than an impediment for specifying that context. The affective resonances

---

19. For two treatments of Israelite diasporic (in the more traditional sense) dynamics see John J. Collins, *Between Athens and Jerusalem: Jewish Identity in the Hellenistic Diaspora* (Grand Rapids: Eerdmans, 2000); and *Diaspora Jews and Judaism: Essays in Honor of, and in Dialogue with A. Thomas Kraabel*, ed. J. Andrew Overman and Robert S. MacLennan (Atlanta: Scholars Press, 1992).
20. To be more explicit here: in concert with the bulk of recent theorizing on affect and diaspora and more generally with postmodern and poststructuralist imaginations of the subject, I assume that what we call "the personal" is never a discrete container of experience shut off from others. It is a function of and deeply embedded in social forces and factors.

of texts are markers or symptoms of social and historical forces. Empire and postcolonial criticisms have painted especially stark and meticulous pictures of Roman rule in the first and second centuries: the enslavement and large-scale displacement of conquered peoples, as well as the sexualized violence and torture, multifaceted acculturation, and economic divestments that went hand in hand with belonging in some way to Rome. Along with these material (and often graphic) reconstructions of the severity of Roman rule, other scholars, especially those in certain strands of postcolonial biblical scholarship, have chronicled the more subtle though no less disquieting effects of imperial life: the allure of imperial prosperity, the way long-term colonial captivity changes the vectors of one's loyalties, and the ever thinning and sometimes non-existent line between resistance and accommodation. While I value and rely on many material reconstructions of the first and second centuries throughout this project, my focus is theoretical and textual, and contributes mainly to the latter task.

Some of the questions I ask here, provoked by diaspora theory and its merging with affect theory, include: How is alienation articulated, and what socio-political echo-effects do those articulations yield? What are the ways that colonial pain lives on in the social body? How can we mark the many complicated and contradictory feelings around the entities to which one (however tangentially) belongs? When can the forgetting of the past be a constructive response to diasporic trauma and loss? What does it mean when passionate imaginations of transcendence are tied to the intractability of social upheaval? Constituting the jumping off point for my constructive re-readings of ancient literature, these questions allow for more dynamic phenomenological descriptions and socio-political readings than the taxonomic, diagnostic, and normativizing terms on which we, as a discipline, have become so reliant: not only terms like *apocalyptic*,

Gnostic, and *supersessionist*, but even *anti-imperial*, *hybrid*, and (of course) *Jewish* and *Christian*. The laying aside of these terms and categories may raise hairs on the necks of some, no doubt, since these have been meaningful indices for trying to understand what, precisely, is at play and what is ethically and politically at stake in that which we call "early Christian literature." I am no less interested in the question of what is at play and what is ethically and politically at stake. I do, however, go at that question through different doors: the basis for each of my constructive re-readings is wondering how these texts variously cope with the diasporic violences and traumas of their context.

While in this project I am quite indebted to postcolonial and empire-critical readings of the Bible, I try to sidestep, reframe, and fill out many of the assessments that empire and postcolonial criticisms employ. The terms *for* vs. *against*, *reproduce* vs. *resist*, and even *mimic* vs. *mock* have felt uncomfortably reductive to me because of their implicit polarities. It is a discomfort I share with or caught from a number of people working in cultural studies.[21] One of the things diaspora and affect theories accomplish is that they engender terms for talking about power that have more texture, more qualitative oomph, and more refined assessments than the fields of New

---

21. Eve Sedgwick's wariness of certain subtle binarisms in contemporary theory particularly resonates with me. She writes, "I would say that [Foucault's] analysis of the pseudodichotomy between repression and liberation has led, in many cases, to its conceptual reimposition in the even more abstractly reified form of the hegemonic and the subversive. The seeming ethical urgency of such terms masks their gradual evacuation of substance, as a kind of Gramscian-Foucaultian contagion turns 'hegemonic' into another name for the status quo (i.e., everything that is) and defines 'subversive' in, increasingly, a purely negative relation to that (an extreme of the same 'negative relation' that had, in Foucault's argument, defined the repressive hypothesis in the first place). It's the same unhelpful structure that used to undergird historical arguments about whether a given period was one of 'continuity' or 'change.' Another problem with reifying the status quo is what it does to the middle ranges of agency. One's relation to *what is* risks becoming reactive and bifurcated, that of a consumer: one's choices narrow to accepting or refusing (buying, not buying) this or that manifestation of it, dramatizing only the extremes of compulsion and voluntary. Yet it is only the middle ranges of agency that offer space for effectual creativity and change" (Sedgwick, *Touching Feeling*, 12-13).

Testament and early Christian studies currently have at hand for describing what it means to live in empire, or what it means to have one's nation in shards at one's feet. Diaspora and affect theories provide not only newly sophisticated analytical concepts, but experientially resonant ones as well. They provide language that communicates the rich, devastating complexity of living, as opposed to the terms and categories I have somewhat polemically listed above which tend, however subtly, to classify, moralize, romanticize, or systematically separate. If affect and diaspora are categories, they are categories of experience, and ones that do not eschew the subjectivity of reading and history in the same way taxonomic and diagnostic categories do.

It is affect and diaspora theories' qualitative descriptions of the rhetoric, creativity, and contradictions of social life that enable me to propose that all of the texts under discussion in this book participate in Israelite diasporic culture—a colonial milieu in which relations to Israel are largely diffuse and interrupted—and that "Christian" is not an overarching category of identity for the texts at hand. If a text shows interest in the temple, priesthood, sabbath, Israelite prophetic history, Judea, Genesis stories, or any number of other elements of Israelite tradition (which all of these texts do), that to me suggests a participation in Israelite diasporic culture. Following the assumptions of diaspora theory, I will elaborate how locating a particular "early Christian" text as more or less Jewish (which usually then implies that it is more or less Christian, or more or less Greco-Roman) is a reproduction of diasporic discourse that defines boundaries of who does, and doesn't, belong. To categorize a text on a scale of Jewishness implies that there is a clear and objective set of criteria for Jewishness. It also denies cultural hybridity (which I assume as a quality of all these texts) and the complex colonial dynamics of crossing cultic and ethnic/national designations that were part and parcel of this period of Roman history.

Within empire and postcolonial criticisms, much energy has been poured into charting the enmeshment of early Christian literature in Israel and in imperial ideology. Yet it seems that there is not, so far at least, a thorough integration of national and imperial belongings, and diaspora theory provides a productive intervention into this problem.[22] Even the ideas of "nation" or "national belonging" as analytical categories for the late first and early second centuries seem vastly underused, likely because the concept of Judaism as a religion has overshadowed scholarship on when and under what circumstances the term *Judaism* comes into existence.[23] Additionally, modern understandings of a nation as an autonomous geo-political entity (i.e., the nation-state) would seem to inhibit the usefulness of that category for the analysis of ancient texts, particularly given the broken condition of Israel and other nations under Rome in the first and second century. I do hear this problem of modern understandings

---

22. This could also be due, in part, to the rise of empire as an optic, which changes the focus to broader, global networks of power, even sometimes supplanting the nation as a category. Vilashini Cooppan sees this erasure of the nation as a category as problematic in the present, because of the persistence of national channels of power, which discourses of globalization sometimes hide. I see this as problematic for the ancient world for different reasons, since the politics and meanings accorded to "nation" are rather different. Because of the Roman Empire's conquest and partial absorption and/or annexing of "nations," it is crucial to ask about the persistence of fragments and attachments to the nation, and how they might be part and parcel of imperial politics. Cooppan, "The Ruins of Empire: The National and Global Politics of the Return to Rome," *Postcolonial Studies and Beyond*, ed. Ania Loomba, et al. (Durham: Duke University Press, 2006), 80-100. For more on Cooppan's rather important and well-thought essay, see chapter 7.
23. For instance there is work such as Shaye J. D. Cohen's, whose collected articles in *The Beginning of Jewishness: Boundaries, Varieties, Uncertainties* (Berkeley: University of California Press, 1999) chart the complexities of Jewish identity, its ostensible distinctiveness, and its cultural hybridities in the ancient world, as well as the relativity of criteria for Jewishness. Notably, however, Cohen also presumes an early and relatively easy distinction between "Jewishness" and "Christianity." The work in the present book is somewhat consonant with Cohen's major thesis, but borrows from diaspora theory to further deconstruct and expansively re-imagine what it meant to belong to Israel's traditions, texts, practices, and/or political pasts.

of nation in particular, so it is important that I clarify what I mean in my use of *nation* or *national haunting*.

In contrast to "the nation-state," and more along the lines of the ancient term *ethnos*, I understand *nation* as a persistent imaginary with political pasts and ongoing effects, geographical referents, and cultural productivity. Although I do intend to imply "peoplehood," I do not wish to suggest a fundamental or monolithic set of shared characteristics—a conceptualization of *nation* that has participated in modern discourses of racial purity. I mean to convey, rather, an uneven and frictive conglomerate tied together through historical, political, and affective factors—including factors that would seem to test the salience of national belonging itself (such as imperial conquest). In fact, as I shall discuss more, it is often the case that colonial and imperial conditions enable or intensify national attachments rather than destroying them. In keeping with diaspora theory, I see the nation as always already composed of strange crossings and colonial entanglements even while the category of nation itself both absorbs and deflects such crossings and entanglements. The nation not only haunts, but is itself also haunted by political conflict and the casualties of its own boundary-marking. In this project, then, I seek to surface the ways nation, empire, and other kinds of belonging inflect and mutually intensify each other, as well as the ways they oppose or chafe against one another.[24]

---

24. These epistemological re-orientations that I have recounted above, including the byways into diaspora theory, are only some of the many and various insights allowed by the broad swath of thinking about affect. There is simply, and thankfully, no unified "affect theory" to pluck out from cultural studies and slap onto the Bible. In fact, it is not clear that one can even use the term "affect theory" in the singular, given the peculiar and gratifying variety of thinking it references. Some people included in this work find themselves theorizing about affects in the plural, and others find themselves theorizing a kind of substantive if mutable force simply referred to as "affect." This difference is described by Melissa Gregg and Gregory Seigworth in the introduction to *The Affect Theory Reader* (Durham: Duke University Press, 2010), 1-28, as due to the two key essays, both published in the same year (1995), and their distinctive theoretical sources, which represent something of a catalyst for the new theorizing on affect. These two essays are Eve Sedgwick and Adam Frank's "Shame in the Cybernetic Fold,"

Haunting turns out to be a recurring theme in this book, and one might very well consider this book something like a haunted history, since I repeatedly seek out lingering effects and wisps of the inconspicuous—things which are "sensed" but perhaps not readily seen. As Avery Gordon remarks, attending to haunting means "putting life back in where only a vague memory or a bare trace was visible to those who bothered to look. It is sometimes about writing ghost stories, stories that not only repair representational mistakes, but also strive to understand the conditions under which a memory was produced in the first place, toward a countermemory, for the future."[25] This book too asks after the spectral conditions of certain representations: I conclude that the notion of a distinct Christian identity in the late first and early second centuries is only possible because of the ambivalent kinds of forgetting associated with trauma and its movement across generations. And while I lay claim to a certain level of referentiality by suggesting my own historical reconstructions as the book proceeds, this is with some irony since my primary historical referents are the thoroughly difficult to document phenomena of trauma and its associated affects.

---

reprinted in *Touching Feeling* which draws on Silvan Tomkins's work in the 1960's, and Brian Massumi's "Autonomy of Affect," now the first chapter in his book *Parables for the Virtual* (pp. 23-45), which depends on the work of Gilles Deleuze and Baruch Spinoza. As a generalized context for theorizing on affect, Michael Hardt has suggested that feminist theory's emphasis on the body and queer theory's interest in the emotions (mainly shame, melancholia, and intimacy) had set the scene for these two essays ("What Affects Are Good For," in *The Affective Turn*, ix full publishing info). I agree that one of the bigger gifts of affect theory is an attention to felt forces that can't be contained (by language or other symbolic systems, by our subjective boundaries, etc.) and an offer of a little bit of a reprieve from linguistic analysis. Though I would add that much of queer theory's interest in the emotions, and much of feminist thinking at large, have drawn their inspiration from psychoanalytic theory. Julia Kristeva's *Powers of Horror: Essays on Abjection* (New York: Columbia University Press, 1987), for example, constitutes something like a psychoanalytic approach to the social life of disgust. Sara Ahmed indeed uses Kristeva's *Powers of Horror* in her work on disgust. Ahmed, *The Cultural Politics of Emotion*, 82-100.

25. Avery F. Gordon, *Ghostly Matters: Haunting and the Sociological Imagination* (Minneapolis: University of Minnesota Press, 1997), 22.

Indeed, attending to ghosts and writing histories of trauma are already compatible, if not linked, enterprises. In the same vein as Gordon, Ann Cvetkovich observes that "because trauma can be unspeakable and unrepresentable and because it is marked by forgetting and dissociation, it often seems to leave behind no records at all."[26] Cvetkovich's book *An Archive of Feelings: Trauma, Sexuality, and Lesbian Public Cultures* plays out the intimate and tangled connections between national traumas and familial relationships, cultural memory and subjective experience, and does so "from the unabashedly minoritarian perspective of lesbian cultures."[27] Cvetkovich performs an "exploration of cultural texts as repositories of feelings and emotions,"[28] finding, among other things, how sexual lives respond creatively to traumatic wounding. She thus archives not just "feeling bad," but other, less obvious emotions that might arise in the whirl around loss and trauma.

While I draw on Cvetkovich's book specifically to better understand the Secret Revelation of John's hard and utopian edges, as well as the combination of pleasure with other more apparently "negative" affects like pain in the Gospel of Truth, I borrow more broadly from her notion of an "archive of feelings" as an approach to history. Creating a lesbian archive of trauma that interrupts equally celebratory accounts of the nation and pathologizing psychoanalytic narratives, Cvetkovich insists on both the difficulties in accounting for trauma and the necessities in doing so. The notion that trauma "puts pressure on conventional forms of documentation, representation, and commemoration" engenders an approach here that seeks out and dilates traces of national and colonial affectivity and reckonings with social confusion and upheaval. Again, I seek

---

26. Ann Cvetkovich, *Archive of Feelings*, 7.
27. Ibid.
28. Ibid.

INTRODUCTION: MAKING SENSE OF OURSELVES

here to create a kind of alternative record, if a partial and ephemeral one, which steps to the side of Christianity's seemingly inevitable dominance or original virtue.[29]

One of the more charming effects of the interdisciplinary interest in affect is a new collision of linguistic registers within theoretical writing. The specialized lingo of high theory has met up with more colloquial intonations, often in the same work, and first-person accounts regularly pepper and even drive abstract or speculative proposals. An apparent consequence of affect, then, perhaps due to its capaciousness as a topic of discussion, has been a renewed interest in being a subject in one's own work, or letting one's affective state(s) into the work, though some have been more tentative and others unequivocal about doing so. Those less interested in personal disclosures still often employ anecdotal narratives of *someone's* experience. What I find so appealing about this is that one can enjoy the allure of heightened theoretical language with the added gratification of closer contact between readers and writers.

This book occasionally aspires to this same idiosyncratic mix of conversational tone and elevated language, first person/anecdotal narrative and conjectural propositions. I hope that it too encourages, in both its theorizing and its style of writing, closer, more sustained contact between readers and writers. While the hope for this kind of contact has often been foreclosed in poststructuralist theory (and, in the greater history of the biblical field, preempted by so much strenuously *un-affected* writing), there has recently been more interest in the way readers and writers are touched and moved, affected, by writing, thus permitting a bit less embarrassment about the desire for this kind of contact.[30] Affected reading and writing in this particular

---

29. Ibid.
30. Sara Ahmed's work on the rhetorical dimensions of affective language and of the place of language in the social world of affects, the stated hopes of Kathleen Stewart to inspire a kind of attentiveness to the intensities and textures of the worlds her readers inhabit, and Eve

19

book thus invites the slip of a return to autobiographical criticism, but a return that does not find itself opposed to poststructuralist complexities, "high theory," or even appeals to rarefied concepts and terms. It is not as much an invitation to self-reveal (though self-revelation might be happily included) as an invitation to sympathize, or "feel with" texts, and to admit that that's part of the reason we read.

By bringing affect back into the picture of reading these texts, I hope not only to sympathetically re-imagine some of these texts, but also to open a route for conversation that does not sharply or qualitatively distinguish what a biblical scholar does from what non-specialists do when they read the Bible: both groups share similar cultural premises and desires for significance.[31] This is not distressing news. It has been a long-running modern and postmodern mistake to think that critical thinking is best represented by hyper-rational modes of analysis; or that this thinking should (or even can) be distinguished from the deep recesses and wide resonances of affect—ever tangled, social, and subjective. What would happen if we could no longer separate knowing or the work of history from their impressionistic foundations, their affective bases? This book is one answer to that question. It is an invitation to consider new ways history, theology, "personal experience," critical thinking, and social critique might more comfortably and more candidly reside together in readings of the strange cluster of texts we have inherited by chance and through the category of "Christianity."

Sedgwick's poignant question "What does it mean to fall in love with a writer?" all might be said to witness in different ways to the affective relationship between readers and writers. See Ahmed, *Cultural Politics*, Kathleen Stewart, *Ordinary Affects* (Durham: Duke University Press, 2007), Sedgwick, *Touching Feeling*, 117.

31. In this vein, Moore and Sherwood propose that the most significant kind of intersection of biblical studies with "theory" would create a disassembling of biblical studies' disciplinary boundaries—that is, the machinery and high walls that keep the field sequestered in hyper-specialized language and practices (Moore and Sherwood, *Invention of the Biblical Scholar*, 130-31).

1

The Force of History

Force is infraempirical. No scientist has ever observed a force . . . Newton did not see gravity. He felt its effect: a pain in the head. The newly visioned blind do not see things. They feel a pain in their eyes . . . With more experience, the feeling of the effect comes to be identified. Reactions in different sense modes are cross-referenced. . . . The experience has been determined, objectified, empiricized . . . With that passage, and that determination, the pain is (provisionally) assuaged. Assuaged: the empirical is palliative.

Brian Massumi, *Parables for the Virtual*

I am convinced that memory has a gravitational force.

Patricio Guzman, *Nostalgia for the Light*

Under the thermal blaze of the sun, a woman carefully examines five tiny white shards in the palm of her hand. She explains that some of these pieces must be from the bones of an arm or a thighbone, because they are flat; the others must be the inside of a bone, because they are porous. "Their whiteness is due to their calcination by the sun," she remarks. In a change of scene, and in a different register, this same woman recalls having found remains of her brother, years before, in a mass grave: some pieces of his skull, a few teeth, a foot. She recounts, "I remembered his tender expression, and this was all that remained.... Our final moment together was when his foot was at my house. That night I got up and went to stroke his foot. There was the smell of decay. It was still in a sock. A burgundy sock. Dark red. I took it out of the bag and looked at it."

In the same expanse of earth where this woman sifts for bones in the ground, hulking telescopes housed in white geometric buildings direct the gazes of some other people upward, rather than downward. This expanse, the Atacama desert in Chile, has zero humidity, and so provides both phenomenally clear skies and an exceptionally slow rate of decomposition, drawing anthropologists, archaeologists and astronomers—as well as survivors of Chile's Pinochet regime, which dumped the bodies of thousands of its political prisoners in this desert. Patricio Guzman chronicles this convergence in his film *Nostalgia for the Light*, framing the Atacama as a "vast open book of memory," both historical and cosmic.[1]

Guzman's film makes connections and distinctions between the various pursuits taking place in the Atacama. For example, stars provided a sense of an outside for prison camp detainees, and astronomy similarly provides a way of working out the question of loss, the past, and memory. According to one astronomer, the questions of his discipline are more abstract and less immediate than the women who search for their loved ones. Guzman interviews him, asking him to describe his work and compare it with the work of those who search the desert for Pinochet's victims:

---

1. Patricio Guzmán, *Nostalgia de la luz (Nostalgia for the Light)*. Directed by Guzman. 2011.

> To compare two completely different things, their process is similar to ours, with one big difference. We can sleep peacefully, after each night observing the past. Our search doesn't disturb our sleep . . . The next day we plunge back, untroubled into the past. But these women must find it hard to sleep after searching through human remains, looking for a past they are unable to find. They'll not sleep until they do so. That is the major difference . . . . I don't know what I would do if a sister, a brother, or one of my parents were lost somewhere in the desert, in this vast expanse. Personally, as an astronomer, I would imagine my mother or father in space, lost in the galaxy somewhere. I would look for them through the telescopes. I would be very anxious as it would be difficult to find them in the vastness.

But by the admission of another astronomer, astronomy helps her address the loss of her parents to Pinochet when she was a year old, and does so by offering a grand-scale perspective. Without resorting to bland reductions like "we all seek answers to our past," Guzman delicately recounts how observing the stars links people in different ways to the trauma of Pinochet's murders.

The irony this film observes is that the apparently less urgent and less proximal work of the astronomers is given more social credibility, technical support, and cash than the women who search for their loved ones. One of the women who has not yet found her brother's body tells Guzman how she does not want to die without having found him: "As I told you the other day, I wish the telescopes didn't just look into the sky but could also see through the earth so that we could find them . . . We would sweep the desert with a telescope. Downwards. And give thanks to the stars for helping us find them. . . . I'm just dreaming."

This film moves me for many reasons; among them, Guzman's generous attentiveness to each person who speaks in the film, and the way he manages to connect bones and stars not only visually and thematically, but even elementally (they are both made of calcium). However I am also struck by the way he treats each endeavor in the

Atacama as reckoning with history's felt forces—even those endeavors which seem least directly involved in the specific and traumatic histories of that geography. The difference is that the more heightened, abstract, and technical language of astronomy as a scientific discipline not only makes it seem loftier, but it also enables distance. One "sleeps better" when removed from the immediacy of such histories.

In a rather different illustration, Brian Massumi also lays out the affective stakes of distanced and grand-scale vision. In his book *Parables for the Virtual,* in a chapter entitled, "Chaos in the 'Total Field' of Vision," Massumi philosophizes on the failures and incidental findings of scientific attempts in the first half of the twentieth century to re-create and isolate visual perception apart from other senses.[2] Not unlike Guzman's understanding of the astronomers in the Atacama, Massumi's chapter tells a story of pain and totalizing, objectifying vision. When scientists tried to reproduce the conditions of pure visual perception, however, subjects in these studies, paradoxically, could not see. They reported experiencing things like "levels of nothingness," and could not tell if their eyes were open or closed.[3] They also experienced strange sensations, including dizziness and out of body experiences. They experienced chaos, not distinct objects. In fact, Massumi tells us, vision is never "pure"—it is always "contaminated by a multisense pastness."[4] It turns out that vision is impossible to isolate and distill, because seeing requires constant cross-referencing between different sensory modes. Seeing is synesthetic, and requires other organs of perception.[5]

---

2. Massumi, *Parables for the Virtual: Movement, Affect, Sensation* (Durham: Duke University Press, 2002).
3. Ibid., 146.
4. Ibid., 155.
5. Ibid.

Subtly disabling the priority and presumptions of objectivity that vision has acquired, Massumi describes visual perception and organization as not only compensatory, but also nearly artistic in its attempt to render experiences comprehensible. Vision is not only an experience: it requires some *abstraction* from experience, and the objects of vision arise out of the chaos of non-separation between the sensing and the sensed. In a rather poetic turn, he summarizes, "The newly visioned blind do not see things. They feel a pain in their eyes . . . With more experience, the feeling of the effect comes to be identified. Reactions in different sense modes are cross-referenced . . . The experience has been determined, objectified, empiricized . . . and . . . the pain is (provisionally) assuaged. Assuaged: the empirical is palliative. The anesthetic is the *perceived*, as distinguished from the perceiving . . . What could this be other than the aesthetic: the pain is the beauty of the world emergent."[6]

Guzman and Massumi together encapsulate the broadest theoretical argument of this project: the discipline of (capital-H) History, with all its abstract, heightened and technical language, arrives to intervene in the felt forces of (small-h) history. It performs the quelling, redirection, or displacement of affect through organized observation. What might proceed from imagining history to be, like gravity, an infraempirical force? What if instead of prioritizing a carefully classified, comprehensive vision, or alongside of the usual inquiries about what happened and how it happened, we attended to history's affective potencies and vicissitudes: its felt effects?

This project nonetheless does not renounce, nor is it especially embarrassed by, a tenacious attraction to the discipline and practices of History in all their limitation. This project is not an apologetic for those various practices themselves. It is, however, a sympathetic

---

6. Ibid., 160-61.

response to them, and even a playful participation in them. It is a project fostered by the mostly speculative assumption that these practices arrive out of, and attempt to cordon off, the vast and overwhelming swampland of affective experience. History is felt as much as it is made.[7]

The notion of history as a felt force is not exactly new. Already insinuated in Jacques Derrida's description of spectrality in *Specters of Marx* is the idea of history as an ongoing force rather than a set of clear events.[8] Both Wendy Brown and Carla Freccero have found Derrida's work on haunting to be productive for rethinking history as emphatically present, if elusively so.[9] Others have tried to account for the ghostly and diffuse energy of primarily traumatic pasts, and have done so in a way that moves to the side of the very fraught and inevitably unanswerable questions of "what really happened."[10] Mourning, melancholy, grief, and trauma appear in this work as affective language for ways that pasts haunt.

The last twenty-five years or so of scholarship in the field of New Testament and early Christianity has nominally accepted the

---

7. The notion that history is felt as well as made is a New Historicist formulation, if perhaps one that is not necessarily obvious or deliberate in New Historicist scholarship. While the idea that history is made, rather than simply occurring, is a basic tenet of New Historicism, *feeling* has typically been thought of in terms too referential or too individual(istic) to be compatible with New Historicist interests. At the same time, early New Historicist writings are full of curiosities around and about affect, though, perhaps due to its poststructuralist inheritances, hesitant to theorize more than melancholy, grief and anxiety. See the affectivity of the New Historicist fascination with the anecdote, for example, illustrated in Catherine Gallagher and Stephen Greenblatt, *Practicing New Historicism* (Chicago: University of Chicago Press, 2000), 49-74.
8. Jacque Derrida, *Specters of Marx: The State of the Debt, the Work of Mourning, and the New International* (New York: Routledge, 1994).
9. Wendy Brown, *Politics Out of History* (Princeton: Princeton University Press, 2001); and Carla Freccero, *Queer/Early/Modern*, Series Q (Durham: Duke University Press, 2006).
10. Grace Cho, "Voices from the *Teum*: Synesthetic Trauma and the Ghosts of the Korean Diaspora," 151-169; Jonathan R. Wynn, "Haunting Orpheus: Problems of Space and Time in the Desert," 209-230; and Greg Goldberg and Craig Willse, "Losses and Returns: The Soldier in Trauma," 264-286, all in *The Affective Turn: Theorizing the Social*, ed. Patricia Ticineto Clough and Jean Halley (Durham: Duke University Press, 2007).

felt quality of history, but has laid considerably more emphasis on its made quality.[11] In other words, while New Testament and early Christianity scholarship is by now much more at ease with the conclusion that histories are produced, as well as with critiques of objectivist modes of analysis that claim fastidious detachment from their narratives, it has not itself necessarily waded into the affective murk. The claim that we are living in the stream of the history we are writing rings with a certain dissonance against, say, the meticulous particularizing of cultural localities and the rigorous rhetorical diagnostics of discursive criticism.[12] Even as those of us in the fields of New Testament and early Christianity soften to our own pain and are able to admit more of the ways we have been touched by and conscripted into violence, this waxing on pain and violence often takes place in puzzlingly remote registers. As Guzman's *Nostalgia for the Light* illustrates, the distancing mode of scientism and technical examination (even without objectivist or positivist pretensions) is an understandable, sometimes important move. But it is not an uncomplicated one.

This chapter addresses "Christian identity" as one particular instance of the field's simultaneous acknowledgement and allaying

---

11. As Moore and Sherwood suggest, "Theory" has been a scapegoat or magnet for this realization, even while philosophy arrived in biblical studies long before deconstruction or New Historicism: "Adapting strategically to the demands of this very particular (and rather peculiar) disciplinary context, Theory in biblical studies found itself repeatedly unveiling, with fitting rhetorical flourishes, the discoveries that objectivity is a myth; that interpretation is necessarily an infinite enterprise; that exegesis cannot be cleanly separated from eisegesis, nor theology from ideology; and that even our most cautious historical reconstructions are first and foremost imaginative creations. The Theory-redolent name of Hayden White was regularly intoned over the last of these discoveries in particular, but the basic position enunciated in the discovery was a commonplace in history departments even in the pre-Theory era, being a fundamental facet of the understanding of historiography expounded by less glamorous names, such as R. G. Collingwood and E. H. Carr" (*The Invention of the Biblical Scholar: A Critical Manifesto* [Minneapolis: Fortress Press, 2011], 100).
12. For a critique of such meticulous particularizing of cultural localities from an epistemological perspective, see Rey Chow, *The Age of the World Target: Self-Referentiality in War, Theory and Comparative Work* (Durham: Duke University Press, 2006).

of the affective potencies of different pasts, teasing out some of the contradictory historical implications of "Christian identity" as an analytical lens. Now a rather fashionable term, "Christian identity" represents something like the cutting edge of New Testament and early Christianity historiography.[13] Judith Lieu, often credited with putting the term into circulation, evokes it in her 2004 book (*Christian Identity in the Jewish and Graeco-Roman World*) to give full due to the variety of practices, positions, and locations represented by the New Testament and related texts.[14] Since then, the term generally signifies a collective weight-shift from essence to practice, universal to local, unity to diffusion, and referential to discursive. In other words, "Christian identity" has become a kind of metonym for a loosely poststructuralist historiography.

Christian identity's first and most influential proponents used it in the service of larger projects deconstructing the categories of orthodoxy, heresy, Gnosticism, and the model of a "parting of the ways" between Christianity and Judaism. More candidly, it was used to go for the jugular of modern, dominant Christianity via its undergirding master narrative.[15] Thus while Christian identity

---

13. For a very brief sampling of the huge volume and variety of recent titles in the fields of New Testament and early Christianity which take up "Christian identity" as an analytic (other than Lieu, King and Boyarin), see V. Henry T. Nguyen, *Christian Identity in Corinth: A Comparative Study of 2 Corinthians, Epictetus and Valerius* (Tübingen: Mohr Siebeck, 2008); Mikael Tellbe, *Christ Believers in Ephesus: A Textual Analysis of Early Christian Identity Formation in a Local Perspective* (Tübingen: Mohr Siebeck, 2009); William S. Campbell, *Paul and the Creation of Christian Identity* (London: T & T Clark, 2008); Bengt Holmberg, ed., *Exploring Christian Identity* (Tübingen: Mohr Siebeck, 2008); Denise Kimber Buell, *Why This New Race?: Ethnic Reasoning in Early Christianity* (New York: Columbia University Press, 2005); and Torrey Seland, *Strangers in the Light: Philonic Perspectives on Christian Identity in 1 Peter* (Leiden: Brill, 2005). Related to associations and meals, and under more specific discussion below, see Philip Harland, *Dynamics of Identity in the World of the Early Christians* (New York: Continuum, 2009); and Hal Taussig, *In the Beginning Was the Meal: Social Experimentation and Early Christian Identity* (Minneapolis: Fortress Press, 2009).
14. King, "Which Early Christianity?" in *The Oxford Handbook of Early Christian Studies*, Susan Ashbrook Harvey and David Hunter, eds. (Oxford: Oxford University Press, 2010), 66-84. Taussig (*In the Beginning Was the Meal*), and Harland (*Dynamics of Identity*) all credit Lieu with this observation.

addresses the mishmash of values, kinds of belonging, and cultural forces at work in the ancient world, it also addresses the social fractures of the present, providing a way to come to grips with histories of Christian violence (colonial, imperial, and anti-Jewish, among others). Karen King, one of the earliest and leading proponents of Christian identity as an optic, explicitly describes her work as "hearing alternative voices," and, perhaps most significantly, as putting another nail in the coffin of "impersonal objectivity," allowing space for "grief, uncertainty and injustice" against the vehement and melancholic suppressions of the modern historian.[16] In fact, most of the leading scholars whose work falls under the aegis of Christian identity are not shy about their political commitments or their grief, though sometimes such politics and affectivity are played out with aching specificity, and other times they are simply implied through vague references to fundamentalism or Christian dominance.[17] In any case, the facing of pain, mess, and violence has

---

15. King describes the master narrative of Christian origins as asserting "an unbroken chain, stretching from Jesus to the apostles and on to their successors in the church—elders, ministers, priests, and bishops—guaranteed the unity and uniformity of Christian belief and practice. This chain links modern Christianity securely with its historical origins in the life and deeds of its founder, Jesus Christ. The correct form of this belief is 'orthodoxy.' It is inscribed in the New Testament canon and the Nicene creed and enacted in ritual performances such as baptism, the Lord's supper or Eucharist meal, and ordination." King, "Christianity Without Canon," Paper presented at the Fall meeting of the Jesus Seminar. New Orleans, 1996, 3.
16. Karen King, "Factions, Variety, Diversity, Multiplicity: Representing Early Christian Differences for the 21st Century," *MTSR* 23 (2011): 216-37 (230).
17. Lieu ends her book by linking her historical work with the current moment, "where we are being urged to discover and to honour the value of difference and diversity, to give ear to the voices from the margins, to acknowledge the integrity of the 'other,' and our need for them, and, only so, to affirm our own as well as their integrity . . . [T]he exposure of rupture and the undermining of stability, which perhaps lies at the heart of any searched-for 'essence', forbids any form of fundamentalism, whether textual or institutional" (*Christian Identity in the Jewish and Graeco-Roman World* [Oxford: Oxford University Press, 2004], 316). King's turn to thinking about the construction of Christian identity appears as another dimension of her focus on taking responsibility for what meanings are generated through historical claims and reconstructions, and on surfacing the lost possibilities and quiet victims of dominant narratives through the integration of non-canonical ancient texts into historical reconstructions. King also writes that "It may be that a complex and partial history of Christian beginnings could lead to critical and constructive reflection on our own theologies and practices in their specifically

been the veritable engine of work on Christian identity, and dealing with grief one of its main ethical motivations.[18]

Rightly so: grief does, or at least can, have ethical reverberations.[19] But it is worth inquiring about what we imagine the relationship between grief and ethics to be. Is the ethics to be found in the simple recognition of grief in the wake of violence or injustice—having witnessed it, having felt its affects, having been part of it?[20] Is the posture of grief an inherently more vulnerable, less defensive one (thus interrupting cycles of violence)?[21] If the project of history, or of writing at all, is always already bound up in loss and death, as Michel Foucault and Michel de Certeau have suggested,[22] how does an admission of grief change the writing of history? And what other,

contemporary contexts, of wealth and poverty, of privilege and deprivation, of natural beauty and environmental disaster, of truth and justice. It could open up new possibilities for appreciating the diversity of forms that modern Christianity has taken globally, and for how Christianity has been enriched through contact with a wide variety of cultures in its 2000 year history" ("Christianity Without Canon" Paper presented at the Fall meeting of the Jesus Seminar. New Orleans, 1996, 21). King's and Lieu's ethical longings are resonant with feminist historiographical ones—particularly in the appeal to silenced voices—a connection that Shelly Matthews is more specific about in her work on Acts and Christian identity. Cf. Matthews, *Perfect Martyr: The Stoning of Stephen and the Construction of Christian Identity* (New York: Oxford University Press, 2010), 3-26. I will discuss this book in more detail in the next chapter.

18. Regarding the master narrative of Christian origins, Hal Taussig writes: "Obviously, even though it covers a relatively short period of time, this master narrative took a long time to come into being. It depends not only on unquestioned and covert mythical thinking but also on cunning calculations that simultaneously preserve, hide, and rationalize the prerogatives of Christian dominance in our day. It is told today—at least in part—to compensate mythically for the messy situation in which Christianity find itself as a worldwide dominant culture." Taussig also describes the "failures of Christianity to provide sufficient authority for negotiating (post)modern life" (*In the Beginning Was the Meal*, 11-13). Daniel Boyarin prefaces his book *Border Lines* with an even more ardent sense of disappointment and heartbreak, expressing how tormented he is by modern Christian and Jewish violence.

19. As David Eng and David Kazanjian write, "Avowals of and attachments to loss can produce a world of remains as a world of new representations and alternative meanings." They suggest an "apprehension of loss as creative," and that keeps loss "steadfastly alive for the political work of the present" (*Loss: The Politics of Mourning* [Berkeley: University of California Press, 2003], 5). For Eng and Kazanjian it seems then that the ethics of grief is tied into the ongoing life of a particular loss or trauma.

20. For an extended discussion of (in)justice and "feeling bad," see Ahmed, *The Cultural Politics of Emotion* (New York: Routledge, 2004), 191-203.

21. As Judith Butler has theorized in much of her work. See, for instance, "Beside Oneself," in *Undoing Gender* (New York: Routledge, 2004), 17-39.

unacknowledged affects might be tagging along behind (or even giving fire to) the apparently more ethically respectable grief?

Grief, after all, hardly appears alone, and the naming of any affect is a dicey matter. Do we always know exactly what we are feeling? What happens when we name an experience as love, sadness, or embarrassment, for example?[23] I find King's choice of words appealing for the complexity they render as a trio: the cluster "grief, uncertainty, and injustice" suggests perhaps not three separate items, but three hazy and overlapping experiences. For instance, grief sometimes accompanies—or is accompanied by—a sense of having been wronged. So what happens when grief bleeds into the more ethically fraught righteous anger? How might we negotiate the grief that is paired with guilt? The pair "grief and uncertainty" is especially shrewd since, as Judith Butler has remarked, "Freud reminded us that when we lose someone we do not always know what it is *in* that person that has been lost."[24]

Butler's repeated writing on grief and mourning has contended that grief reveals an intrinsic susceptibility, that we are "given over from the start" and "undone by each other;" therefore, claiming our grief means accepting that susceptibility.[25] But to claim one's grief, is, as Butler recalls from Freud, not the same as knowing all the facets of one's grief. Admitting to grief is simply admitting to unfinished

---

22. As for instance Michel de Certeau and Michel Foucault have suggested. Michel de Certeau, *The Writing of History* (New York: Columbia University Press, 1992); and Michel Foucault, "What is an Author?," in *Language, Counter-Memory, Practice*, ed. Donald F. Bouchard (Ithaca: Cornell University Press, 1977). In a consonant way, Stephen Greenblatt begins his book *Shakespearean Negotiations* with this line: "I began with the desire to speak with the dead" (*Shakespearean Negotiations: The Circulation of Social Energy in Renaissance England* [Berkeley: The University of California Press, 1989], 1).
23. Massumi, *Parables for the Virtual*, 1-22.
24. Butler, *Precarious Life: The Powers of Mourning and Violence* (London: Verso Press, 2004), 21. She also deconstructs the difference between mourning and melancholia, but I am not as much talking about mourning vs. melancholia as about "grief" as the affect that might be said to connect the two and that crosses the shaky line between conscious and unconscious processes.
25. Butler, "Beside Oneself" in *Undoing Gender*, 17-39.

business, an entry into a cloudy process. We are stripped of knowing how to proceed, in addition to not always being clear on what we are grieving. So any ethics of grief is complicated by both grief's proximity to other affects and the problem that we do not always know what we are grieving. It seems, then, that if grief is part of an ethics of history, one is obliged to the indefinite, amorphous, and elusive dimensions of pastness—not only the spectrality of pasts, but their often ambiguous affects.[26] This is the obligation that I hope to meet, opening the question of how certain pasts might be haunting us, and doing so by risking naming some of the barely-claimed affective stakes of histories of early Christianity.

*   *   *   *

Christian identity has come to replace Christianity as the object of analysis for many scholars in the field—Christianity now signaling an almost wistful imagination of theological and social coherence. Curiously, though, Lieu begins her book by mulling over the *limits* of the term "Christian identity," and they are not all that different from problems with the term "Christianity." For one, the word "Christian" hardly appears in any New Testament literature, making it an obvious anachronism there. But she also concedes that "[t]here is an

---

26. Carla Freccero, reading Butler's work on grief alongside Derrida's hauntology, offers a queer ethics of history that tries to account for the ongoing affective force of the past. As Freccero notes, "The past is in the present in the form of haunting. This is what, among other things, doing a queer kind of history means, since it involves an openness to the possibility of being haunted, even inhabited, by ghosts" (*Queer/Early/Modern*, 80). This "penetrative reciprocity" of haunting embraces an erotic *jouissance* of history, and resists the melancholic entombment and memorializing of history (typically conceived), which treats the past as resolved and over. De Certeau, in *The Writing of History*, describes Western practices of historiography in precisely the language of entombment and memorialization as Freccero (cf. Freccero, *Queer/Early/Modern*, 70-72). Wendy Brown has also written on "Resisting Left Melancholia" in *Loss: The Politics of Mourning*, ed. David L. Eng and David Kazanjian (Berkeley: The University of California Press, 2003). Freccero does not address specifically the problem of grief's unknowability, or present much of an affective range beyond grief and *jouissance*.

admitted but unavoidable contradiction in accepting even a broad classification of 'Christian' while also seeking to subvert its unity and differentness."[27]

Lieu adopts "Christian identity" to address local difference and, she admits, suggest translocal connections. But Lieu also observes a similar set of problems with the term "identity" as with the term "Christian(ity)". Not only does "identity" tend to suggest sameness and stability, but it too has its anachronisms, implying as it does a post-Cartesian individualistic self-consciousness.[28] With both "Christian" and "identity" qualified, she nonetheless goes on to chronicle "Christian identity," the goal of which she describes as this: "to explore, through the texts generated within the movement initiated in different ways by the life and death of Jesus of Nazareth, how they construct a distinctive identity. It is an identity that in the end we agree to label 'Christian,' so long as we forswear further categories such as 'orthodox' or 'heretical'."[29] Despite her own reservations about unity and essences, Lieu refers here to a *singular phenomenon*, a "movement," even if it is initiated "in different ways," with a primary catalyst—the life and death of Jesus. Amidst a wariness of singularity, a surprising point of reference materializes, one that is not unique to Lieu. The uncertainties and deadlock of terms (in other words, the attachments) in Lieu's introduction dramatize a more general set of conflicts. "What do we call it?" is not a question of precision, but of preservation: that is, how to keep the "it" alive.[30]

---

27. Lieu, *Christian Identity*, 24.
28. Ibid., 12. She clarifies that this anachronism in the term "identity" is less at issue in her study, however, because she has her eye on belonging and group consciousness—the construction of belonging through tropes and discourses, and the management of boundaries and difference.
29. Lieu, *Christian Identity in the Jewish and Graeco-Roman World*, 12.
30. Karen King notes this dynamic in which even "critics of normative identity projects" resist giving up the problematic terminology of "Gnosticism," and perhaps even more to the point, have trouble coming up with alternatives ("Factions, Variety, Diversity, Multiplicity," 220).

Like Lieu, so many of the scholars who use something like the construction of Christian identity as an optic use it against the force of their own analyses. Work done by Hal Taussig, Philip Harland, and Richard Ascough on Greco-Roman associations and association meals has collectively illustrated that what we call "Christian gatherings" were formed on the association model. But that model actually disallows for any single or exclusive identifications, and this work additionally suggests that translocal links between associations that bore similar identifications were often spotty, weak, or even non-existent.

So although it is easy to imagine, for instance, a gathering of ethnic Jews[31] oriented toward Israel as homeland, and with Yahweh as exclusive patron deity, or perhaps a mix of Jews and non-Jews joined on the basis of a kind of exuberant loyalty to Christ, Ascough's work shows that such imagination is complicated by a number of factors. First, there is evidence of Jewish involvement in associations with non-Jewish deities as patrons.[32] Second, diaspora Israel links to Jerusalem, for example, were often reticent at best, especially during periods of social distress, such as the rebellions of the mid-first century, and in general associations with homeland or geographical links were often multiethnic or multinational in composition.[33] Within New Testament literature specifically, it is clear that at least some of those who gathered around Christ (e.g., the Corinthians) were hesitant to see themselves as translocally affiliated.[34] Ascough

---

31. On the complications of even this imagining of something like an ethnic Jew, see Cynthia M. Baker's essay, "'From Every Nation Under Heaven': Jewish Ethnicities in the Greco-Roman World," in *Prejudice and Christian Beginnings: Investigating Race, Gender and Ethnicity in Early Christian Studies* (Minneapolis: Fortress Press, 2009), 79-100, in which she notices that the Pentecost narrative of Acts is not a specifically Christian universalist construction, but rather a deeply Israelite (and diasporic) imagination in which affiliation, and even homeland in some sense, is shared but not necessarily on the basis of ethnicity/nationality.
32. Richard S. Ascough, "Translocal Relationships among Voluntary Associations and Early Christianity" *JECS* 5, no. 2 (1997): 236.
33. Ibid., 231, 236.

also raises the strong possibility that Paul's Thessalonians, for instance, were an existing group of craftsmen who met together as a group before encountering Paul, and for whom Christ was secondary (perhaps incidental?) to their gathering.[35]

This relativization of Christ as a singular or fundamental basis for affiliation is confirmed by Harland, who has shown that "Christ associations," like others, drew their members from five overlapping networks: professional organizations, households, neighborhoods, sanctuaries or temples, and shared homeland or ethnic identity.[36] Judean associations were not only formed around the more predictable ethnic and cultic networks, but they also found definition through shared neighborhood, occupation, and geographic origin (which was not necessarily Israel), and so were regularly composed of people that fit neither cultic nor "ethnic" parameters for "Judean." Such circumstantial kinds of belonging meant tension, but it also meant a merging of practices and affiliations that might normally (or categorically) seem to be at odds with one another.[37] Hal Taussig's study of "early Christian" associational meals suggests, in fact, that negotiations of class, gender, and imperial loyalty, among others, were primary to these gatherings; and Christ, or being "in Christ," at least for Pauline groups, worked to smooth or amplify other tensions of belonging.[38] In other words, for the first hundred years of what we

---

34. As Ascough notes, "Meeks points to Paul's collection as indicating translocal obligations to other Christians. However, Paul's troubles with raising the money promised, and his rhetorical strategies in his letters to the Corinthians (II Cor 8.1-15; 9.1– 5), suggest that they, at least, remained unconvinced that they had a social and religious obligation to an otherwise unknown group. What confuses the Corinthians is not necessarily the fact that they have to donate, but that the monies are going to Jerusalem rather than the common fund of the local congregation. Also, the financial support for the Jerusalem church came from the newer, Pauline churches (not the reverse), which would have gone against expectations. In a translocal organization the established center usually supports the struggling, newer organizations" ("Translocal Relationships," 237).
35. Richard Ascough, "The Thessalonian Christian Community as Professional Voluntary Association," *JBL* 119, no. 2 (2000): 311-28.
36. Harland, Ibid., 1; and Taussig, Ibid., 35.
37. Taussig, Ibid., 35.

call "early Christianity," "Christian" was not *itself* a kind of belonging to be worked out.[39]

Yet despite the contingencies and textual problems, Taussig, Harland, and Ascough all use the term "Christian" to describe the social gatherings represented by New Testament literature. The only real sense of social coherence apparent in their analyses, though, is effected through the very use of the word "Christian." Even for scholars such as Karen King and Daniel Boyarin, whose work has repeatedly unhinged notions of continuous social or theological content for the groups we call ancient Christians and deconstructed clear distinctions between ancient Jewish and Christian identities, the term "Christian" has a curious stability about it. For King, the category "Christian" still figures as that which contains all the social and theological diversity. For Boyarin, although "Christian" is not a category mutually exclusive to "Jew," it is still nonetheless a pertinent category as early as the Gospel of John.[40] Not only is the "Christ" in Christian not a universal appellation for Jesus, posing the question whether so-called Christ people and non-Christ Jesus people would even recognize themselves as belonging together,[41] it is also far from obvious that the sudden "all of you out there" appeals and grand

---

38. Ibid., 183-84.
39. Ibid. For Taussig, it appears that "Christian" is the category that facilitates the working out of other differences. In other words, it seems to create the space for negotiation. Cf. 145-172.
40. Cf. Boyarin, *Border Lines*, 89-111, in which he discusses "The Intertextual Birth of the Logos."
41. The concentration of New Testament literature arriving from Asia Minor and the eventual dominance of the very term "Christian" may have created a false sense that "Christ" language itself is universal among people interested in Jesus. It is an open question how "Jesus people" who were not using the rhetoric of Christ at all—as indicated by Q, the Gospel of Mary and the Gospel of Thomas, for instance—may have related to the term "Christian" as invoked by authorities or others. My questions on this are provoked by a set of reflections in *Redescribing Christian Origins,* ed. Ron Cameron and Merrill P. Miller (Atlanta: Society of Biblical Literature, 2004). I am particularly interested in the insight, first made by Burton Mack but later elaborated by Merrill Miller, that "Christ" language was not universal to people interested in Jesus, and the implications that might have for assumptions that Jesus was "originally" understood as a messianic figure. Neither Miller nor Mack think much about what this might mean in terms of the ceding of these non-Christ traditions to "Christ" traditions, either in the canon or in history. See Merrill Miller, "The Problem of the Origins of a Messianic Conception of Jesus,"

perspective of early second-century literature are more than hyperbolic imagination—or that they imagine the same "you."[42] There are ways to understand the appearance of the term "Christian" in the late first and early second centuries, as well as ways to understand relationships between texts, without presuming a unitary, translocal phenomenon that finally comes to be named. In fact, many of these scholars have already proposed ways to do this (see chapter two), which makes the problem of their reifications of the figure of "the early Christian" through the optic of Christian identity all the more engrossing. However wary of referentiality so many contemporary historians of early Christianity seem to be, "the Christian," as a subject, remains recalcitrantly referential.

"Christian identity" is a strategic term, if epistemologically contradictory, indexing universality and continuity as well as the impossibility of the same. As such, it seems to house the contradictory longings and dissatisfactions of a (post)modern diaspora: senses of belonging and estrangement, guilt and latent triumphalism, which may, by the way, do as much to instantiate each other as to cancel each other out.[43] For instance, as an instrument of politicized historiography, the Christian identity optic has been party to an increasingly obsessive cataloging of ideology in ancient texts, a

in *Redescribing Christian Origins*, 301-36; and Burton Mack, *A Myth of Innocence: Mark and Christian Origins* (Philadelphia: Fortress Press, 1988).

42. I will say more on this in the next chapter regarding Ignatius. This language/construction of a multitudinous readership appears in, 1 Pet. 1:1, James 1:1, Eph. 1:1, and Rev. 1:4, for instance. In Revelation, for example, the addressees are 7 "churches," but 7 is perhaps too symbolic of a number to be an actual referent to a number of gatherings..

43. Perhaps obviously, estrangement no less implies belonging, since that which you are estranged from still has a claim on you. It is tied painfully to you, or you to it, through the very feeling of estrangement. Colonial belonging lives eerily on in this manner, imposing its belonging most forcefully through a sense of estrangement, even in what is experienced as self-estrangement. Frantz Fanon chronicles something like this in his book *Black Skin, White Masks*, trans. Richard Philcox (New York: Grove Press, 2008.) On latent imperial desires, see Erin Runions, "Empire's Allure: Babylon and the Exception to Law in Two Conservative Discourses," *JAAR* 77, no. 3 (2009): 680-711.

suspicious ferreting out of any possible violence (anti-Jewish rhetoric, valorization of masculinity, imperial mimesis, etc.) covertly nestled in the text. However crucial such work is for certain ends, this vigorous attachment to a hermeneutics of suspicion—this "paranoid imperative"—given so much prestige in contemporary criticism has affective as well as ethical reverberations. As Eve Sedgwick points out, not only does the hermeneutics of suspicion typically refuse its own affectivity, but it additionally contains a kind of obsessive impulse to forestall surprise: "The first imperative of paranoia is *There must be no bad surprises.*"[44]

According to Sedgwick, it is not incidental that the injunction of paranoid practices to anticipate violence and pain runs so strongly in queer theory, given the depths of pain animating and contiguous to queer theory (the AIDS crisis, homophobic violence and exclusion, for example). However, for contemporary Christians with visceral memories (that is, sensory, but not necessarily conscious ones) of colonial missions, holocausts, and various crusades into the Middle East,[45] such paranoia may have other valences along with grief, the specificities of which depend on one's proximity or generational relationship to such violences. Such paranoia may also contain guilt, anger, loss, shame, and embarrassment, for example. It is possible that some of this guilt, shame, loss, etc., are more quiescent factors in the American right-wing Christian defensiveness that, against all odds, continuously insists on purity and its own moral justifiability. But for so much liberal and progressive scholarship, it is hard to ignore the moral satisfaction of implicitly scolding the aggressive threads, ancient or otherwise, of the very tradition that one has inherited, however one has inherited it (and boy, is this satisfying, trust me).

---

44. Sedgwick, Ibid., 130.
45. By memory, I do not mean to consign these events to the past as if they are "over and done with," but rather to evoke the haunted traces and ongoing persistence of certain traumas, as the literature on loss, haunting, and spectrality cited above suggests.

Do such demonstrations of righteousness and outrage interrupt or consolidate a sense of Christian exceptionalism and ethical achievement? Though different in tactic, compulsive scrubbing and exposing dirt have a common source of anxiety.

Christian belonging, however unsettled or fractious, has been generated and regenerated through violence. But the relationship between any belonging and violence may be less straightforward than identity models might have us believe. In Althusser's famous model of interpellation, the "subject" is produced through the formative, symbolic, and inherently violent act of being hailed by the Law (represented by any number of figures), and turning in acknowledgment. This notion of "subjectivity" as being formed in power has been a dominant understanding for identity for the last forty years, as seen in the work of Michel Foucault, Judith Butler, and Gayatri Spivak, among many others. Althusser's interpellation and its theoretical elaborations suggest the content of subjectivity/identity is not natural or stable, but rather "socially constructed," contingent, and even fragile. I am in full accord with the constructedness of the subject—that is, its constitutive sociality—but I am additionally wondering if the interpellational model and language of subjectivity does not undercut the very contingency that notions of the constructedness of identity wish to highlight. What's more, violence has other, less predictable effects, and ones that don't always relate to the maps and grids of identity. For example, the visceral haunting of violence can seal even warring factions together,[46] creating entanglements that not only set limits on but scramble identity categories or models of interpellation.[47]

---

46. For instance, Jacqueline Rose writes about the way Palestinians and Israeli Jews are joined through the haunting of violence in a "monstrous family of reluctant belonging." See *States of Fantasy* (Oxford: Clarendon, 1996), 30-31. More will be said about this concept in chapter three.

What is more, as much as Christian identity arises out of postmodern suspicion of the category of religion for the ancient world,[48] the term "Christian" still signifies, like religion, a category that supersedes geographic, cultural, and ethnic differences in order to generate another kind of particularity. It may be that Christian identity does not work as well as one might like for either ancient or contemporary people, and what we call Christian identity blinds one to all kinds of intricate relationships around the perimeters of the category "Christian," or investments in Christian texts and history that both weaken and intensify the category's affective pull.

Aside from imputing a basic stability, "identity" emphasizes the work of the ego ideal—in Freudian terms, the coherent vision of oneself to which one aspires—giving it a distinctly unattainable quality.[49] This is especially true of interpellational models following from Althusser, since Althusser is an explicit interpreter of psychoanalyst Jacques Lacan. It might be worth recalling that even Judith Butler and Julia Kristeva, who use interpellational and Lacanian models respectively, give an account of how identity is affectively imbued.[50] Identity is not only ideal (or, to emphasize its

---

47. See Louis Althusser, *Lenin and Philosophy and Other Essays* (New York: Monthly Review Press, 1971).
48. For instance, both Boyarin and King expressly question traditional understandings of the category of religion, in *Border Lines* and "Factions, Variety, Diversity, Multiplicity," respectively.
49. For Lacan, it would seem subjectivity is bound up with the symbolic, or the Law, and thus the ego ideal. In his discussion of the mirror stage, on the other hand, what apparently emerges as identity is bound more to the ideal ego and the Imaginary. The relationship between subjectivity and identity is not typically strongly differentiated in contemporary theories, and even regularly interchangeable. I myself am not all that interested in differentiating the two. Althusser, for instance, makes no distinction between subjectivity and identity, relating both to ideology (which for him is of the Imaginary order). His now well-known scene of the police officer hailing the subject, a scene cast as exemplary of the dynamics of interpellation, is based on Lacan's mirror stage. Although the work of Judith Butler and Michel Foucault, for instance, both depend on Althusser, the notion of "discursive construction" of the subject seems to be an assumption leaning more heavily on the symbolic. See Jacques Lacan, "The Mirror Stage as Formative of the I Function as Revealed in Psychoanalytic Experience," in *Écrits: The First Complete Edition in English* (New York: W. W. Norton and Company, 2007), 75-81.

affective dimensions, aspirational). It is also linked with disgust and melancholy, which continue to join one to what one ostensibly is not.[51] Affect theory has expanded on this observation by pointing out how affectivity beyond melancholy and disgust "sticks" people together, claiming that some of the queerness of affect is how it binds people in ways that muddy lines of identification, even rendering such lines incomprehensible.[52]

Daniel Boyarin's *Border Lines*, a book that impressively makes the case against any distinctly Jewish or Christian theological content through late antiquity, leans heavily on Althusserian epistemologies. But despite or alongside his reliance on identity construction as a framework, Boyarin also hints at other ways of understanding belonging and social life. For instance, his lyrical preface not only cops to a love of Christianity (in addition to Judaism, which he considers more "his own"), it additionally draws a complex illustration of what might be imagined as some of the felt terms of his affiliation to Christianity. "As long as I can remember I have been in love with some manifestations of Christianity . . . " he writes. He goes on to contextualize this love within a relationship to a Judaism tormented by Israeli policy and practice toward the Palestinians, or,

---

50. Butler has regularly written on Althusser's interpellational model, and both Kristeva and Butler write on Lacan. Lacan has a crucial and contested place in Butler and Kristeva's respective work, and they both challenge the centrality of the father/phallus/Law in Lacan, though in very different ways. Kristeva challenges Lacan particularly by theorizing the more primary place of the mother's body in language (the semiotic, as opposed to Lacan's symbolic). Butler on the other hand challenges the normative heterosexual positioning of subjects in the Lacanian scheme, as well as Lacan's opposing of desire and identification. See Judith Butler, *Bodies That Matter: On the Discursive Limits of "Sex"* (New York: Routledge, 1993), 93-120.
51. Primarily Judith Butler, "Melancholy Gender-Refused Identification," *Psychoanalytic Dialogues* 5, no. 2 (1995): 165-80; and Julia Kristeva, *Powers of Horror: An Essay on Abjection* (New York: Columbia University Press, 1982).
52. Cf. Ahmed, Ibid., on the "stickiness" of affect, as well as Puar on affect and contagion in her *Terrorist Assemblages: Homonationalism in Queer Times* (Durham: Duke University Press, 2007), esp. 172-74.

more pointedly, within a relationship to those Jews who label him as "anti-Semitic" for not aligning with Israeli policies and ideologies:

> On the stairs of my synagogue, in Berkeley, on Rosh Hashanah this year, I was told that I should be praying in a mosque, and versions of this, less crude perhaps, are being hurled at Jews daily by other Jews. I don't wish to romanticize my situation. It is not I that is suffering; my only personal pain is the pain of living on the margins, and that, too, has its privileges. More piercing to me is the pain of watching a tradition, my Judaism, to which I have dedicated my life, morally disintegrating before my eyes. It has been said by many Christians that Christianity died at Auschwitz, Treblinka, and Sobibor. I fear—G-d forbid—that my Judaism may be dying at Nablus, Daheishe, Beteen (Beth-el), and al-Khalil (Hebron).[53]

Boyarin's alienation from Judaism is itself evocative, as an alienation that nonetheless attaches him all the more to its history. But I am for the moment more interested in the way this story figures within the context of Boyarin's self-proclaimed love of Christianity. Figured within the tense, nasty, and periodically bloody relationship between Christians and Jews, Boyarin's love of Christianity is likened in this preface to the love shared by a couple in an abusive relationship (for which he puts the term *love* in quotes).[54] He describes hearing *In the Garden* sung by Tennessee Ernie Ford on TV as a child and being moved to tears,[55] an example that offers much in the way of understanding how love of traditions works through affective attachments to specific, if often quirky, multivalent moments or elements, then treated as metonyms for a larger abstraction. It is not clear what about *In the Garden*, sung by Ford, moves Boyarin, and rightly so. Just as in grief, in love we do not always know what it is in the beloved that we love.

---

53. Boyarin, *Border Lines*, xiv.
54. Ibid., xiii.
55. Ibid., ix.

Boyarin's love for Christianity demands being seen as more than an outsider's romanticism. The passage above casts his outrage and disillusionment with Judaism in parallel relation to a post-Holocaust Christian sadness and disillusionment. While testifying to the complicated and contradictory facets of his love, in the context of a kind of love letter, it implies one of the terms of his association with Christianity is surprisingly through a parallel experience of Jewish and Christian ethical failure. Boyarin suggests his love is "queer" for its transgression of identity boundaries,[56] though it would seem his love illustrates instead how the terms of identity actually oversimplify the complexities of social-affective investments which are contradictory and multidirectional from the get-go. Boyarin nearly admits as much, writing, "Judaism is not the mother of Christianity. They are twins, joined at the hip."[57] Rather than separate kinds of belonging, the collection of terms, practices, texts, and people abstracted into Judaism and Christianity belong in specific ways to each other.[58] It is no wonder then that the trend in which Boyarin participates is invested in parsing out precise ideological relationships between ancient Jews and Christians. As I will elaborate in further chapters, such a trend may indeed be expressing and giving organization to uneasy, visceral dimensions of belonging—forms of affection, admiration, repugnance, guilt, embarrassment, estrangement, and more.

This is not to say that Boyarin (or anyone else) is "mistaking" the felt present for ancient history. The question of whether affective

---

56. "Why does my book want me to 'come out'? Why do I need to tell about the love that (almost) would not dare to say its name, the love of this Orthodox Jew for Christianity?" Boyarin asks (Ibid., xi).
57. Ibid., 5.
58. By "belonging to each other" I mean not simply that they are more responsible to each other than, say, to any other collectives. Rather I mean to do justice to Boyarin's own sense, expressed not only in the conjoined twins analogy but his entire thesis, that Judaism and Christianity have specific, messy, and long-term entanglements in history, including extremely strained and violent ones, that problematize their ostensible separateness.

investments are projected back into history to work out the present, or whether the present is an enactment with variation of older relationships and discourses, is not only not resolvable, it may not be the most pertinent question, since both ways of framing the problem rely on a certain untenable linear temporality. History is felt as much as it is made, but the feedback loop between the feeling and making is a delicate circuit, full of live wires.[59] At the same time, though, ironically enough, the conundrums of Christian identity challenge the bracketing of referentiality in poststructuralist historiography, not because there are Christians "back then" who need only to be located or described; but because, despite our best efforts, we cannot leave referentiality behind.[60] It may be more critical to ask where one's referentiality lies, and what it means, rather than how to get rid of it.

Besides, if reference on some level is inevitable, what better provocation could there be to periodically change reference points, or even dream up some new ones? The ironic necessity of a historical searching for something or someone in the face of an ever expanding unknowing, having only pieces in unsure relation to you and to time, is that it becomes a way, though maybe not necessarily the only or best way, of learning how to live with the ghosts and glimmers of nebulous forces that loom and outstrip you. The pursuits of the discipline and practice of History are futile only if judged in terms of the accuracy of their results. As an address to the engulfing and ever

---

59. That is to say, history is not felt *before* it is made (into History), as I think a literal reading of Massumi would demand. Massumi is more attached to the idea that there is something pre-linguistic to affect (though not pre-social). As I expressed in the introduction, I find the notion of "pre-linguistic" to be a challenging, if not troublesome, assumption, however I do find the idea of affect as having an indeterminate relation to language compelling. Similar to Massumi, Charles Shepherdson, in a Lacanian vein, suggests affect be taken as coextensive with the real (an "effect of symbolization"), whereas emotion falls into the category of the symbolic. See Shepherdson, *Lacan and the Limits of Language* (New York: Fordham University Press, 2008), 94.
60. Cf. Rey Chow's almost scouring critique of poststructuralist epistemology, particularly the bracketing of referentiality, in her book, *Age of the World Target*, 1-24.

widening resonances of affect, however tentative, roundabout, and fraught that address may be, these practices and pursuits of History tell a different story than the one they would seem to be writing. By chronicling the haunted present, they offer a deeply subjective and indirect route—but a route nonetheless—to the very pasts that haunt.

In the next chapter, I inquire about the affective stakes, as well as the historical and ethical-political implications, of one particular imagining of early Christian identity: early Christian identity as in some way queer. But I also continue to foreground loss and its affects, and national and imperial haunting, making them my reference points as I bring affect and diaspora to bear on some of the very texts through which so many histories of Christian identity are narrated—the letters of Ignatius and 1 Peter.

2

On the Historical Queerness of Christianity

In some of the most cutting edge historical work in the fields of New Testament and early Christianity, early Christian identity has been associated with queerness. This association is made either because of the crossing or disruption of identity categories present in "early Christian" literature, or because of the kinds of apparently transgressive social performances that coalesce around these texts. But, as I'll argue in this chapter, there are historical and theoretical problems as well as some surprisingly double political alignments embedded in this association. So what collective affective investments might this association between transgressive queerness and Christian identity in historiography signal? Can queerness be useful in our renderings of ancient sociality as represented in "early Christian" literature? How might we consider the social-affective landscape of the late first and early second centuries *without* Christian identity or an essential Christian transgressiveness?

The association of Christian identity with queerness first stirs up some matters about the relationship between queer theory and

Christian historiography. Queer theory, roughly emerging in the early 90's as a confluence of poststructuralist theory, LGBT activism, and feminist theory, has arrived only recently in the disciplines of New Testament and early Christianity. Ten years or more had gone by after Eve Sedgwick's *Epistemology of the Closet* and Judith Butler's *Gender Trouble* (two signal texts of what was, after their writing, designated queer theory)[1] before the fields of New Testament and early Christianity had shown any marked interest in gender, identity, or bodily life as social/discursive constructions, or in early Christian texts in the context of the history of sexuality.[2] By now, following trends in gender theory and cultural studies that have started to theorize queerness as "anti-identity" or non-normed identity rather than as sexual identity, there have been a number of recent projects within the fields of New Testament and early Christianity that have adopted this model for understanding "early Christians" or their assumed prototypes as queer in the sense of defying ancient identity categories.[3] Several of these projects revolve around Galatians, specifically emphasizing the baptismal formula "neither Jew nor Greek, slave nor free, male and female" in Galatians 3:28.[4] Others

---

1. Neither Judith Butler nor Eve Sedgwick describe anything like "queer theory" in these books, and the term "queer" barely appears in them. The term "queer theory" however does go into circulation in the early 1990's. Sedgwick reflects much more at length on the implications of "queer" in *Tendencies* (Durham: Duke University Press, 1993).
2. Though this is not to say that the question of homosexuality as a historical category for ancient Christianity was not addressed before the last decade or two. Cf. John Boswell's *Christianity, Social Tolerance, and Homosexuality* (Chicago: University of Chicago Press, 1980). Stephen Moore, describing queer theory as "a poststructuralist 'take' on sex (homosex but also heterosex), sexuality, and sexual identity that argues (or assumes) their invariable instability, their de-essentializing fluidity, their contingent status as discursive constructions and/or products of performance," notes that the interest in queerness in biblical studies has hardly been poststructuralist in orientation. Moore, *The Bible in Theory Critical and Postcritical Perspectives* (Atlanta: Society of Biblical Literature, 2010), 225.
3. This is a group of which I consider myself a part. My own work on *The Thunder: Perfect Mind* postulates that the text is both a Christian text and a queering of identity categories. See Hal Taussig, Jared Calaway, Maia Kotrosits, Celene Lillie and Justin Lasser, *The Thunder: Perfect Mind: A New Translation and Introduction* (New York: Palgrave Macmillan, 2010).

have pointed out that the term "Christian" seems to appear in contexts of violence and public shame (in martyr narratives, for example), noting the wildly complicated gender performances that also occur in these contexts.[5] Thus "queer" has become an historical category for understanding the emergence of the term "Christian" and even Christians themselves. Queer itself is not an uncontested term, however, having come to indicate both LGBTI identities[6] (being "queer identified") and that which is inimical to identity. It appears now that in contemporary historiography "Christian," like

---

4. Daniel Boyarin's *A Radical Jew: Paul and the Politics of Identity* (Berkeley: University of California Press, 1994), for example, includes a chapter entitled, "There Is No Male and Female: Galatians and Gender Trouble." Davina Lopez's work in *Apostle to the Conquered: Re-Imagining Paul's Mission* (Minneapolis: Fortress Press, 2008), consonant with Boyarin's, describes Paul's ideological work in Galatians as a kind of anti-identity (86-105). While Brigitte Kahl's reading of Galatians similarly gestures to queer theoretical conceptualities of anti-identity, Lopez specifically describes Galatians in terms that evoke gender-queerness. For Kahl's reading, see, *Galatians Re-Imagined: Reading With the Eyes of the Vanquished* (Minneapolis: Fortress Press, 2010).

5. Virginia Burrus's *Saving Shame: Martyrs, Saints and Other Abject Subjects* (Philadelphia: University of Pennsylvania Press, 2008) associates the shame of being persecuted "for the name" Christian with queerness (12-14). Burrus similarly uses queerness to unearth and refigure the erotic force of hagiographical literature in *The Sex Lives of Saints: An Erotics of Ancient Hagiography* (Philadelphia: University of Pennsylvania Press, 2004). In this earlier book, however, she does not associate a particular queerness with Christian identity. Melanie Johnson-Debaufre uses the term "queer" to describe the *ekklesiai* in Acts, but it is unclear whether she intends that queerness to indicate identity or anti-identity. She does, I think, make room for the possibility that I will pose later in this essay, that the *ekklesiai* in Acts are no queerer than anybody else, through her strategic choice of the term *ekklesia* over "Christians." However, her thematic use of "coming out" imagery as an analogy suggests she means the queer *ekklesiai* to have implications of a particular identity. Johnson-Debaufre, "Inside Out and Upside Down: Acts 17:1-8 and the Outing of the Thessalonian *Ekklesia*" (paper presented at the annual meeting of the Society of Biblical Literature, New Orleans, La., November 2009). On the queer gender performances of martyrs and saints, see, for example, Elizabeth Castelli, *Martyrdom and Memory: Early Christian Culture Making*. (New York: Columbia University Press, 2007), 33-103. Paul Trebilco notes, based on the use of "Christians" by Agrippa in Acts 26:28 and the use in 1 Peter, that "it is used in an outsider-facing situation" and in a "mocking" or "pejorative" sense, which later became "insider" language. See Trebilco, *The Early Christians in Ephesus from Paul to Ignatius* (Tübingen: Mohr Siebeck, 2004), 554-56. He does not use the word "queer" but his description easily resonates with it.

6. Queer is the shorthand for the growing acronym: gay, lesbian, bisexual, transgender, intersex (the acronym usually also includes "queer," i.e., LGBTQI); it sometimes also appears as lesbian, gay, bisexual, two spirit, trans and gender non-conforming.

queerness, imparts ambiguously a particular identity and anti-identity, in any case carrying queerness's implications of subversion.

The life of queer theory in Christian historiography is a bit surprising given the strained relationship (to say the least) between so many queer-identified people and numerous forms of contemporary Christianity: homophobic rejections of queer-identified clergy, and evangelical and conservative lobbying against marriage equality, for example. But that strained relationship is indeed the space into which the affinity between Christian historiography and queer theory apparently wants to burrow. What could be more troubling to bigoted anti-gay Christians than to hear the word *queer* tossed in the direction of their origins?[7] Queerness importantly disjoined early Christianity from the fantasy ideal of modern American middle-class mores, values, and family life, but it joined it to another fantasy ideal—that of the (post)modern progressive American malcontent. Of course, the historical queerness ascribed to "the early Christian" represents a fairly important disruptive strategy. But these strategic uses of queerness perhaps represent less a radicalizing of Christian historiography than the widespread conventionalization of queerness. *Even early Christians* are queer these days, solidifying queer's trendiness and intellectual cachet.[8]

---

7. Illustrating the tension in using queerness as a descriptor of early Christians, Melanie Johnson-Debaufre aptly writes, "I borrow some of this theoretical material fully aware that implying that the Thessalonian *ekklesia* are a bunch of queers might be insulting to either Christians or historians. But it likely will be even more insulting to queers" (Ibid., 1).
8. One must note, however, that this cachet around queerness in academic circles happens alongside the deepening material hazards of queer existences, and continual queering of new populations. Rosemary Hennessy, in *Profit and Pleasure: Sexual Identities in Late Capitalism* (New York: Routledge, 2000), argues from a materialist perspective that an increasing middle-class of queer-identified folks and commodification of queerness participates in and masks some larger (and gendered) dynamics of exploitation. In a similar vein, Jasbir Puar (*Terrorist Assemblages: Homonationalism in Queer Times* [Durham: Duke University Press, 2007]) discusses "exceptional queers" being folded into model citizenship, which can hide the violence and disenfranchisement of the greater majority of LGBTI individuals.

There are other ways that the term *queer* serves Christian historiography. *Queer* as nearly synonymous with subversion means that the queer "early Christian" is positioned—almost by definition—as out of alignment with and even in opposition to the Roman Empire in some way.[9] Although in many cases this arrives from admirably close readings of textual imaginations,[10] and though it may offer inspiration or complications for contemporary Christians living in and with American or western imperialism (more on that in the next chapter), the effect of this particular collective sensibility is what Jasbir Puar terms "queer exceptionalism." In her book *Terrorist Assemblages: Homonationalism in Queer Times*,[11] Puar brings analyses of sexuality and gender to the problem of U.S. exceptionalism (claims to excellence and transcendence), observing a kind of "U.S. sexual exceptionalism" operating in the current cultural moment. She reflects on the images of sexualized violence from Abu Ghraib and the circulation of other eroticized and violent nationalist images after 9/11, drawing attention to the ways the nation is founded through the queering of certain populations who are cast as a perverse "threat to life" (or to "our way of life"). Such programmatic torture occurs simultaneously with U.S. claims to be a paragon and defender of human rights, and is justified through the "exceptional circumstances" of the war on terror. Puar notices how sexual exceptionalism is deployed by the U.S. and is perpetuated by

---

9. I should note that a queerly subversive relationship to "power" is not reducible to an oppositional stance against a single political entity such as the Roman Empire. Although it does seem that the Roman Empire in so much contemporary scholarship tends to signify not just a political entity, but more broadly a confluence of discourses, norms, and systems at play in the ancient Mediterranean.
10. That is, even in texts such as Revelation, in which it is fairly apparent that a kind of hatred, disgust, or otherwise affective form of refusal of empire is present, it may take texts too much at their word to assume this constitutes a monolithically subversive posture toward empire, or that such texts manage to be cleanly extricated from the lures, attractions, and deep formative effects of empire.
11. Puar, *Terrorist Assemblages: Homonationalism in Queer Times* (Durham: Duke University Press, 2007).

individuals and collectives within the nation who identify with such claims. In particular she challenges the intensive focus on Arab or Muslim homophobia by some LGBTQI political groups, a focus which reinstalls the colonialist civilized vs. uncivilized binary underwriting so much U.S. nationalist violence.[12] When queerness is cast as essentially or monolithically subversive, she argues, it in effect masks the racial inflections and nationalist alliances promoted in these kinds of LGBTQI political interests.

With eerie congruence to U.S. sexual exceptionalism, the notion of "the early Christian" as historically queer establishes an idealized, even unique, resistance somewhere within the emergence of "Christian" (ever in quotes at this point) rhetoric and social practice, preserving something of an original virtue for Christianity. Of course, U.S. exceptionalism has been chained from the start to biblical exceptionalism through narratives of perfection and distinctiveness paired with a destiny associated with land. But while the historical queerness of early Christians by virtue of their Christianness is a trope that may cause visceral upset for some contemporary people, or may interrupt some consolidations of Christianity with normativity, it also, sadly, broadens U.S. and biblical exceptionalisms. The ambiguity of whether "Christian" signifies an identity or anti-identity has settled into the idea of the people we call "early Christians" as being *queer subjects*. Yet the very notion of a "queer subject" has an unfortunate contradiction about it. As Puar notes

---

12. Puar writes, for instance, that "The secular gay and lesbian human rights framing of Islamic sexual repression mistakes or transposes state repression for sexual repression, essentially denying any productive effects of juridical structures (replaying again the repressive hypothesis Foucault warns against). This contemporary version of repression does not contradict colonial fantasies of Orientalist sexual excess, perversity, and pedophilia. Working in tandem, the proper modern gay or lesbian subject is foreclosed, while the terrorist is forever queer, improperly sexual, embedded in an 'always already homosexualized population' . . . .Queer secularity is constitutive of and constituted by the queer autonomous liberal subject against and through the reification of the very pathological irrational sexualities that are endemic to discourses of terrorist culpability." Ibid., 14-15.

in her conclusion, "[d]espite the anti-identitarian critique that queer theory launches (i.e., queerness as an approach, not an identity or wedded to identity), the queer subject, a subject that is against identity, transgressive rather than (gay or lesbian) liberatory, nevertheless surfaces as an object in need of excavation, elaboration, or specularization."[13]

I wonder if the work of summoning Christian subjects not only as queer but as "objects in need of excavation, elaboration, and specularization" *at all* is likewise closely tied to the perpetual lean in the fields of New Testament and early Christianity towards our exceptionalist imaginations of the first century. Where there are ancient Christian subjects, no matter how diverse, diffuse, or intricately configured, what often follows is a description of the unique positioning of these subjects in history, a claim about their very atypical deployment of discourse, or a contention that these subjects are peak innovators or distinctively transgressive.[14] The current fixation on empire risks embarrassing contradiction unless it attends to the sometimes subtle braiding of exceptionalism and the search for and description of ancient Christian subjects. The very desire to target and describe particular ancient subjects as Christian is itself knit into U.S. imperialism, given the larger colonial problem of trying to make Christians out of unwitting or unwilling others.

Although it may at the moment appear otherwise, I am criticizing neither fixations on empire nor the practice of borrowing from queer theory for historical ends. This very book testifies to my own fixation on empire, as well as to a deep attachment to queer modalities of

---

13. Puar, Ibid., 206.
14. Burton Mack makes this larger point about exceptionalism in his conclusion to *A Myth of Innocence: Mark and Christian Origins* (Minneapolis: Fortress Press, 1988), 351-376. Even Boyarin (*Border Lines: The Partition of Judaeo-Christianity* [Philadelphia: University of Pennsylvania Press]), whose work deconstructs the theological uniqueness of Christianity, upholds a certain exceptionalism—particularly in his claim that the invention of religion disembedded from culture is Christian."

history. But the nodes of empire and queerness tie together a whole host of fears, complaints, and yearnings about our own collusions in power, and these nodes can be engaged more scrupulously.

Puar's *Terrorist Assemblages* is full of cautionary tales, as well as numerous compact creative propositions for rethinking social life, whether ancient or contemporary. For one, Puar puts affect to work with the Deleuzian notion of assemblages,[15] assuming a fully diffuse concept of subjectivity. She suggests that even more complicated models of identity like intersectionality, which theorizes the collusion of various systems of domination and focuses on multiple, intersecting forms of categorical difference, actually miss new fissions and fusions of gender, sexuality, and race that arise in an atmosphere of U.S. sexual exceptionalism and homonationalism.[16] Demonstrating the limits of identity and intersectional analyses, Puar suggests re-

---

15. As I understand it, the term *assemblage*, as described in Gilles Deleuze and Felix Guarttari's *A Thousand Plateaus: Capitalism and Schizophrenia*, translation and foreword by Brian Massumi (Minneapolis: University of Minnesota Press, 1987), refers to heterogeneous conglomerations and patched together elements that form entities, events, and even complex agencies. The term emphasizes dispersion, miscellany, and change.
16. Following Massumi, Puar suggests that intersectionality still assumes a certain solidity of categories, and forces the inchoate confusion and momentary contingencies of identity into stabilizing frameworks: "As opposed to an intersectional model of identity, which presumes that components—race, class, gender, sexuality, nation, age, religion—are separable analytics and can thus be disassembled, an assemblage is more attuned to interwoven forces that merge and dissipate time, space, and body against linearity, coherency, and permanency. Intersectionality demands the knowing, naming, and thus stabilizing of identity across space and time, relying on the logic of equivalence and analogy between various axes of identity and generating narratives of progress that deny the fictive and performative aspects of identification: you become an identity, yes, but also timelessness works to consolidate the fiction of a seamless stable identity in every space. Furthermore, the study of intersectional identities often involves taking imbricated identities apart one by one to see how they influence each other, a process that betrays the founding impulse of intersectionality, that identities cannot be so easily cleaved. We can think of intersectionality as a hermeneutic of *positionality* that seeks to account for locality, specificity, placement, junctions. As a tool of diversity management and a mantra of liberal multiculturalism, intersectionality colludes with the disciplinary apparatus of the state—census, demography, racial profiling, surveillance—in that 'difference' in encased within a structural container that simply wishes the messiness of identity into a formulaic grid, producing analogies in its wake and engendering what Massumi names 'gridlock': a 'box[ing] into its site on the culture map'" Puar, *Terrorist Assemblages*, 212. Massumi, *Parables for the Virtual: Movement, Affect, Sensation* (Durham, NC: Duke University Press, 2002), 3.

thinking queerness *as* assemblage, which "moves away from excavation work, deprivileges a binary opposition between queer and not-queer subjects, and, instead of retaining queerness exclusively as dissenting, resistant, and alternative (all of which queerness importantly is and does), it underscores contingency and complicity within dominant formations."[17] An assemblage is an "affective conglomeration that recognizes other contingencies of belonging," a "series of dispersed but mutually implicated and messy networks," which foregrounds the receptions and receptiveness of bodies, the production of populations, and new modes of belonging that do not just cross but effectively scramble identity categories.[18]

The language of affect and assemblage would seem to address Judith Lieu's worry about the lack of precision of the term *identity* for describing social self-understanding in the ancient world. Lieu fumbles for language in and around the texts she studies, and indeed repeats variations of a particular locution: a "sense of identity" ("a sense of being Christian," "a sense of Jewishness"). If identity has the effect of fixity, something like the "sense of identity" may very well kill some of that effect. A "sense of identity" lends a vagueness to terms that would otherwise convey clarity, however constructed. Lieu's repetition of "sense," cast through the glass of affect, offhandedly evokes things like prickly skin sensations, bodily extensions in space, charged affinities to certain people or things, and other indistinct aspects of subjective/collective experience, the momentary incidents and confusions of which muddle identity's implied locational grid.[19]

17. Ibid., 205.
18. Ibid., 211.
19. As Brian Massumi writes, "The body came to be defined by its pinning to a grid. Proponents of this model often cited its ability to link body-sites into a 'geography' of culture that tempered the universalizing tendencies of ideology. The sites, it is true, are multiple. But aren't they still combinatorial permutations on an overarching definitional framework?...Is the body as linked to a particular subject position anything more than a local embodiment *of* ideology? Where has

If we take analyses of social formations and power seriously, mimicking the imperial will-to-knowledge through the precise charting of subject positions and locations may not be very useful, as Puar suggests.[20] But like Lieu, Lieu's colleagues in the Christian identity crowd have already begun to recount such alternate ways to think about ancient sociality within or between the lines of their more explicitly subject-centered work. The picture of associational life drawn collectively by Richard Ascough, Hal Taussig, and Philip Harland is already one of a "sense" of belonging rather than obvious boundedness anyway. Social life was "permeable" and involved "multiple group belonging," a belonging that was "elaborated" and "negotiated," and often imbued with an erotic charge.[21] Add in the possibility that these ostensibly Christian groups had a basically circumstantial relationship to Christ and an often reticent, or even non-existent, relationship to each other,[22] then what we have is exactly, as Puar suggests, "a series of dispersed but mutually implicated and messy networks" where any number of specified

---

the potential for change gone?...How can the grid itself change?..." Massumi, *Parables for the Virtual*, 2-3. Massumi is thus theorizing how to restore movement to theories of embodiment, i.e., taking seriously the poststructuralist interest in the radical instability of the body, though through a Deleuzian affective framework.

20. Puar, Ibid., 203-222.
21. Taussig is particularly fond of the terms elaboration and negotiation. On the erotic charge of the meal, see Jennifer A. Glancy, "Notes on Early Christian Responses to Corporeality, Intimacy and Sexuality in Dining Culture" (paper presented at the annual meeting of the Society of Biblical Literature, Meals in the Greco-Roman World Seminar, New Orleans, La., November 2009). Glancy importantly notes a wider tradition of early Christian defensiveness about the intimate and sexual elements of the symposial setting. Cf. Carly Daniel-Hughes "The Sex Trade and Slavery at Meals" (paper presented at the Society of Biblical Literature Annual Conference, Meals in the Greco-Roman World Seminar, Boston, Mass., November 2008) and "Bodies at Rest, Bodies in Motion: Status, Corporeality, Sexuality and Negotiations of Power at Ancient Meals" (paper presented at the annual meeting of the Society of Biblical Literature, Meals in the Greco-Roman World Seminar, New Orleans, La., November 2009). On the affective context of the symposial meal of the Corinthians, see Maia Kotrosits, "The Rhetoric of Intimate Spaces: Affect and Performance in the Corinthian Correspondence," *USQR* 62, no. 3-4 (2011): 134-51.
22. Ascough, "Translocal Relationships Among Voluntary Associations and Early Christianity," *Journal of Early Christian Studies* 5:2 (1997): 223-241.

articulations of belonging are born, intensify, or die. One might perhaps notice the looseness of connection implied by the word *association* itself, or even that *assemblage* bears more than a minor resemblance to the meaning of the word *ekklesia*.[23]

This is not to say that identity and interpellation analytics are without their uses. The sudden imperial ethnography on Christians in this period and its beginning use as a self-designation may very well validate those models, however epistemologically compromised, to an extent.[24] But identity has a way of crowding out other models for understanding belonging, social relationships, and circuits of power.[25] When identity is the primary object in view, it curbs our capacity to understand the deep but indefinite sociality of self-

---

23. Thanks to Brigitte Kahl for noticing this. Though *ekklesia* is often translated as "church," Philip Harland, Hal Taussig, and other members of the SBL seminar on Greco-Roman meals, in line with its ancient uses, treat this as simply common language for associational social gatherings. Taussig, *In the Beginning Was the Meal Social Experimentation and Early Christian Identity* (Minneapolis: Fortress Press, 2009), and Harland *Associations, Synagogues and Congregations: Claiming a Place in Ancient Mediterranean Society* (Minneapolis: Fortress Press, 2003).

24. I mean, what is not epistemologically compromised? I am simply pushing back here against the ironic naturalization of identity as an optic for understanding social relations.

25. Part of what Boyarin and Karen King have shown is that even in texts for which "constructing identity" is a vehement enterprise (heresiological literature, e.g.), the connections and affiliations between ostensibly separate groups were (are) still operating in complex and quite unpredictable ways. While Boyarin's *Border Lines* and *Dying for God: Martyrdom and the Making of Christianity and Judaism* (Stanford: Stanford University Press, 1999) both track the intricate entanglements between what are later termed "Judaism" and "Christianity," *Border Lines* suggests the very categories of orthodoxy/heresy are a covert and almost ironic shared heritage of Christian and Jewish self-definition. In *Dying for God*, Boyarin proposes a late antique turn toward specifically martyrological discourse as the shared field through which Jewish and Christian identities articulated themselves. King's work at large surfaces close resonances and tight differentiations between social groups and their texts, highlighting their struggles to answer the same difficult questions, such as how to approach gender and women's leadership (*The Gospel of Mary of Magdala: Jesus and the First Woman Apostle*. [Santa Rosa: Polebridge Press, 2003]), how to make sense of a world that has strayed from one's own ideals and is run by corrupt rulers (*The Secret Revelation of John* [Cambridge: Harvard University Press, 2006]), and how to cope with persecution ("Toward a Discussion of the Category of 'Gnosis/Gnosticism': The Case of the *Epistle of Peter to Philip*" in *Jesus in apokryphen Evangelienüberlieferungen: Beiträge zu ausserkanonischen Jesusüberlieferungen aus verschiedenen Sprach- und Kulturtraditionen*, ed. Jörg Frey, Jens Schröter, and Jakob Spaeth [Tübingen: Mohr Siebeck, 2010], 445-65. Cf. also Karen King and Elaine Pagels, *Reading Judas: The Gospel of Judas and the Shaping of Christianity* (New York: Viking, 2007).

understanding, the accidents of proximal relations, and the haphazard mobility of collectives.

For instance, the correspondence between the governor Pliny and the emperor Trajan, in which Pliny asks what he should do about those hard-to-locate but superstitious Christians and the rumors being spread about them (Pliny, *Ep.* 10.96-97), is regularly cited in order to produce a distinct constituency of troublesome and pious believers. Among other things in this exchange, Pliny claims that while he is not sure exactly how concerned to be about Christians, he has figured out that torturing a few people named as "Christians" sure whips the larger public back into shape (i.e., traditional cultic practice) quickly. But rather than reading Pliny as testifying to the subversiveness and counter-imperial practices of Christians in Asia Minor, Harland and Ascough suggest that this exchange actually deconstructs notions of Christians as either unique or comprising a universal constituency. Harland sees this exchange as demonstrating how very ordinary Christians were in terms of their practice and being on the receiving end of the slander of "superstition."[26] Ascough reads Pliny's concern about the desertion of temples quite locally, suggesting that there was an interruption of local merchants' business due to the regional popularity of Christian associations.[27] It is not a given, however, that Christian associations are so popular that they are driving people away from temples. It could be that the return to local temples after the punishment of some named as "Christians" may be more about the general worry or fear of retribution amongst those who were now more interested in showing their relationships to traditional cults.[28] If it is true that this specific exchange shows the unexceptional and local nature of Christian associations, then it is

---

26. Harland, *Dynamics of Identity*, 42-43.
27. Ascough, Ibid., 241.
28. Joseph J. Walsh, "On Christian Atheism" *VC* 45, no. 3 (1991): 255-77 (259).

quite possibly overemphasized with respect to other portions of the correspondence. Maybe the most illuminating portion of this Pliny/Trajan exchange for "Christian identity" is that it makes no mention of Christians at all.

In fact, Pliny shows concern not just over Christians, but associations at large. He asks whether there should be a guild of fire fighters, for example, which includes the seemingly peripheral promise that he will take care to ensure no one who is not a fireman joins such a guild. Trajan unilaterally refuses, noting how quickly such associations drift away from their ostensible purposes and become political.[29] Trajan seems to be worried about associations because their composition is not manageable from an imperial standpoint. Is it this very mixing of people, this mobility of affiliation, that gives them a "political" valence? Given the kind of broad imperial demands placed on associations and their gatherings—requiring libations be made to the emperor, occasional bans on associations, regulations on who could join associations[30]—Rome's relationship to associations shows, more than anything, angst about the general conundrums of loyalty and affiliation.

The question remains, then: how might we understand the indeterminate quality of associations alongside the apparent identification of "Christian" evoked by Pliny? The new appearance of "Christians" on the imperial map may not be explicable solely through Acts' apologetic that this is simply a very popular and attractive movement. People get fused together in multitudes of queer ways without any kind of chosen or shared self-understanding.

---

29. Pliny *Ep.* 10.33-34.
30. Cf. Taussig, Ibid., 118-25; and Wendy Cotter, "The Collegia and Roman Law: State Restrictions on Voluntary Associations, 64 BCE-200 CE," in *Voluntary Associations in the Graeco-Roman World*, ed. John S. Kloppenborg and Stephen G. Wilson (London: Routledge, 1996), 74-89.

One word for this is "racializing."[31] Are there truly ready-made Christians, understanding themselves as such, hiding out everywhere around the Mediterranean, negotiating survival as a new cult? It rather seems that the appearance of the term "Christian" in this particular period represents a standard and imperializing tactic of grabbing onto rhetoric and applying identity categories where the messiness of belonging fails to produce any obvious delinquents.[32]

The modern waxing on Christian identity reflects the imperial problem: Who are "these people"? What are "they" about? How can we understand this as a movement? How do we pinpoint groups with hard-to-define loyalties? Christians as historically queer is one possible answer, but the very questions over-determine the answers. Even aside from the ideological problems of exceptionalism that plague the notion of historically queer Christians, the rhetoric of queerness in the ancient world encompassed a huge swath of sexual and ethnographic discourses on peoples (Amazons, Jews, Gauls, etc.), making the notion that "Christians" were a kind of specifically queer group hard to claim as a specified historical description.[33]

In other words, the people we want to call "early Christians" do have a kind of queerness about them, but only if we abandon the idea of their uniqueness and their transgressiveness. Their social life

---

31. Again, this relies on her redefinition of queer-as-assemblage, focusing on mobility, populations rather than individuals, and both subversion and complicity within social formations, against notions of queer as only subversive or associated with particular subjects.
32. Since the term *christianus* is a Greek word with a Latin suffix, the term may very well have originated in an imperial context. The suffix tends to indicate "belongs to," which is a kind of possessive, and was often used with reference to students of particular teachers. Tertullian thus parallels the moniker with Epicurians and Platonists. Tertullian, *Apology* 3. Cf. Elias J. Bickerman, "The Name of the Christians," *HTR* 42, no. 2 (1949): 109-24.
33. See Trebilco, *The Early Christians in Ephesus*, 554-57, on the internalization of an "outward-facing" designation. Again, I am not separating sexual and ethnographic discourses in part because of the racializing dynamic of "queering" of certain populations (ancient and modern) who are seen as a threat to life/civilization, as well as the tendency for Romans in particular to represent conquest of ethnically-specified people in terms of sexual penetration. Cf. Davina Lopez, *Apostle to the Conquered*; and Joseph Marchal, "Bio-Necro-*Biblio*-Politics?: Restaging Feminist Intersections and Queer Exceptions" in *Culture and Religion* 15, no. 2 (2014): 166-76.

could hardly be classified as transgressing anything but our own contemporary stakes in identifying them.[34] That is to say that the historical queerness of Christians is fairly unexceptional.

This inquiry into theoretical problems with distinct or queer content to "Christian identity" provokes a re-reading of some of the signal texts for demonstrating the presence of a particular and troublesome Christian identity. In the rest of this chapter, I will be addressing 1 Peter and the letters of Ignatius.[35] While both 1 Peter and Ignatius use the word "Christian," and both discuss pain and suffering at some length, "Christian" figures quite differently in each text, and it is far from obvious that 1 Peter and Ignatius fit the usual narratives that there were people in this period targeted for an already assumed Christian identity. Read through affective and diasporic lenses, what these texts offer instead of an account of Christians is an understanding of the more fractal ways violence might have generated the conditions of possibility for a *later* "sense" of Christian belonging. Even more importantly, I think, they illustrate the various and terrifying distortions and new vectors of sociality that occur when the recalcitrance of national belonging meets colonial losses and violence.

*   *   *   *

In a short, public audience article on 1 Peter, Paul Achtemeier narrates a broad context in which to place the text:

> Large size is not always an advantage. This was especially true of the nascent Christian movement toward the end of the first century A.D. During its initial decades, it had been a small movement, often confused

---

34. I do not mean to say that no Christians have ever participated in transgressive social practices. Rather, I am trying to deconstruct the idea of "Christian" practices as somehow distinctly transgressive.
35. I will be re-reading Acts along these lines in chapter 3.

with the Judaism from which it sprang, regularly ignored. But its popularity fueled a steady growth, until the point was reached when people realized Christians had a radically different set of values than the ordinary resident of the Roman Empire. At that point, a radically conformist society began to demand of the Christians that they act like anyone else in their neighborhoods—taking part in festivals that included sacrificing to local gods, sharing in banquets where the meat served came from animals sacrificed to pagan deities, burning a pinch of incense before a bust of the emperor and declaring "Caesar is Lord"—things faithful Christians could not do. It got to the point where even the title "Christian" was enough to generate hostility.[36]

Without using the word "queer," Achtemeier tells the story of a non-conformist movement with an initially "confused" or confusing identity. He is writing about the history leading up to 1 Peter, a turn-of-the-century text that contains one of the earliest known evocations of the word "Christian." But while Achtemeier's subtext may be queer, his story is hardly unorthodox, and its individual elements are echoed by scores of other scholars: 1 Peter represents communication between people who primarily identify as Christians, whether Jewish or gentile, and the theme of suffering in the letter suggests that they are suffering as Christians (meaning suffering for being Christians), whether in households[37] or in the framework of Roman persecution.[38] These Christians are distinctive for their counter-cultural values,[39] and 1 Peter represents a compromise of those ethics in order to conform to Greco-Roman behavioral

---

36. Achtemeier, "Between Text and Sermon: 1 Peter 1: 13-21," *Interpretation* 60:3 (July 2006): 306-308, esp. 306.
37. Cf. David Balch, "Hellenization/Acculturation in 1 Peter," in *Perspectives on First Peter*, ed. Charles H. Talbert. (Macon: Mercer University Press, 1986), 81-101.
38. Cf. Boris A. Paschke, "The Roman ad bestias Execution as a Possible Historical Background for 1 Peter 5:8," *JSN* 28, no. 4 (2006): 489-500.
39. Cf. Balch, "Hellenization/Acculturation in 1 Peter"; Achtemeier, "Between Text and Sermon: 1 Peter 1: 13-21"; and Charles H. Talbert, "Once Again: the Plan of 1 Peter," in *Perspectives on First Peter*, 41-51.

standards (as seen in the household codes) because of outside pressure.[40]

The story of persecution and counter-cultural resistances has understandably felt a little too romantic to some. For instance, Ben Dunning worries that scholarship has taken the appeals in 1 Peter to an alien and outsider status far too literally.[41] Placing himself as a Foucaultian/New Historicist reader of texts as cultural poetics, Dunning instead understands the letter as part of a larger discourse of Christian identity that constructs the Christian self as other/outsider in ancient Mediterranean culture. Indeed, Dunning not only means to temper socio-historical scholarship and its attempts to sketch an actual social location for the audience of 1 Peter by treating the language of "aliens" and "outsiders" as literal or legal descriptions. He also seeks to interrupt the narrative of a low and outside Christian identity that inevitably finds its way to the very privileged center of the Roman Empire.

While Dunning does not oppose his rhetorical work to socio-historical work on "grids" and "groups," he does cast it as a more careful consideration of the text and its possible relationships to the people implied by the text.[42] Yet because the term "Christian" is never scrutinized for its own socio-historical interests or implicit referentiality, there still remains in Dunning's reconstruction of ancient rhetoric a *historical Christian identity*.

---

40. Lieu, *Neither Jew Nor Greek? Constructing Early Christianity* (London: T & T Clark International, 2002), 182.
41. Benjamin H. Dunning, *Aliens and Sojourners: Self as Other in Early Christianity*. (Philadelphia: University of Pennsylvania Press, 2009), 1-24. He comments largely on John Elliot's *A Home for the Homeless: A Sociological Exegesis of 1 Peter, Its Situation and Strategy* (Eugene, OR: Wipf and Stock, 2005). However, Dunning also worries that metaphorical readings of the outsider language in 1 Peter do not fully appreciate the ways this language might work for those who employ it.
42. Ibid., 14. Dunning quite moderately imagines a scenario in which one might be able to draw concrete sociological conclusions about an ancient audience, but notes that the sources required to do this work are "sadly lacking."

The idea that the sender and recipient of the letter should be seen as identifying as Christians, however, hits more than a few bumps in the road. On the most basic level, 1 Peter contains near-constant appeals to the scripture, tropes, and rhetorical strategies of ancient Israel.[43] It is fictively attributed to Peter known as the "apostle to the circumcised" (cf. Gal. 2:8) who is supposedly writing from Babylon (Israel's encoded reference to Rome). It seems worth considering that the explicit recourse to exile, foreignness, and diaspora are not just rhetorical adjustments on or appropriations for a Christian self-understanding,[44] especially since the only time the word "Christian" is used it is a tiny and circumstantial notation: "those suffering as Christians" is only listed in the letter as one of among many kinds of suffering (such as slaves being treated cruelly by masters in 2:19, and intra-community abuse in 3:9).[45] Israel is the organizing concept for the people in 1 Peter, as 2:9-12 so vehemently demonstrates:[46]

> But you are a chosen race, a royal priesthood, a holy nation, God's own people, in order that you may proclaim the mighty acts of him who called you out of darkness into his marvelous light. Once you were not a people, but now you are God's people; once you had not received mercy, but now you have received mercy. Beloved, I urge you as aliens

---

43. Elisabeth Schüssler Fiorenza, "The First Letter of Peter," in *A Postcolonial Commentary on the New Testament Writings*, ed. Fernando Segovia and R. S. Sugirtharajah (Bloomsbury: T & T Clark, 2009), 380-403. Schüssler Fiorenza nonetheless participates in this identity-based debate by claiming the recipients are Jewish Christians.
44. Most crucially, perhaps, the text is addressed to the "chosen exiles of the diaspora" (*parepidemos diasporas*) (v. 1). However, see also 2:9-12, which I discuss below.
45. As Denise Buell suggests, "While the term *christianos* appears as a charge for which a reader might suffer (1 Peter 4:16), there is no indication that it is either the term readers used for themselves or that this term marked collective belonging apart from Judaism." See Denise Kimber Buell, "God's Own People: Specters of Race, Ethnicity and Gender in Early Christian Studies," in *Prejudice and Christian Beginnings: Investigating Race, Gender, and Ethnicity in Early Christian Studies*, ed. Laura Nasrallah and Elisabeth Schüssler Fiorenza (Minneapolis: Fortress Press, 2009), 159-90, 182.
46. Schüssler Fiorenza, "First Letter of Peter," 388. Philip Harland similarly describes the way in which the author of 1 Peter "draws heavily on Judean ethnic identities," however he sees this as being put to use "to express self-understanding of these non-Judean (gentile) followers of Jesus" (*Dynamics of Identity*, 17).

and exiles [*paroikous kai parepidemous*] to abstain from the desires of the flesh that wage war against the soul. Conduct yourselves honorably among the gentiles, so that, though they malign you as evildoers, they may see your honorable deeds and glorify God when he comes to judge.

Taking the language of diaspora literally or referentially on certain levels doesn't mean it cannot also be read rhetorically on others, of course. In fact I would like to highlight some of the diasporic rhetoric in 1 Peter so as to intervene constructively not only in the older questions about whether 1 Peter is directed at "gentile Christians" or "Jewish Christians," and 1 Peter's place in the story of a queer constituency gone straight, but also in the notion that 1 Peter invests itself in Christian belonging at all. The somewhat simple premise of taking 1 Peter's language of exile and diaspora at face value gives way to more complicated accounts of belonging and violence, both in 1 Peter and at large.

Even though 1 Peter assumes an audience of diasporic Israel, there is still a sense of contingency of belonging, and the hinge on which this belonging rests is obedience. While some have suggested that the apparent cultural accommodations in the text are survival strategies, this is at odds with the claims of the author of the letter, since this good behavior does not preserve them from harm at all. It simply vindicates them in the eyes of their god and makes their abusers look foolish (e.g., 2:29-20; 3:17-20). 1 Peter does not see pain and abuse as avoidable, so what kind of "survival" would these ostensible compromises effect? Of course, this good behavior supports a survival of the Christian name and/or reputation, some argue.[47] But again, "those suffering as Christians" is only listed in the letter as one of among many kinds of suffering.

Throughout chapter 2 of the letter, the goading towards obedience is interlaced with the language of chosenness, throwing an additional

---

47. Lieu, *Neither Jew Nor Greek?* 182.

wrench into the idea that the obedience demanded by the household codes and the imperative to honor the emperor are some kind of survivalist accommodation. In fact, in 1 Peter 2:9, 2:13, 2:15, and 2:20, Israel's god is implicated in the calls to obedience. Even alongside the rhetoric of living "among gentiles" (2:12) and having escaped from living "like gentiles" (4:3), the author casts their Israelite exceptionalism in a gentile mold. More specifically, in the section forbidding adornments on women in chapter 3, "Peter" writes: "It was in this way long ago that the holy women who hoped in God used to adorn themselves by accepting the authority of their husbands. Thus Sarah obeyed Abraham and called him lord. You have become [Sarah's] daughters doing what is good, not fearing intimidation" (v. 6). These women have earned a precarious place in Israel as Sarah's daughters, but it is a place dependent upon their obedience and submission to the values of the household codes.[48] If these household codes are deeply Greco-Roman in form and moral orientation as some have suggested,[49] how is it that *conforming* to them has earned these women a crucial spot among Israel's chosen?

The language of chosenness and turning away from gentile practices amidst a *collusion* of Israel's chosenness with gentile practices represents a familiar course for diaspora belonging. Diaspora belonging is always expressed through dominant values and discourse from the start, captivated by the ideological mapping of colonial territorialization.[50] In fact, the very project of reconstitution of

---

48. There is nothing specifically anti-Greco-Roman about the prohibition to adorn, since, as Alicia Batten has found, there is already a certain Greco-Roman cultural ambivalence around women's adornment. Alicia Batten, "Neither Gold nor Braided Hair (1 Timothy 2:9; 1 Peter 3.3): Adornment, Gender and Honour in Antiquity," *NTS* 55, no. 4 (2009): 484–501.
49. Most influentially, Elisabeth Schüssler Fiorenza, *In Memory of Her: A Feminist Theological Reconstruction of Christian Origins* (New York: Crossroad, 1994).
50. Hall describes how part of the work entails "imposing an imaginary coherence on the experience of dispersal and fragmentation." See Stuart Hall, "Cultural Identity and Diaspora," in Braziel and Mannur, *Theorizing Diaspora* (Malden, Mass: Blackwell Publishing, 2003), 234–35.

diaspora identity is a project of creating underlying unity, as Stuart Hall suggests, in order to "restore an imaginary fullness or plenitude to set against the broken rubric of [the] past."[51] Reflecting on black Caribbean self-understanding, Hall writes that, while so much effort and creativity has been spent by colonized peoples trying to "recover" and "research" an identity that has been "distorted" by colonization, cultural identity is made in the recovery process itself. He notes, "What we share is precisely the experience of profound discontinuity…it was the uprooting of slavery and transportation and the insertion into the plantation economy (as well as the symbolic economy) of the Western world that 'unified' these peoples across their difference, in the same moment as it cut them off from direct access to their past."[52] Diaspora belonging is engendered less by a shared past before colonization or an originating geography than by a similar positioning vis-à-vis the West.

More to the affective point, however, Hall also discusses Africa as an essentialized place of origin for those in the African diaspora, one which gathers intense affective and figurative value. It is a place that cannot be returned to, strictly speaking, at the very least because it risks reifying the western image of Africa as primitive and frozen in time. In diaspora, one's loyalties are necessarily doubled and conflated, ever in unexpected ways—even through claims to origins, purity, continuity, or exclusive loyalty over and against a dominant culture. For Hall, "the origin" in diaspora belonging is not always or necessarily a place; it is, however, a "reservoir of representation," an "imaginary plenitude."[53]

This is to say that engagement in diasporic rhetoric indicates less some kind of social-locational specificity than a felt reality and set

---

51. Ibid., 235-36.
52. Ibid., 238.
53. Ibid., 245.

of relational triangulations. The question of whether the audience in 1 Peter might be understood as "Jewish" or "gentile," for instance, ignores the basic assumption that even the very term "gentile" (which I further complicate in the next chapter) denotes that this is Israel's own discourse. Like all discourses of diaspora in which the question of who "really" belongs is endlessly debatable, since "gentile" and "Jew" were imagined, negotiable, even overlapping designations.[54]

There may also be ways to think about the pain, violence, and collectivity in 1 Peter, and Christ's relationship to them, without assuming either a collective Christian identity, or that there is some sort of rebellious threat to imperial status quo igniting revenge.[55] Not only is the kind of pain referenced in 1 Peter fairly diverse, but disproportionately severe, random, and preemptive violence were par for the course at this moment in the Roman Empire.[56] What if, for instance, Christ was not the cause for their pain, but the lens through which they organized and focused it?[57] The repetition of "in Christ" and "through Christ" in the letter already gestures toward Christ as a kind of capacity or productive space, rather than simply an object of

---

54. Shaye Cohen has shown with rather specific illustrations a number of the ways the gentile/Jew boundary was confused or crossed, and this involved not just expressing loyalty to Israel's god, but also to becoming a member of a Jewish community (through slavery, for example) without any kind of conversion, per se. What Cohen makes abundantly clear, however, is that these boundaries were not by any means hard and fast, and usually involved community negotiations (with sometimes unclear results). They are, in short, anecdotally particular. See his "Crossing the Boundary and Becoming a Jew," *HTR* 82, no. 1 (1989): 13-33.
55. Many scholars may be quick to say that there were no widespread persecutions of "Christians" by the imperium at the time of 1 Peter. However, they nonetheless often hold to the assumption that the main suffering in 1 Peter is about being a "Christian" and thus an outsider. Cf. Gerald Downing "Pliny's Prosecution of the Christians: Revelation and 1 Peter," *JSNT* 34 (1988): 105-23; and Achtemeier, "1 Peter 1:13-21."
56. See the following works: Thomas Africa, "Urban Violence in Imperial Rome," *The Journal of Interdisciplinary History* 2, no. 1 (1971): 3-21; John H. Elliott, *1 Peter: A New Translation with Introduction and Commentary*, The Anchor Yale Bible Commentaries (New York: Random House, 2000), 94-102; and John Dominic Crossan, *The Historical Jesus: The Life of a Mediterranean Jewish Peasant* (New York: HarperOne, 1993), 168-206.
57. Hal Taussig and I elaborate on the notion of Jesus as a lens for focusing pain at length in our co-authored monograph, *Re-reading the Gospel of Mark Amidst Loss and Trauma* (New York: Palgrave Macmillan, 2013).

piety or worship (though I certainly would not want to make those mutually exclusive).[58] As an affectively jammed site of investment, Christ is a figure for (in this case) pain, estrangement and grandiosity, one effect of which is a consolidation not only of the legendary, if conditional, aggregate of Israel, but also of imperial-belonging.

The feedback loop between violence and belonging is a complicated one, and is probably least well understood through recourse to chicken-or-egg theories of causation and identity. Even when identity is evoked in the injury, torture, or murder of people, it serves no one to claim that the relationship is straightforward—particularly in the case of something like popular imaginations of Christian martyrdom, in which violence is refigured (not unproblematically) to fortify moral triumphalism, whether as innocence or its subtler equivalent, pure subversion.

The Pliny-Trajan correspondence has taken on a kind of assumed relationship to the death and writings of Ignatius of Antioch, for example, and produced an imagination that Ignatius dies in Rome, under Trajan, for being a Christian. This is derived from the account of Eusebius,[59] for whom the interest in Christian martyrs and his alliances with Constantine already produces its own acute questions about the mutual investments, affective and otherwise, of empire and innocence.[60] Ignatius's death under the apparent persecution of

---

58. Cf. 1 Pet. 1:3, 21; 3:16, 21; 4:11; 5:10, 14.
59. Eusebius, *Hist. eccl.* 3.22.36. Skeptical of Eusebius's account, R. H. Hübner and Thomas Lechner have suggested a late second century dating and pseudepigraphal status for Ignatius's letters. Hübner, "Thesen zur Echtheit und Datierung der sieben Briefe des Ignatius von Antiochien," ZAC, 1 no. 1 (1997): 44-72; and Lechner, *Ignatius Adversus Valentinianos? Chronologische und Theologiegeschichtliche Studien zu den Briefen des Ignatius von Antiochien*, (Leiden: Brill, 1999).
60. I am indebted to a conversation with Richard Ascough for this thought. I am unsure which of us said this, probably him. I find Jeremy Schott's work on the rhetorical and postcolonial dynamics of the "Christianizing of the Roman Empire" very helpful. See Schott, *Christianity, Empire and the Making of Religion in Late Antiquity* (Philadelphia: University of Pennsylvania Press, 2008). Eusebius, in the *Life of Constantine*, reports that Constantine ends persecutions and praises martyrs for their endurance. Eusebius is, among other things, trying to portray Constantine as less tyrannical than previous imperators, so it would seem that he is using

Christians by Trajan is historically unpersuasive not only because of Eusebius's various agendas, but because Trajan is hardly bothered by the Christians; the problem is Pliny's, and Pliny doesn't seem to have any trouble killing people off himself. He sends only Roman citizens to Rome, and it is unlikely they would be sentenced, like Ignatius, to die so spectacularly in the arena.[61] Trajan says nothing in this or any other public record available that would indicate an interest in executing "Christians" in the arena. In fact, in this exchange, he even specifies that the "Christians are not to be hunted out." So either some informal process has changed by the time Ignatius is (in his words) "condemned," or he is condemned for some reason that is not quite about being a Christian.

In fact, Ignatius never quite says he dies for being a Christian.[62] How Ignatius associates his death with Christ and Christianity

---

contrast to full effect here. Cf. Schott's discussion (122-26) of how Eusebius's larger tactic is also showing the consonance of empire and Christianity from their nearly contemporaneous inception. What I am curious about is not so much the overt discourse of consonance between Eusebius's Christianity and empire, but rather what kind of affective implications might be drawn from the work of Eusebius in describing an imperial Christianity with emphasis on martyrdom.

61. Romans had more respectful punishments, since the Valerian laws established during the Roman Republic offered special protections for those who had Roman citizenship (see also Acts 22:25).

62. Ignatius states that he is being brought to Syria "on behalf of the name and hope that we share" (*uper tou koinou onomatos* . . .), although the Loeb edition of Ignatius has this translated as "because." To die as a representative of, or on behalf of, is not the same as being executed *for* something, and notably he does not say what that name is. It is not that being a "Christian" is the *cause* of his death, but rather it seems it is that he represents the name of Jesus Christ in his death, just as he states elsewhere: "My chains exhort you; I bear them on account of Jesus Christ" (*Trall.* 12.2). The inflections of these statements will be explored below. Other places where Ignatius evokes "the name" without naming the name are: *Eph.* 7.1, and *Magn.* 1.2. In *Magn.* 10.1, he states, "For this reason, since we are his disciples, let us learn to live according to Christianity. For whoever is called by a name other than this does not belong to God." Again, the referent of "this name" is not entirely clear, since it does not seem that "Christianity" is a name. In the greeting to the letter to the Romans, he speaks of an *ekklesia* that "bears the name of the Father." When he does talk about "being Christians," it is not in the context of his death, but rather in the context of obedience to the bishop (*Magn.* 4.1). It may be that Ignatius is read through the lens of later martyrological scripts and narratives (the *Christianus sum*, e.g.), which themselves are not transparent accounts of events.

(*christianismos*) has a remarkable subtlety and resourcefulness about it that is lost in a reading of Ignatius as an early stop on the path towards orthodoxy and standardized martyrological narratives. While the timing of Ignatius's death is not otherwise verifiable, entertaining the relative concurrence of Ignatius's letters and the Pliny-Trajan correspondence does provide some material for re-casting the relationship of violence and Christian belonging.

* * * *

> "And so it is fitting not only to be called Christians [*christianoi*], but also to be Christians . . ." (Ign. *Magn.* 4.1).

> "It is outlandish to speak Jesus Christ and judaize [*ioudaïzein*]. For Christianity [*christianismos*] did not believe in Judaism [*ioudaïsmos*], but Judaism in Christianity—in which every tongue that believes in God has been gathered together" (Ign. *Magn.* 10.3)

In Ignatius's letter to the Magnesians, he crafts a number of temporally and otherwise counter-intuitive formulations. Not only does he claim that the most godly prophets of Israel were persecuted for "living according to Jesus Christ" (Mag. 8.2), but also that "judaism" believed in "christianity." What we might take those two terms to mean, and, more precisely, what Ignatius means by them, seem to be the more prominent questions these days, rather than why Ignatius makes this formulation or what immediate effect it has. The reason for this is that Ignatius's ontological prioritizing of "christianity" over "judaism" and his re-reading of Israel's prophetic history through Jesus Christ ring as straightforward supersessionism and fulfillment theology, the latter histories of which include many subtle reinforcements and breathtaking damage. What more could there be to say about that?

But it is worth separating the long-term ideological effects of Ignatius's words from their more proximate affects, at least to restore some of the dynamism and creativity of Ignatius's letters, if not also to shake off some of our doomed sense of inevitability regarding supersessionism. Indeed, apart from the ready interpretations of martyrdom and supersessionism, Ignatius' letters mark an awfully queer slip of history in the sense that his inversions of time and his flamboyant imagination are eventually conscripted into, and even become, a new imperial normativity. While this conscription is not totally accidental, neither is it an expected development resulting from an embedded ideological program in Ignatius's letters: it rather points to the surprising force of affect—especially the affectivity that coalesces around violence—in binding and rending collectives.

Ignatius's always already existent Christianity is only possible through the merging of various, if sometimes linked, imperial cruelties.[63] As Lieu finds, *christianismos* in Ignatius's writing appears as something of a counterpart to *ioudaïsmos,* though she also notes that "Jew" and "Christian" are not used oppositionally in Ignatius.[64] *Ioudaismos,* first seen in the literature associated with the Maccabees, is evoked not as a distinct religion per se, but rather as the abstracted entity justifying—in the sense of giving purpose and meaning to—one's murder, patterned on the "noble death" literary tradition.[65]

---

63. Ignatius is also apparently challenged on his archaizing techniques. In *Phil.* 8-9 he writes, "For I heard some saying, 'If I do not find it in the ancient records, I do not believe in the gospel.' And when I said to them, 'It is written,' they replied to me, 'That is just the question.' But for me, Jesus Christ is the ancient records; the sacred ancient records are his cross and death, and his resurrection, and the faith that comes through him—by which things I long to be made righteous by your prayer. The priests are good, but the high priest who has been entrusted with the holy of holies is better; he alone is entrusted with the hidden things that belong to God. He is the door of the Father, through which Abraham and Isaac and Jacob and the prophets and the apostles and the church enter."

64. Lieu, *Christian Identity in the Jewish and Graeco-Roman World* (Oxford: Oxford University Press, 2004), 252.

65. Lieu, *Neither Jew Nor Greek,* 59. There is a huge range of opinion on what the term *ioudaioi* indicates. This term is historically imagined as an overarching religious or faith-based identity.

"Perhaps inevitably," Lieu writes, "bound up with the threat of martyrdom there developed an understanding of Judaism and of the Jewish people set over against a hostile world bent on its destruction. Judaism demanded a loyalty of belief and life that could lead to death itself and set the Jewish people apart from all other peoples. It provided a citizenship or city life of its own, even when circumstances gave this no political reality."[66]

Importantly, then, *ioudaismos* arose as a negotiation of diaspora-belonging—but as Lieu notes, one that eschews place of origin as its referent. In fact, recent theorizing about diaspora has suggested that place is overemphasized in traditional thinking about diasporic belonging, especially because geography and homeland are themselves discursively made, not foundational realities.[67] The production of diasporic identity is not always or primarily about land or hope for return; it is also about constructions of corporeality, affect, and temporality, in which violence is a catalyst for belonging, not an impingement on it.[68] While Jerusalem and the larger place of Israel still held sway for many (and still do), obviously, "judaism" did

---

However, some recent scholars, perhaps most famously Boyarin (*Border Lines*), Steve Mason, "Jews, Judeans, Judaizing, Judaism" *JSJ* 38 (2007): 457-512, and Philip Esler, *Conflict and Identity in Romans* (Minneapolis: Fortress Press, 2009), have importantly challenged that notion of a faith-based identity, suggesting that it disembeds cultic practice from geographic, ethnic, and cultural contexts.

66. Lieu, *Neither Jew Nor Greek?*, 59. Other modes of articulating citizenship will be explored further in chapters 4 and 5 with regard to the Secret Revelation of John and Hebrews.
67. See, for example, Stuart Hall, "Cultural Identity and Diaspora"; and Rey Chow, *Writing Diaspora: Tactics of Intervention in Contemporary Cultural Studies* (Bloomington: Indiana University Press, 1993), 27-54, 99-119.
68. Brian Keith Axel, *The Nation's Tortured Body: Violence, Representation and the Formation of a Sikh "Diaspora"* (Durham: Duke University Press, 2001); and "The Diasporic Imaginary," *Public Culture* 14, no. 2 (2002): 411-28. Axel writes, "I am concerned that the field [of diasporic studies]'s emphasis on an analytic model of *place*—central to many studies—will ultimately preempt any serious accomplishments. Place has primarily been developed to identify a diasporic people's 'place of origin.' This very common analytic posits that a homeland is originary and constitutive of a diaspora, and very often it supports an essentialization of origins and a fetishization of what is supposed to be found at the origin (e.g. tradition, religion, language, race)," 411.

the work of homeland when the viability of attaching to a physical place was strained for whatever reason.

In the early second century, more than just place was strained for those with connections to Israel and its traditions, however, and Ignatius's evocation and eschewing of *ioudaismos* should be rethought with these conditions in mind. In a post-70 C.E. world in which Jerusalem, its temple, and so much of its leadership had been destroyed, and there was ongoing disagreement about what to make of this violence (or even who to blame for it), a repudiation of *ioudiasmos*—signifying a lively if abstracted diaspora collective—is not necessarily surprising. Israel's defeat was definitive, and even somewhat anomalous in Roman military history, as Milton Moreland has emphasized: the public parading of Israel's cultic objects, which were procured during the looting of the temple at the end of the war, was an especially sharp jab, one that heightened the already flashy Roman victory processional to an additional level of humiliation for conquered peoples. And if it was out of the ordinary for the Romans to completely destroy temples, it must have seemed particularly grim that decades later the temple had not been rebuilt.[69]

The specificity of that very spectacular embarrassment of being dispossessed of one's most treasured sacred objects may inhabit Ignatius's writing. Ignatius of course stages his own journey to Rome as a kind of procession with himself as the "God-bearer" (*theophoros*) and his Ephesian readers as the "*agiaphoros*," or holy object bearers (*Eph.* 9.2). Allen Brent has argued that Ignatius, in evoking this language, specifically echoes the scene of Roman forces parading with cultic objects from the temple in Jerusalem as depicted on the Arch of Titus (or one could probably also say he echoes the memory produced by the Arch itself).[70] Such a connection to the

---

69. Moreland, "Jerusalem Destroyed," in Penner and Dupertuis, *Reading Acts in the Second Century* (Durham, UK: Acumen Publishing, 2012), 55-56.

imperial processions might automatically be read as a woefully (anti-) imperial identification and stark instance of Christian triumphalism. But others have been more cautious about such a clear connection, noting not only the regularity with which processional imagery was used to express devotion to gods, but the lack of direct reference in Ignatius to the imperial procession.[71] In any case, the notion that Ignatius imagines/dramatizes the march to his death in Rome as a procession in honor of Israel's God with the Ephesians as carriers of key cultic objects—all in the wake of the destruction of Jerusalem and the temple—need not be a specific enactment of the Roman victory procession to be haunted. In that post-war context, Ignatius' imagery would seem to be neither a standard processional imagination nor an especially triumphal or subversive one. Indeed, the march toward Rome in honor of Israel's god might be more delicately understood as a complicated, pained, and ghostly embodiment of Israel's collapse.[72]

This is not to say that Ignatius' attachment to Israel isn't thoroughly ambivalent. Indeed Jerusalem and its temple were objects of intense ambivalence already, for economic and colonial reasons at least. Given the catastrophic losses embedded in the destruction of Jerusalem, its ruling class, and so many Israelite practices, one can easily imagine *ioudaïsmos* hardly felt useful to some as a way of making one's death meaningful in the early second century.[73] It is

---

70. Allen Brent offers an analysis of the resonances of Ignatius's procession with Roman victorial processions in his "Ignatius of Antioch and the Imperial Cult," *VC* 52, no. 1 (1998): 30-58. Brent builds on the work of William Schoedel, *Ignatius of Antioch: A Commentary* (Philadelphia: Fortress Press, 1985), who has remarked not only on the stagey character of Ignatius's journey but its dissonance with Roman values and geography.
71. Cf. Philip Harland, *Dynamics of Identity*, 52-59. In line with his book's thesis, he discusses the procession in Ignatius as an enactment of Christian identity, but offers an importantly wider ancient context for Ignatius' recourse to procession language.
72. Returning to Freccero, it would seem then that Ignatius is haunted by losses of Israel in that he is spectrally animated by them. *Queer/Early/Modern* (Durham: Duke University Press, 2006).
73. On the "shattering" of Jerusalem already after 70 C.E., see Seth Schwartz, *Imperialism and Jewish Society: 200 BCE to 640 CE*, (Princeton: Princeton University Press, 2009), 101-176. "Though the hope of some Jews for their immanent revival ended only with the failure of the Bar Kokhba

within the swirl of affects around diasporic hopelessness and imperial and national hauntings that Ignatius evokes *christianismos*, as seen in Ignatius's other well-known statement on *ioudaïsmos* and *christianismos*:

> But if anyone should interpret *ioudaïsmos* to you, do not hear him. For it is better to hear *christianismos* from a man who is circumcised than *ioudaïsmos* from one who is uncircumcised. But if neither one speaks about Jesus Christ, they both appear to me as monuments and tombs of the dead, on which are written merely human names. (*Phil.* 6.1)

Ignatius' statement that those who don't speak of Jesus Christ appear to him as "monuments and tombs" suggests that his rhetoric depends heavily on the sense of a "dead" Israel. But again, it is not that Christian belonging or piety is the source of Israel's apparent death in Ignatius' letters. It is rather that the political death of Israel, the sense that belonging to Israel or to "judaism" was a moot point, that gives life to Ignatius' "christianity." Placed in the context of diasporic trauma, the word *christianismos* exhibits traces of ambivalent dependence on Israel's history and literature, as Ignatius's recourse to Hebrew scriptures underscores,[74] and suddenly *christianismos* begins to swell with a disappointment in the apparent demise of *ioudaismos*. *Christianismos* in the letters of Ignatius functions as a rhetorical flourish, and the force and impulse for this flourish is derived from the clustered affectivity surrounding Israel's various and dramatic imperial confrontations.

Crucially, *christianismos* is attested nowhere earlier than Ignatius, and the term is so immediately handy for Ignatius, given his famous obsessions with social oneness,[75] as to press the possibility that he

---

revolt in 135 C.E., the centralizing and integrating tendency of the Roman Empire made such a revival unlikely from the start" (105).
74. In fact Isa. 66:18 is evoked in Magnesians 10, quoted above. For a more direct appeal to Hebrew scriptural authority for legitimization of Ignatius's gospel, see *Phil.* 8.2.

coins it.[76] As Lieu writes, "It is its strategic use rather than its frequency that demonstrates how important 'Christian' was as a term of self-definition for Ignatius; its absence from elsewhere among the Apostolic Fathers—including from Polycarp's own letter, despite his knowledge of Ignatius—probably shows how much he was innovating."[77] "Christianity" is a serious rhetorical concoction, though, regardless of how standardized and taken for granted it has become. It puts to work senses and memories of Israel's violent imperial confrontations in visceral ways through its generative entanglement with the word *ioudaismos*, not to mention that the word "Christian" is already thick with the tension of imperial relations given its emergence in, as I have described it, the crosshairs of imperial violence and racializing rhetorics. To this very point: in the letters of Ignatius, being "called" a Christian and being "found" a Christian do not always appear in predictable relationship to one another:

> For me, ask only that I have power both inside and out, that I not only speak but also have the desire, that I not only be called a Christian but also be found one. For if I be found a Christian, I can also be called one and then be faithful—when I am no longer visible in the world. Nothing that is visible is good. For our God Jesus Christ, since he is in the father, is all the more visible. The work is not a matter of persuasion, but Christianity is a matter of greatness, when it is hated by the world (*Rom*. 3.2-3).

Ignatius's letters, like 1 Peter, use the word "Christian" without quite owning it. If in 1 Peter "Christian" is a marginal notation, Ignatius's more invested sense of being Christian is both anticipatory and

---

75. See, for instance, John-Paul Lotz, *Ignatius and Concord: The Background and Use of the Language of Concord in the Letters of Ignatius of Antioch* (New York: Peter Lang, 2007); and Allen Brent, *Ignatius of Antioch: A Martyr Bishop and the Origin of the Episcopacy* (New York: Continuum/T & T Clark, 2007), 14-43.
76. Lieu indeed suggests he coins it (*Christian Identity*, 251-52).
77. Ibid., 252.

retrojective, but still never a given.[78] The idea that Ignatius's Christian-ness is (anticipatorily) "revealed" in the arena,[79] though, in addition to not being related to why he dies, may not necessarily be about a martyrological devotion to and consolidation of self-articulated identity, or a deployment of that identity in counter-imperial directions. To my mind, it speaks more to the way Ignatius is moved by the imperial panoptic targeting (that is, bringing into being) of populations that are, not incidentally, assembled through the wreckage of other social demolitions. It attests to the way violence can arouse and intensify identitarian attachments in general, energizing desires for recognition: not only is Ignatius revealed in the arena, becoming what he truly is in and through the architecture of the imperial gaze, but his god is the invisible-made-visible, even hyper-visible ("all the more visible"), the spirit of which exposes the truth (*Phil.* 7.1).[80] Ignatius' excitement at spectacle and plays on visibility suggest this craving for recognition; a desire to *be seen*, at the same time as violence supposedly obliterates subjectivity.[81]

---

78. Elizabeth Castelli's lovely close reading of the letters of Ignatius treats his language of selfhood as a transformation that is "continuously in process" (*Martyrdom and Memory*, 82). I do not dispute this. However, I am interested in the curious way in which time figures in this process of selfhood—especially since his letters are riddled with confusions of time. When exactly does Ignatius become a disciple? On the one hand, Ignatius has yet to "attain God," or become a disciple (for this language, cf. *Eph.* 1.2, 12.2; *Magn.* 9.2; *Trall.* 5.2; *Rom.* 8.3). Yet in *Magn.* 10.1, Ignatius claims that because they *are already* disciples, they should learn to live "according to *christianismos*." In *Romans* 5, it seems that his mistreatment by the soldiers is what makes him a disciple, but it is not clear. In general, although his letters already presume belonging to Jesus Christ, he emphasizes that it is particularly in suffering that he belongs to Jesus Christ (*Rom.* 4.3). He also makes some more direct statements that his death reveals whether Christ's life *has been* in him (*Magn.* 5.2). This more explicit anticipation/retrojection also occurs elsewhere: although not referring necessarily to himself, Ignatius claims "a tree is known by its fruit, so those who profess to belong to Christ will be seen by what they do" (*Eph.* 14.2).
79. Castelli, *Martyrdom and Memory*, 81. Virginia Burrus suggests that "double vision" is required for the viewing of the martyr: "When Ignatius's body has disappeared—when his shaming has been perfected—his identity will be rendered transparent" (*Saving Shame*, 21).
80. For a particularly close study on the dynamics of seeing and the arena, see Christopher Frilingos, *Spectacles of Empire: Monsters, Martyrs, and the Book of Revelation* (Philadelphia: University of Pennsylvania Press, 2004).

For Ignatius, as in 1 Peter, Christ is an affectively saturated figure that rehashes and cuts across patterns of belonging. But while Ignatius and 1 Peter both make recourse to Christ for framing and directing fear, pain, loss, blustery arrogance, and more, the orientation of that work is not shared. For 1 Peter, Christ extends an investment in belonging to Israel. For Ignatius, that investment lives on only hauntedly (since Israel feels dead to him) in his *christianismos* and in his procession towards dying. So rather than extending an investment in Israel, Ignatius's self-understanding as Christ's perfect disciple—or even as Christ—in his death, manages to conduct the investment towards himself:[82]

> I am writing all the gatherings and giving instruction to all, that I am willingly dying for God, unless you hinder me. I urge you, do not become an untimely kindness to me. Allow me to be bread for the wild beasts; through them I am able to attain God. I am the wheat of God and am ground by the teeth of the wild beasts, that I may be found to be the pure bread of Christ. Rather, coax the wild beasts, that they may become a tomb for me and leave no part of my body behind, that I may burden no one once I have died (*Rom.* 4).

By imagining himself as wheat ground in the teeth of the beasts, soon to become the "bread of Christ," Ignatius not only reads his rather mundane execution through the cosmic hyperbole of suffering that is Jesus Christ, he also renders himself the sober center of the meal practices of the assemblies. He hyperbolizes the tiny assemblies along with himself by borrowing the organizing and cohering mechanism

---

81. Castelli also waxes eloquent on the tension between Ignatius's bodily destruction and his visibility. She suggests there is a "deep-seated tension in Ignatius' letters between notions of presence and absence, visibility and identity, the body and language. At a critical point in his plea to the Roman church not to save his life, Ignatius suggests that the destruction of his own body will render him an incorporeal word of God" (*Martyrdom and Memory*, 80-81). To me, Ignatius not only seems haunted here, but even becomes a ghost himself.
82. Cf. *Trall.* 2.1 for the merging of Ignatius and Jesus Christ and its implications for social unity.

of the arena to rhetorically construct his various letter recipients as a social whole, thereby giving the effect of a massive crowd.[83]

This strongly rhetorical and de/reconstructive reading of Ignatius places him and his strivings in dynamic relation to his context and interpretational history, rather than as an always already exemplar of now dominant Christian ideology. While being strongly rhetorical, I also intend it to be sympathetic without (I hope) instantiating Christian narratives of innocence and victimization by entering the allure of martyrological narratives. Such a reading need not rely on dating Ignatius to the early second century, although I am interested in that possibility. What I am proposing is, in the event of the specific affective context of the early second century, exploring *what else* might be read in Ignatius' letters, what other configurations of violence and belonging might emerge, beyond the persecution of Christians because of who they are or what they ostensibly believe, thus also treating violence as a more diffuse, elusive, and intricate force in imaginations of selfhood and belonging.

This is to say that *christianismos* was from the beginning a diasporic figuration in that it constructs belonging through corporeality, temporality, and affect. Like *ioudaïsmos*, *christianismos* is not itself national, but is beset with the losses of the nation. Unlike *ioudaïsmos*, however, *christianismos* overtly refuses Israelite diasporic

---

83. Likewise, he starts his letter *To the Ephesians* thus: "Ignatius, who is also called God-bearer, to the church that is blessed with greatness by the fullness of God the Father, a church foreordained from eternity past to obtain a constant glory which is enduring and unchanging, a church that has been unified and chosen in true suffering by the will of the Father and of Jesus Christ, our God . . ." As the SBL Greco-Roman meals seminar now broadly assumes, the size of associational gatherings was remarkably small, given that the typical dining room and triclinium fit a dozen or so diners snugly. This material reality is quite contrary to most (superimposed) imaginations of "church" gatherings. Cf. Brigitte Kahl on the "horizontal social integration" (and social stratification) inherent in the arena game setting; *Galatians Re-Imagined*, 148-67. Kahl produces this analysis through a close reading of the poet Martial's *Liber de spectaculis*. The notion of the integrative function of the arena is also a central thesis of Allison Futrell, *Blood in the Arena: The Spectacle of Roman Power* (Austin: University of Texas Press, 1997).

configurations of belonging (even while being one). It is the abstraction of a social body whose vague and reticent sense of connectivity is amplified and conducted through the conflation of Christ and Ignatius's body, and presumed through the future perfect in anticipation of imperial violence ("when I suffer, I will have been . . ."). To what extent Ignatius is alone in his imagination of a *christianismos*, and to what extent his recipients in the assemblies/assemblages are, like him, swept up in the spectacular promises of Christian identification, cannot be known. Such are the quandaries of belonging. Hanging heavily over Ignatius, no less than the modern wish to locate and describe Christians, is the problem that belonging cannot be strictly measured.

Rather than being an inevitable and descriptive development, *christianismos* crops up at the eventful collision of colonial affects and circumstances, including diasporic hopelessness and, in the face of that hopelessness, Ignatius's pining for meaning and recognition. Reading Ignatius affectively also invites imagining Israel, *ioudaïsmos*, and the eventual currency of *christianismos* as nodes of attachment rather than entities or phenomena, in that they act as magnets for what might otherwise seem to be surprisingly mixed and conflicted constituencies. Instead of taking the representational dimension of these terms at face value and extrapolating their content (however constructed), we might seek out their "affiliative powers," asking not what they mean but why and under what circumstances they might have become meaningful.[84]

---

[84]. I am condensing and appropriating Jasbir Puar's elaboration of Axel's work here. She notes that "to shift away from origin for a moment allows other forms of diasporic affiliative and cathartic entities . . . to show their affiliative powers . . . Furthermore, an unsettling of the site of origin (i.e., nation) as one of the two binding terms of diaspora de facto wrenches ancestral progression out of the automatic purview of diaspora, allowing for queer narratives of kinship, belonging and home" (*Terrorist Assemblages*, 171). Puar's elaboration of Axel also shifts emphasis from the representational to the affective: "We move from What does this body mean? To What and who does this body affect? What does this body do? While the notion of contagion is slightly

Identity language and analytics do not adequately account for the multiple and seemingly contradictory affiliations that are embedded in diaspora conditions, or, we might say, the very condition of being social itself. They also tend to interfere with the very present and palpable awareness that belonging is remarkably subjective and qualitative, a "sense" that one has or gets, a sense that can change in inflection as well as thrust. The senses of belonging are much more expansive than simply the success and failure or the "in" and "out" of identity, especially because any identity category represents gnarls of particular elements, the associations with and attachments to which vary wildly from person to person.[85] Not just unstable, belonging is thick with—or even forged through—chance relationships and haphazard investments. Social bodies, meaning both intersubjectively constituted "individuals" and those collectivities of which they are a part, are dynamically experienced and unevenly transferable; and because of their uneven transferability, they defy easy containment.

The affective life of social bodies requires us to reframe the question of "how Jewish, how Christian, etc., are they?"--a question which demands not only positional charting but also some kind of objective rubric for judgment of what counts as Christian or Jewish. Such rubrics and judgments can only be made by entering the discourse of belonging itself. That problem of entering the discourse, though, is exemplary of the very queer way the ancient bodies "of"

---

overdetermined in relation to unwanted and afflicted bodies, in this case I am suggesting not that specific bodies be read as contagions, but that all bodies can be thought of as contagious or mired in contagions: bodies infecting other bodies with sensation, vibration, irregularity, chaos, lines of flight that betray the expectation of loyalty, linearity, the demarcation of who's in and who's not" (172).

85. Cf. Carolyn Dinshaw, *Getting Medieval: Sexualities and Communities* (Durham: Duke University Press, 1999). Karen King has suggested thinking of "Jewish identity" as tactically and rhetorically defined by and contingent on location, interests, practices, and relationships of the person claiming such an identity, which reflects an indebtedness to Judith Lieu's work. Karen King, "The Problem of Jewish Christianity or How to Represent the Diversity of Early Christianity" (paper presented at the annual meeting of the Society of Biblical Literature, Early Jewish-Christian Relations Section, Washington, D. C., 19 November, 2006).

the texts and bodies apparently "outside" the texts mingle and coalesce, affectively passing into and out of one another, creating forms belonging along and across other lines demarcating not only identity, but time and place.[86] In fact, that "christianity" contagiously takes on a life of its own and becomes *operative* as a node of attachment—gathering into it not just the near-hopeless grasping and beguiled insistence of Ignatius, but also such a wild assortment ranging from the supra-national aspirations and smug superiority of empires, to the melancholy of modern historians, and the pious convictions of church people across ages and continents—may be one of the queerer turns of Christian history yet.

---

86. I am here indebted to Jane Gallop, *The Deaths of the Author* (Durham: Duke University Press, 2011) and Carla Freccero's notion of "queer spectrality" in her book *Queer/Early/Modern* (Durham: Duke University Press, 2006), and much more will be said about this subject in subsequent chapters, particularly my final chapter.

3

Reading Acts in Diaspora

Reading for affect, and reading affectively, reorients one to texts and history by cueing one into the indefinite, turbulent, and immersive qualities of bodily and social life. While possibly the most recognizable qualities of bodily and social life, these qualities are also the most unsettling. Affect indeed unsettles in more literal ways: constantly bringing people into new and different vicinities, changing the charge of old relationships, confounding self-understandings, and expanding perceptions of relationship. This instability and flux is where diaspora meets up with affect—drawing attention to the unsettled and mobile dimensions of belonging of all kinds, as well as to the way nations and empires haunt, enliven, and re-form collectives, often in surprisingly deep and subtle ways.

Reading for affect and diasporic sociality has so far surfaced the longings and attachments giving energy to the historical analytic "Christian identity," and it has reframed the social life of 1 Peter and Ignatius's letters, allowing for more intricate and intimate dynamics of violence, imperialism, and belonging to emerge. In this chapter,

I bring an affective reading to bear on the Acts of the Apostles to entertain the book as something other than a highly elaborate imagination of Christian origins, charter document for Christianity, or a construction of Christian identity—all of which assume Christian-belonging to be the central social interest of the book. Beginning with some objections to reading Acts as a construction of Christian identity, I suggest not only that "Christian" is a much more fraught, marginal, and ambivalent notion in Acts than is generally assumed, but that the question of social belonging at large in Acts is fraught and ambivalent. In my reading, Acts is a diasporic account of the very strange confederations and rivalries constitutive of colonial life, and a melancholic epic of imperial romances and disappointments.

A discussion of Acts, however, is never only about Acts, since Acts' story is nearly inseparable from our long-view imaginations of Christian history.[1] Church and scholarly readers alike have invested in Acts as *the* "Christian story," however ideal or menacing: the notion of a popular and controversial movement radiating out from Israel and making its way in and through the Roman Empire is nothing if not an Acts-funded story. Achtemeier's description of the backdrop for 1 Peter, for example, charted a rough trajectory from

---

1. As Richard Ascough writes, "Luke has served a paradigmatic role in subsequent understandings of how Christianity developed, with an emphasis not only on accuracy, but also on logical order. Even today among biblical historians, Luke's approach is taken at face value as the way in which history is to be narrated. The isolation of key events or key figures leads to theories of monocausality. In subsequent debates, the central issue at stake becomes whether one or another cause led to subsequent events. When theological assumptions are brought into play—as they are in Luke-Acts and much of Christian historiography—the monocausality points in the direction of divine intervention, or at the very least the suggestion that God's guiding hand has given direction to the events. In the case of Christian events, they are taken to be exceptional or unique" See his "Bringing Chaos to Order: Historical Memory and the Manipulation of History," *R&T* 15, no. 3-4 (2008): 280-303 (281). Although taking up a very different set of theoretical frameworks than I do here, this article is helpful in both its encapsulating of the investments of contemporary Christian historiography and its imagining of epistemological alternatives.

a small movement fully embedded in (or at least easily "confused" with) Israel and at odds with the values of its world, which eventually achieved full assimilation to Greco-Roman social norms. The problem is that such a narrative of early Christian history curiously suggests that the content of Christianity or Christian identity has been betrayed before the terms "Christian" or "Christianity" have even been invented. Such readings of Acts as "the Christian story" additionally push the entirety of the text through the sieve of a term that may not be central to the book in its ancient historical moment.

Despite the fact that Acts' panoptic view parallels modern historiographical practices,[2] it has become clear that Acts is not interested in doing history the way modernity has defined it. Acts' story has long been under scrutiny not only for its "inaccuracy" but for a whole host of other reasons, and many critiques have not only focused on its order or description of events, but also its ideological investments in and ascription of particular content (utopian, anti-Jewish, empire-friendly, etc.) to Christian identity.[3] Yet the notion

---

2. As Melanie Johnson-Debaufre writes, "Our scholarly practices reproduce the shape and order of the past in the same way it is conceptualized by Acts itself—from the beginnings to now, from Jerusalem to Rome in centrifugal but distinctly westward leaning motion. This synching between historical narrative and time-space movement in Acts' narrative produces a model of history that marches forward." See her "Inside Out and Upside Down: Acts 17:1-8 and the Outing of the Thessalonian Ekklesia," (paper presented at the annual meeting of the Society of Biblical Literature, New Orleans, La., 2009).
3. While the genre of "history" for Acts still has a large number of advocates, the kind of history Acts seems to write has not been specified, and the genre of history is not seen as coextensive with facticity. See, e.g., Martin Dibelius, *The Book of Acts: Form, Style, Theology*, ed. K.C. Hanson (Minneapolis: Fortress Press, 2004). David Aune has extended the Acts-as-history thesis, though not as an objective narration of events. He rather contends that Acts is a history giving content to group identity. See David E. Aune, *The New Testament and Its Literary Environment* (Philadelphia: The Westminster Press, 1987). David Balch has similarly described Acts as a "political history" in "The Genre of Luke-Acts: Individual Biography, Adventure Novel or Political History?," *SwJT* 33, no. 1 (1990): 5-19. For a helpful summary of Acts relative to the fact/fiction of history debate, see Loveday Alexander, *Acts in its Ancient Literary Context: A Classicist Looks at the Acts of the Apostles* (New York: T & T Clark, 2005), 135-55. Acts has long been a site for articulating utopian imaginations of Christian practice, particularly Acts 2-4, especially given the references to sharing all goods in common (2:44-45). For Acts as Christian and anti-Jewish, see Richard Pervo, "The Gates Have Been Closed (Acts 21:30):

that it charts a popular and controversial movement rarely gets questioned. Contemporary readers seem to have caught Acts' epic imagination, its desire for social significance of mythic proportions—so much so, in fact, that even historical and ideological interrogations of Acts' story leave intact its monumental vision of a definitive social movement finding its bearing in the world. What is more, Acts' epic imagination—its large-scale perspective and penchant for the legendary—is so spellbinding, so alternately vexing and satisfying to contemporary Christians, that it not only drives historiographical subtexts, but also pulls nearly all of Acts' critical attention away from the muddier and decidedly more pained and mundane social landscape of the text.[4]

That is to say, changing our orientation to Acts has implications for more than just the book itself. Although Acts may not be all that interested in Christian identity, contemporary Christian historiography inadvertently expresses, through its Acts-funded story of Christianity, an affectivity that is awfully close to Acts. If Christian historiography at large assumes not only an ancient movement with

---

The Jews in Acts," *JHC* 11 (2005): 128-49. For Acts constructing Christian identity as anti-Jewish and empire-friendly, see Shelly Matthews, *Perfect Martyr The Stoning of Stephen and the Construction of Christian Identity* (New York: Oxford University Press, 2010), which is discussed in detail further on in this chapter.

4. In addressing the force of Acts' linearity and its effect on imaginations of Christianity, Johnson-Debaufre ("Inside Out and Upside Down") suggests going queerly off the main roads in Acts, as well as moving to the side of the linear temporalities of traditional history to produce alternate imaginations of early Christian social life. Ascough ("Bringing Chaos to Order"), drawing from chaos and complexity theories, begins with Acts' "ordered" account to suggest something similar: "Unlike historicism, an approach that embraces non-linear dynamics builds on quantum physics, describes 'a world that is cloudy and fitful.' The challenge of non-linear dynamics lies in the recognition that the world is in constant flux, with change the norm, and any lasting sameness the result of very special local conditions maintained at a cost." This has a certain resonance with Brian Massumi's complaint that the state of contemporary theorizing on social relations and identity does not account for change and movement, even though movement is the clearest given. Massumi, *Parables for the Virtual: Movement, Affect, Sensation* (Durham, NC: Duke University Press, 2002). From yet another theoretical standpoint, Stephen Moore counter-reads Luke-Acts poststructurally so as to disable some of its forces of coercion, particularly those to which the reader is subjected (*Mark and Luke in Poststructuralist Perspectives* (New Haven: Yale University Press, 1992), 87-143.

deep historical import, but one that is given over to empire as or before it reaches its full bloom, then maybe it has noticed Acts is not only a story of epic significance or utopian or counter-cultural impulses, but also a story of arrested possibility, of regrettable coalitions with dominant structures and systems, of sighs and reflections that it should have been some other way. I want to propose not only that Acts, like Ignatius and 1 Peter, points to rather incidental and frictive conditions around the historical emergence of the term "Christian." I additionally want to suggest that the affective drifts in our renderings of Acts actually bring us to considerations of belonging within and around the text that are more pressing than "Christian identity": the strange gatherings and haunted sociality of life within empire.

* * * *

The word "Christian" appears twice in Acts, and both instances relate to Paul. In the first, it is mentioned almost offhandedly that "the disciples were first called Christians" (11:26) at Antioch, where some go to teach "the Hellenists" after Stephen's death. The second occurs near the end of Acts in a scene between Paul and Agrippa:

> [Paul said,] "King Agrippa, do you believe the prophets?" And Agrippa said to Paul, "Are you so quickly persuading me to make me a Christian?" Paul replied, "Whether quickly or not, I pray to God that not only you but also all who are listening to me today might become such that I am—except for these chains" (Acts 26:28-29).

Taken together, these two moments in the text would seem not only to speak back to all of Acts but also to early Christian self-conception in broad strokes: in 11:26, Antioch and Paul seem to encapsulate the Christian "mission to the gentiles," and in 26:28-29, Paul's recounting of the purpose for his journey is the apparent content of Christian confession. The problem is that not only does no one in the text claim the C-word for themselves, but Paul even sidesteps the question posed by Agrippa, perhaps suggesting hesitation in Acts about the name itself.[5] Paul is not afraid to claim other ostensible identity categories, though, and variously refers to himself as a Jew, Pharisee, and Roman citizen in Acts. These two instances do confirm the picture of the term "Christian" suggested by the Pliny-Trajan correspondence, however: that the term "Christian" is a form of imperial slander—or at least a passive designation—and likely appears first in Asia Minor.[6]

Acts is typically understood as narrating (whether fictively or accurately) Paul's apparent change of allegiance in Galatians 1:13-14 as a change of identity: he becomes a Christian. Not just in traditional interpretation but more recent scholarship as well, Paul is often seen as "converting" from Jewish identity to Christian identity, and so representing a larger set of bipolar loyalties and ideological positions in Acts. For proponents of the new perspective in Pauline studies beginning with Krister Stendahl, Paul has not converted to anything like a distinct religious identity, but rather retains his Jewish identity with a "call" to the gentiles, a distinction that emphasizes the total entrenchment of Christian identity within Judaism.[7] Paul's status as Roman in Acts, signified not only by his repeated claiming of Roman citizenship but also by his name change after an encounter with a Roman proconsul named Sergius Paulus (13:7), has been similarly

---

5. As Richard Pervo suggests, *Dating Acts: Between the Evangelists and the Apologists* (Santa Rosa: Polebridge Press, 2006), 168-69. Matthews concurs (*Perfect Martyr*, 7). More will be said about the specificity of their arguments, which nonetheless propose a Christian identity despite this hesitation in Acts.
6. I suggest that Acts confirms the coincidence of the term "Christian" with Asia Minor not only because the location of this first instance of "Christian" is Antioch, but also because of Acts' clearer understanding of Asia Minor's geography. Acts' use of "Christian" is archaizing, and Acts seems to have a need to account for it. That said, I would argue that "Christian" is not more than incidentally important for Acts, as I will outline in more detail below.
7. Krister Stendahl, *Paul Among Jews and Gentiles* (Philadelphia: Fortress Press, 1976), 1-77.

read as representing Acts' friendliness to empire, if not read as truly biographical.[8]

But Paul's change in Acts may not fall so easily along identity/categorical lines. It is worth scrutinizing the scene of Paul's vision of Jesus in Acts 9:

> Meanwhile Saul, still breathing threats and murder against the disciples of the Lord, went to the high priest and asked him for letters to the synagogues at Damascus, so that if he found any who belonged to the way, men or women, he might bring them bound to Jerusalem. Now as he was going along and approaching Damascus, suddenly a light from heaven flashed around him. He fell to the ground and heard a voice saying to him, "Saul, Saul, why do you persecute me?" (Acts 9:1-4).

Whether read as a conversion or more softly as a turn towards "the Way," Paul's vision is usually interpreted as a signal moment in the making of Paul's identity: Paul goes from being allied with temple officials and synagogue instigators who provoke Stephen's death, to proclaiming the name of Jesus "before gentiles and kings and before the people of Israel" (9:15). In other words, he goes from being a "zealous Jew" to a gentile affiliated/inclusive Jew, i.e., a Christian. Yet the subtexts of this scene muddle any kind of patent change of allegiance on the part of Paul. Both Stephen's death and Paul's vision are heavily inflected with intertextual connections to

---

8. For instance, Brigitte Kahl suggests that it is at this moment of name change when Paul is "baptized" into the Roman order. See her "Acts of the Apostles: Pro(to)-Imperial Script and Hidden Transcript," in *In the Shadow of Empire: Reclaiming the Bible as a History of Faithful Resistance*, ed. Richard A. Horsley (Louisville: Westminster John Knox Press, 2008), 145. Kazuhiko Yamazaki-Ransom, however, sees Saul becoming Paul not as a moment of identity "change" for Paul, but rather simply indicating Paul's always already colonial condition. He argues, "Luke's use of the double name does not merely signify the Greco-Roman setting of the narrative, it also indicates the socio-political relationship between Sergius Paulus and Paul. The use of two names for an individual, one in his native language, the other in the language of the colonizers, points to the reality of the imperial domination of other cultures. In Luke's narrative, this is Paul's first encounter with a Roman official, and therefore the use of his Roman name is appropriate . . . Thus the relationship of Sergius Paulus and Paul is that of colonizer and colonized." See his *The Roman Empire in Luke's Narrative* (New York: T & T Clark, 2010), 119.

2 Maccabees. Shelly Matthews, in her recent reading of Acts in *Perfect Martyr*, sees Stephen's death and its importance in Paul's later story in Acts as a strong rhetorical overturning of Maccabean martyr traditions.[9] Acts sets up a parallel between Paul and the story of Antiochus IV's persecution of the Jews in 2 Maccabees 9, and likewise links Stephen's death to Zechariah's in 2 Maccabees 24.[10] Kazuhiko Yamazaki-Ransom writes of the former parallel:

> Not only are both Paul and Antiochus characterized as persecutors, the overall structures of their accounts are remarkably similar. In both Acts 9 and 2 Macc. 9, the persecutor rushes to a location in order to harm the people of God (Acts 9:1-2; 2 Macc. 9:1-4). On his way, he is struck by divine intervention and falls to the ground (Acts 9:11-12; 2 Macc. 5-10). In both accounts, the persecutor prays (Acts 9:11-12; 2 Macc. 9:13-17). In both accounts, there is a reference to conversion and mission (Acts 9:15-16; 2 Macc. 9:17).[11]

As Yamazaki-Ransom points out, this last parallel is especially striking for its resonance with Paul's mission: "and in addition to all this he also would become a Jew and would visit every inhabited place to proclaim the power of God" (2 Macc 9:17).

If Paul undergoes a conversion, it is not a Christian conversion. Yamazaki-Ransom differentiates the accounts of Paul and Antiochus by suggesting that Acts "gives it a crucial twist" to "redefine the idea of 'the people of God' with a Christological focus," since Antiochus is a gentile persecutor of Jews, and Paul is a non-Christian Jewish persecutor of Jewish Christians.[12] Yet this intertextuality would seem

---

9. Matthews, *Perfect Martyr*, 99-130.
10. This link is also made to Jesus in Luke. Thus Stephen's death resonates with both Zechariah's and Jesus' deaths.
11. Kazuhiko Yamazaki-Ransom, "Paul, Agrippa I, and Antiochus IV," in Rhoads, Esterline and Lee, *Luke-Acts and Empire, Essays in Honor of Robert L. Brawley*. (Eugene, OR: Wipf and Stock, 2011), 116. Though, as Yamazaki-Ransom also notes in this essay, there may be other literary resonances with Acts 9, including with the figures of Heliodorus in 2 Maccabees 3 and Apollonius in 4 Maccabees 4.
12. Ibid., 119.

to interfere with those categories. Paul is first allied with the temple authorities in this portion of Acts, and, because of Roman presence in the temple in the first century, this is already a Roman (i.e., gentile) inflected alliance. There is no doubt that Paul is a Jew before his vision of Jesus, but this link to Antiochus, and more generally to the tropes and interests of 2 Maccabees (e.g., the critique of Hellenization and the pollution of the temple), confounds the idea that in this moment Paul goes cleanly from one set of loyalties to another. Instead, he goes from being one kind of "zealous Jew" affiliated with gentiles to another.[13]

Shelly Matthews's *Perfect Martyr* offers one reading of Acts as being, or containing, a signal moment in the making of Christian identity, and it is worth discussing her work at length—in part because it is so well executed –to show how such readings disambiguate the social dynamics represented by and in proximity to the text. On the one hand, Matthews repeatedly notices the deep entanglements between Acts and Israelite Scriptures and tradition. She notices for instance that Stephen's speech criticizing the temple is fully embedded in Israelite prophetic traditions, and that his death is not only imagined in the form of Jesus' death, but also closely linked to Zechariah's death in 2 Maccabees 24.[14] She also notes that Acts does not embrace the term Christian, and likewise gives an account of the social ambiguities represented in text. For example, she discusses the scene in Acts 18:24-28 where Apollos, described as a Jew, publicly "refutes the Jews":

---

13. Likewise, if Paul is the Antiochus Epiphanes figure at whose feet Stephen is murdered, would not this intertextual echo cause Stephen's death (and critique of the temple) to resonate, at least minimally, with that of the Maccabean martyrs? This literary echo is ironic too, of course, since one thrust of Maccabees is the problem of the violation of Jewish food customs, a cause for which Eleazar dies (cf. 2 Macc. 6:18). But the irony only underscores the point that this text defies simple categorization of Stephen and Paul, as well as their alliances.
14. Matthews, *Perfect Martyr*, 99-130.

> It could be said that the rupture enacted by "the Jew" upon "the Jews" in this particular passage ... captures precisely both the split Acts asserts and the confusion the narrative has in naming it. Acts is a book in which individual Jews – Stephen, Apollos, Peter, and, quintessentially, Paul – "vehemently refute the Jews" by proving Jesus is Christ. While asserting two distinct groups, Acts still has not embraced unequivocally the name by which Jesus believers will come to be named.[15]

But it is in scenes such as this one in Acts where the use of "Christian identity" as an optic, or the assumption of a first- or second-century movement wanting exclusive identification as "Christian," clashes with Matthews's delicate textual work. Matthews notices the confusion in the narrative, but, again, for me it is these very moments of confusion that thwart the notion of "two distinct groups." Christian identity as a filter for the text leads Matthews to read Luke-Acts as redeploying Israel's traditions to violent ideological ends by putting them to use for the dichotomization of Jew/Christian: "Acts underscores the gospel accusation of prophet persecutors as *other* in even bolder lines by offering Stephen up as the embodiment of the persecuted prophet, while aligning his murderers with ancestors that he does not share."[16] Her logic for why Acts does not embrace the term "Christian" is that "Luke fears its sectarian connotations. The author does not see his social group—'the Christians'—as one among many factions within Judaism, merely standing alongside the Pharisees and the Sadducees, but rather the 'true' Judaism, or true Israel itself."[17] Casting "Christian" as both an obvious and reticently

---

15. Matthews, *Perfect Martyr*, 7. Matthews also writes, "Adopting the model and terminology employed by Boyarin, one might say that the author of Acts is an early border agent working to fix barriers and hence construct two unified and distinct social/religious entities called Judaism and Christianity (or better, working to fix barriers between his version of Christianity, with Judaism on the one side and heresy on the other). But he is an early player, laying bricks in his particular region of the ancient Mediterranean for the "borderline" between Judaism and Christianity that will not be firmly and broadly erected for some centuries" (7).
16. Ibid., 72.
17. Ibid., 88. I agree that Acts lays claim to a true Israel, and I will say more about this in what follows.

claimed identity in Acts may not quite fully account for its complicated and minor role. Perhaps more to the point, the use of Christian identity leads Matthews into a contradiction: she suggests that Christian identity in Acts is an assumption of separateness from Jews, while she also suggests that Acts' equivocation about the name "Christian" is that it connotes something other than true Judaism.

Matthews likewise describes Acts as "part of a developing supersessionist rhetoric" which enfolds converted Jews only to distinguish them from angry mobs of unrepentant Jews.[18] However, in terms of conversion language and the language of "believers," it is important to note that no conversion language is ever used in reference to a Jewish figure in Acts.[19] It seems "conversion" applies not to being converted to the Way, but to loyalty to Israel's God, and thus Jewish figures would not need to be converted.[20] Matthews is of course right about the stakes of Acts' rhetoric in the history of interpretation, and she is highly attuned to Acts' uneasiness around the term "Christian," as well as to the text's tense social ambiguities. But Matthews' use of Christian identity as an optic for understanding Acts in its immediate historical context ends up erasing so many of the more subtle relational dynamics that Matthews herself unearths.

There are ways to do justice to both the social ambiguities and the claims to the true Israel within Acts. I want to suggest that, rather than ancient supersessionist rhetoric, Acts illustrates the heated discourse of authenticity that is part and parcel of diasporic

---

18. Ibid., 32.
19. Richard Pervo finds this to be a sign of Acts' bias towards them ("The Gates Have Been Closed"). It could be that "believing" does not refer only to followers of "the Way." The Pharisees in Acts 15:5 who disagree with Paul about circumcision are referred to as "believing," for instance. While one might argue that the Pharisees are followers of "the Way," the text does not specify, and I do not think this can be assumed.
20. I am hesitant about conversion language, mainly for its implications of exclusive religious belonging and consciousness change, which is both too modern a conceptuality and at odds with ancient sociality and belonging, as I have suggested in the last chapter. It might be thought more loosely as a signal of (non-exclusive) loyalty or affiliation.

belonging. In her book *Writing Diaspora*, Rey Chow critically examines how those in diaspora within the western academy play into western dynamics of fetishistic particularization and attachments to essentialized, authentic, other-cultural identity.[21] She discusses discourses of Chinese poets and academics, noting how such poets and academics, even amongst each other, often compete for, trade on, or are accused of not being "authentically" Chinese enough, either in their political alignments, theory, or language.[22] Being more authentically Chinese then ironically becomes the mode in which one's status in the western academy is underwritten. Chow sees this happening with all sorts of identities that are considered marginal—feminist, Caribbean, queer—in which appeals to that identity are part of an upward mobility within academic circles.[23] Acts' appeal to "the Way" as true Israel constitutes, like all appeals to the (ever elusive) authenticity of one's own origins, a frightened navigation of its own complicated, hybrid, and confusing diasproric conditions, even while it claims to be, in Chow's words, a defense of the origin itself.[24]

While it does no good to skim the violence from the scenes and rhetoric in Acts (or the place of Jews in it), the landscape of affiliations

---

21. Further, Chow illustrates the western academic self-interestedness in discussions of Third World particularity, "the oppressed," and descriptions of cultural pluralism. The Western academic tendencies in discussions of non-Western people have been either to universalize them regionally or to hyper-particularize them in a fetishistic manner. In the latter tendency, naming cultural particularity has been seen as an ethical redress, but for Chow such almost inevitably becomes a kind of poker-game of Western self-righteous cultural sensitivity, as well as, again, the Western attachment to "authentic" cultural identity. Rey Chow, *Writing Diaspora: Tactics of Intervention in Contemporary Cultural Studies* (Bloomington: Indiana University Press, 1993), 1-26.
22. Ibid., 99-119.
23. Ibid., 68-71.
24. Ibid., 99-119. Tat-Siong Benny Liew has done a beautiful (and regularly first-person and affective) analysis of the diasporic dynamics of interpretation and self-understanding within the category "Asian American" in *What is Asian American Biblical Hermeneutics?: Reading the New Testament* (Honolulu: University of Hawai'i Press, 2008). See his analysis of Luke's appeal to multiple origins and similar appeals made within Chinese America in order to fit in (66-67).

and violent encounters are not easily resolved around identity lines. The text's implicit paralleling of Paul and Antiochus, casting Paul as the "gentile convert," clouds any easy delineations of Israel in the narrative—as does the constituency of Stephen's synagogue antagonists, not insignificantly described as "Cyrenians, Alexandrians, and others of those from Cilicia and Asia" who accuse him of blasphemy (6:9).[25] Simply rethinking the interactions of Paul, who is constantly getting himself into sticky predicaments, generates ways to understand relationships of violence and sociality in Acts without needing to assume that Christian identity is the cause or beneficiary of it. In the harrowing world of Acts, Paul's alliances are not limited to "the Way," his main antagonists are not only Jews, and the apparent trajectory of Acts away from the collective of Israel and towards *imperium* (as if these are totally separable entities) is overestimated.

In Acts 16, for instance, Paul and Silas are in trouble: they are in the Roman colony of Philippi in Macedonia, and they have interrupted the lucrative exploitation of a slave girl by exorcising the demon that possessed her.[26] Her owners, upset about the loss of cash, drag Paul and Silas before the authorities. The charge is that they are Jews inciting practices unlawful for "us Romans" (16:21).[27] They are

---

25. Matthews explains the mixed constituency of Stephen's synagogue opponents as Acts depicting Stephen's Jewish opponents as "from the far reaches of the earth." That very locution, however, already suggests a hybrid condition (*Perfect Martyr*, 4).
26. So much more could be (and has been) said about this passage. For a reading of this passage relative to colonial dynamics, particularly with respect to the good girl/bad girl contrast between Lydia and the slave girl, and the political connection to Mark's Gerasene demoniac, see Jeffrey Staley, "Changing Women: Postcolonial Reflections on Acts 16:6-40," *JSNT* 73 (1999): 113-35. Staley suggests that these two women function to "legitimize the ideological and territorial conquests of a nascent Christianity" (127), but this reading historicizes later categories and colonial dynamics.
27. The charge and the actions do not quite line up, as Craig S. de Vos notices. In his article, "Finding a Charge that Fits: The Accusation Against Paul and Silas at Philippi," *JSNT* 74 (1999): 51-63, de Vos summarizes various theories of how Paul and Silas are charged and why, but it seems the charge is simply a mechanism of revenge for their having interrupted the cash flow from the girl's exploitation.

attacked by an unspecified crowd, beaten, and imprisoned. Paul's appeal to the jailer to set them free is that he and Silas are Roman citizens. While the scenes preceding and following this episode involve baptisms of Lydia's and the jailer's families, respectively, the accusation here has nothing to do with Paul and Silas being followers of "the Way." It is a question of Jewish violation of Roman law.[28]

In the next chapter, another episode of violence unfolds in Thessalonica, and this time it is indeed because of the success of Paul's preaching among Jews and Greeks. The attack is driven by some "jealous" Jews, apparently enlisting the help of some "evil people of the marketplace" (17:5). However, the charge is the same as in the last chapter: they are acting contrary to imperial values. Followers of "the Way" and their violent detractors are, in these episodes, *both* composed of alliances of Jews and gentiles, and the detractors of "the Way" are regularly instrumentalizing Roman anxieties and imperial law in order to accuse Paul and company. To lay these chapters' alliances and hostilities out more succinctly: first, we find Paul and Silas (as Jews) vs. marketplace people allied with Rome; then Paul and Silas are allied with Rome as citizens; and, finally, we find Paul and Silas as followers of "the Way" who attract Jews and gentiles vs. "jealous Jews" and gentile thugs who ally themselves with Roman law.

Affiliations are no less slippery in Ephesus in Acts 19, where it is the Ephesians who are protesting the claims of "the Way"—claims which are, it should be noted, not about Jesus at all, but simply about idols—for being an affront to the city's economic/cultic investments. But Paul is on the side of at least some of the officials of Asia (19:31), and the person who attempts, or is pushed, to make a defense is

---

28. On the explicitly political and legal character of the language in this episode, as well as the heightened sense of Roman conflict with Jews, see Charles Talbert, *Reading Acts: A Literary and Theological Commentary on the Acts of the Apostles* (Macon, Ga: Smith and Helwys, 2005), 152.

a Jew named Alexander (19:33). The text does not clarify whether Alexander is a follower of "the Way" or not, probably because the charge is simply about a thoroughly Jewish position on idols: "gods made with hands are not gods" (19:26).

Neither should Paul's alliances with the Pharisees be downplayed. In the final chapters of Acts, Paul is attacked in Jerusalem at the temple and then sent to Rome. While he is accused of "teaching everyone everywhere against the people, the law and this place," the text emphasizes that the trouble is his relationship with gentiles (21:28; 22:21-22; 26:19-21) and his claim about resurrection (23:6-8; 24:21; 25:19; 26:8). In the assembly, however, Paul reminds the Pharisaic group that "I am a Pharisee" (present tense), and, despite the fact that they had their disagreements with Paul before (15:5), they find nothing wrong with him since, as the text says, Pharisees profess resurrection (23:8). Acts continually portrays the exoneration of Paul in various ways and places, but it is not simply the Roman authorities that it portrays doing so.

The episodes I have recounted are not small exceptions to the larger rule of Jewish opposition to Paul and companions; they represent significant complications that mitigate dichotomizing or exclusive identification of figures in the text.[29] Whether explicitly or more subtly through intertextual association, social groups split, mix, and merge, forming surprising and multidirectional affiliations. These alliances are mainly situational, and based on circumstances varying from economic interests, to philosophical disagreements and

---

29. As Milton Moreland has written, "The very ambiguity and hybridity we find in Luke's story should cause us to question the use of traditional, seemingly well-established categories when speaking of Luke's theology and group identities [in Acts]." See his "Jerusalem Destroyed," in Penner and Dupertuis, *Reading Acts in the Second Century* (Durham, England: Acumen Publishing, 2012), 50-51. Moreland, however, contradicts himself on this point. At once a sensitive treatment of the complexity of Acts' relationship to Jerusalem and a critique of well-established categories, his essay also suggests that Acts is a "narrative reconstruction of Christianity" (58), thus himself employing a well-established category.

resonances, to political hedging and negotiation amidst Roman rule, and they do not occur in any obvious trajectories.

Of course, the rhetoric of Acts is accusatory, and even occasionally rabidly violent towards some Jews in the text—virulent inter-group rhetoric is a familiar, if sad, hallmark of all kinds of belonging. But the notion that Acts is constructing Christian identity is jumbled by the relationships of Paul, the signal character, himself. This notion likewise misses all the puzzling and sinister vectors of power, violence, and sociality that frame, even plague, the story. The charged and confusing social scenes of Acts may actually be a starting point for constructively reconsidering the text. It is a depiction of the pains of imperial social clamoring. Following Milton Moreland's insistence on the late first- or early second-century dissolution of Israel as a historical setting and important subtext for Acts, it is a chronicle of the desperate brokering of fragile agency and inclusion in increasingly broken diasporic conditions.

* * * *

In chapter 17, after the confrontations in Thessalonica, Acts writes that Paul, upon spending time in Athens, is "deeply distressed to see that the city was full of idols" (v. 16). All riled up at the offense to his sensibilities, Paul argues with others in the synagogue, as well as some Stoic and Epicurean philosophers, who find his talk about Jesus novel, and therefore compelling. Standing in front of the Areopagus that overlooks Athens, Paul poetically praises the Athenians for their religiosity, and then cites one altar among many as that of the god he proclaims. He wins a few people over with talk about resurrection, but just as in the synagogues, some leave scoffing at him.

While dramatic for its venue and speech, this episode is remarkably casual in that Paul quite easily finds a place for his god among many gods in Athens, preaches about this god in the mode of a suddenly repopularized cosmopolitanism, and then picks up some philosophically inclined listeners by offering them some new ideas. Paul, ever multilingual in Acts, has put himself, both literally and metaphorically, in the language of the city and the people to whom he speaks. While Paul is not part of a religious entity called Christianity to which someone could be said to convert, "convert" might actually be an incidentally helpful word here, if taken for its non-religious definition: "to adapt."[30] That is to say, given the mode in which Paul speaks his message, is it the philosophers or the message that "converts"?[31]

At the Areopagus, Paul exemplifies the relational dynamics of one of the most paradigmatic stories of Acts:

> When the day of Pentecost had come, they were all together in one place. And suddenly from heaven there came a sound like the rush of a violent wind, and it filled the entire house where they were sitting. Divided tongues as of fire appeared among them, and a tongue rested on each of them. All of them were filled with the holy spirit and began to speak in other languages, as the spirit gave them ability. Now there were devout men, Jews from every nation under heaven living in Jerusalem. And at this sound the crowd gathered and was bewildered, because each one heard them speaking in the native language of each (Acts 2:1-4).

Pentecost, as an inversion of Babel, is compact diaspora-mythology. The apostles are gathered in Jerusalem, as are Jews from every *ethnos*,

---

30. This scene has directly been described by some as a model of interreligious dialogue. See, e.g., Khiok-khng Yeo, *What Does Jerusalem Have to Do with Beijing? Biblical Interpretation from a Chinese Perspective* (Harrisburg: Trinity International, 1998), 165-97. In Liew's discussion of Yeo, he disagrees, suggesting Acts is about "conversion, not conversation" (*What is Asian American Biblical Hermeneutics?*, 67). Beverly Roberts Gaventa however, sees this scene as interfering with any "conversion or conversation" theme as that might be applied to Acts, suggesting instead that it shows "the adaptability of Paul's witness to varying circumstances." See her "Witnessing to the Gospel in the Acts of the Apostles: Beyond the Conversion or Conversation Dilemma," *WW* 22, no. 3 (2002): 240.
31. The question of who gets converted in colonial interaction is a basic and rhetorical one in postcolonial theory, one that points to Bhabha-ian notions of ambivalence and hybridity.

who speak separate languages (2:5). Even with this brief information, we already come upon a diasporic negotiation of continuity and discontinuity: despite being from "every nation under heaven" and having different native languages, they are imagined as one devout population gathered in Jerusalem. The resonances of *ethnos* shouldn't be taken for granted, either, since belonging to Israel is commonly described with this word. They share an affiliation, but not on the basis of nation or ethnicity.

Indeed, Luke is only one of a number of ancient writers assuming a multi-ethnic Jewish population,[32] and this description of a community as both particular and universal is a standard tactic of diasporic belonging, which despite its ostensible interests in specified "particularism," appeals to a universalizing whole (ethnic, geographical, political and/or religious).[33] Put differently, national, ethnic, or religious particularity (the true Israel, e.g.) is not the opposite of universalism, but rather does its own universalizing work as a kind of oneness produced in diaspora that elides all kinds of other boundaries and differentiations.[34] So in Acts, the people at Pentecost

---

32. As Cynthia Baker finds, Luke, like Philo and other writers of Greco-Roman antiquity, recognized a world of ethnoracial diversity among Jews of their era. These writers assumed no definitional conflict or categorical contradiction in imagining Jews as belonging to a vast multiplicity of *ethne* ("nations," "homelands," "peoples") through *genos* ("birth," "race") and ancestral *synegeia* ("kinship"). See Baker, "From Every Nation under Heaven," in Nasrallah and Schüssler Fiorenza, *Prejudice and Christian Beginnings: Investigating Race, Gender and Ethnicity in Early Christian Studies* (Minneapolis: Fortress Press, 2009), 95. Baker also observes that Acts' Pentecost scene has tied a number of scholars in "exegetical knots," because it does not assume a "Jewish ethnoracial particularlism" that contrasts with a universalizing Christian mission or identity: "Jews thus provide Luke's *model*—not merely his *foil* or *counterpoint*—for imagining a universal, multiethnic spirit-filled community" (95).
33. Rey Chow likewise notices that the terms "universal" and "particular" tend to be treated as separate, mutually exclusive categories even as these terms, when viewed as conceptualities, actually reinforce and supplement each other. She quotes Naoki Sakai: "They are never in real conflict; they need each other and seek to form a symmetrical, mutually supporting relationship by every means in order to avoid a dialogic encounter which would necessarily jeopardize their reputedly secure and harmonized monologic worlds. Universalism and particularism endorse each other's defect in order to conceal their own; they are intimately tied to each other in their accomplice. In this respect, a particularism such as nationalism can never be a serious critique of universalism . . . "(5).

are connected by the term "Jew" and through a temporarily shared geographical location. It is clear that "Jew" here refers not to an overarching essential religious similarity, as in a faith-based personal piety that transcends culture or place, but to a set of loyalties that is ambiguously ethnic and transethnic, and is seated in a constructed (or better: fantasized) geography that simultaneously relies on specified shared homeland and defies it.

In this idealized vision of Pentecost, though, it is not the case that they all begin to speak the same language through the holy spirit. Rather, the apostles find *themselves* translated; their message rendered in the native tongues of others. Acts both imagines wholeness in Jerusalem and sees that idealized wholeness as only possible through an elaborate set of fissions and crossings of cultures and loyalties. What does Paul's mission to the *ethnē* mean in light of this diasporic ambiguity? The fact that Paul's mission to the *ethnē* in Acts is comprised almost entirely by time spent in diasporic synagogues suddenly seems less contradictory.[35]

Acts' vision of wholeness lasts for an entire chapter, but never again pans out in the text. By the end of the story, these instances of strange bedfellows and momentary mergers of cultural and political loyalties have come to look less ideal. As Paul's travels show, those moments of solidarity and in-gathering are haunted and enabled by violence. Not to mention that they are, as Paul's appeals to Roman citizenship show, often grounded in ambivalent protections from further harm.

Indeed, Paul's Roman citizenship, while often interpreted as representative of Christianity's increasing ascendency, does not get him very far in Acts. The book ends practically anticlimactically, with

---

34. Chow also wants to interrogate how solidarities are formed, on what bases, and what forms of power/identity those solidarities take up.
35. The fact that Paul spends most of his time in diaspora synagogues is often explained through the merging of Peter's and Paul's respective actions—Peter has the table vision, Paul mostly spends his time with Jews. I do not think that explanation excludes my reading though.

Paul testifying to an only partly convinced group of Roman Jews. He has, through his repeated invoking of citizenship, landed himself in the dubious place of awaiting a session before the emperor in Rome. He seems to consider this safer than being given over to the officials in Jerusalem. It is true, he is not executed at the end of Acts, but rather proclaims the Lord Jesus Christ "with all boldness and without hindrance," a statement ironized by the fact that he does so in chains. In his confrontation with Agrippa, in fact, the moment in which Paul is named as a "Christian," it turns out that his affiliation with Rome and Roman authority is a one-way street: they feel no affiliation with him. His claim of belonging to Rome is dwarfed by his pathetic status in the face of Agrippa, who seems to blame Paul's naiveté about Roman justice for his continued detainment. In the face of Paul's guilelessness, Agrippa's verdict ripples with sarcasm: "I would let him go," he says, "if he had not appealed to the emperor" (26:32).

The entire exchange between Paul and Agrippa, though short, is soaked in dark humor. It exudes and deflects anxieties around loyalty and its contingencies. Agrippa is making fun of Paul's outlandish brazenness and propensity for persuasive rhetoric, mocking him with the slander "Christian." Paul responds in the kind of bitter double-tongue usual for tense interactions with authorities. The affective complexity and tenor of this scene, accomplished by its anti-climactic irony, combined with the fact that Paul does not die at the end of Acts, means that the term "Christian" does not take on anything like the formulaic freight of later martyrological declamations. Paul is denied real vindication in the text, ending up as a sad sap who sold himself out only to be held in long-term detention.

"Christian" in this exchange is therefore a flippant smear, a momentary designation that worriedly puts a kind of upper limit on the contingencies of affiliation. Again, alongside of Ignatius and 1 Peter, this scene seems to confirm "Christian" as an imperial slander:

Acts is archaizing and particularizing the scene by placing it in the story of Paul. Acts' earlier use of the term in 11:26, then, amounts to a similarly archaizing use of the term. I would emphasize that this use, particularly as a passive construction, is still conflicted, and not indicative of any program for Acts or of any comprehensive understanding of identity.[36] "Christian," in Acts' historical place and moment, is both marginal and necessary to account for; both wounding and beside the point.

*   *   *   *

Acts' narrative and social world is steeped in danger, and rings with a deep sense of Israel's futurelessness[37]—so much so that Acts is seemingly obsessed with security.[38] But as a story that depicts instance after instance of securitizing gestures and close calls, it seems that Acts

---

36. The Greek reads: *Chramatisai te protos en antioxeiai tous mathatas christianous*. Judith Lieu sees Acts' use of the term "Christian" as comprehensive, but she notes that in other texts which represent early uses of the term "Christian" seem to exhibit a "double-edged defensiveness and pride" (*Christian Identity*, 253). I myself am less sure that Acts exhibits pride around the term, though it does seem to want to positively incorporate the slander.
37. Moreland ("Jerusalem Destroyed") presses that the seeming futurelessness of Israel be taken more seriously in shaping the text, and proposes that Luke-Acts' connections to Israel are, in the face of the fractured relations between Rome and Israel, a risky move that others like Marcion were unwilling to make. Moreland is clearly assuming a second-century dating for Acts, as am I. He follows Richard Pervo's proposal in *Dating Acts: Between the Evangelists and the Apologists*. (Santa Rosa: Polebridge Press, 2006), which has been highly influential on the work of the Westar Institute's Acts Seminar. In a summary of the Acts Seminar's conclusions, Dennis Smith writes: "There has been a scholarly consensus for some time that Luke-Acts as a two volume work was written in about the year 80 CE. This dating has been fundamental for all proposals regarding the historical reliability of Acts, using arguments ranging from the view that the author was a companion of Paul to arguments that the reliability of Acts is proven by how well it tracks with the story of Paul's mission as found in his letters. Early on in its research the Acts Seminar, led by the seminal work of Richard Pervo and Joseph Tyson, overturned that consensus and found instead that Acts was written in the early second century. This conclusion has significantly undermined a vast segment of Acts scholarship that has relied on the 80 CE dating." See Dennis E. Smith, "Top Ten Accomplishments of the Acts Seminar" (paper presented at the Westar Acts Seminar, spring 2012).
38. Brigitte Kahl, highlighting the thematic nature of the language of Luke's prologue, describes Acts as "security-minded" (*asfaleia*): "Beyond blaming Luke as an apologist or romanticizing him as a revolutionary, one has to realistically assess how far Luke went in the transformed historical situation that imposed severe limits on what was safe" ("Acts of the Apostles," 156).

does nothing but muddy the waters regarding which affiliations are safe and which are hazardous. Neither Rome nor Israel appears to be unilaterally safe or risky, and they turn out not to exclude each other as affiliations, either.

In fact, Acts bitterly demonstrates the ways in which securitizing gestures offer the hope and possibility of safety, but often only achieve "toleration" or marginal protections, if any at all.[39] The love and loyalty that compose patriotism, especially among populations who are disenfranchised by the very nation to which they confess their loyalty, promises upward mobility that is only accomplished in certain token or exemplary cases.[40] National love even thrives, ironically, on its unrequited nature, endlessly extending one's investment with the continued hope of getting a return.[41] Thus Paul's endless captivation with being Roman, it seems, culminates in nothing less than his captivity by the Romans, even though the authorities repeatedly say he has done nothing wrong.[42]

It is a profoundly expressive turn of Acts to follow the scene between Paul and Agrippa with a trip to Rome that is a tumultuous journey over stormy seas, one that results, no less, in a shipwreck. The larger story of Luke-Acts begins, we might remember, with a set of innocent-seeming solidarities. The Gospel of Luke is constantly

---

39. As Kahl suggests regarding Acts: "It is true that, thanks to interventions both by divine and Roman powers, Paul eventually reaches Rome safely and is able to preach there 'without hindrance' (Acts 28:31). But for the communities of Jesus' followers this expression at the end of Acts is an awkward fulfillment of the 'security' promised in Luke 1:4. It signals a rather fragile status of toleration that is nothing like full acceptance and approval on the side of the Roman authorities, especially as Luke mentions that a soldier is securing Paul's door all along. Paul remains a prisoner of Rome to until the end" (ibid., 151).
40. Ahmed, *The Cultural Politics of Emotion*. 130-31. Puar, *Terrorist Assemblages*. 37-78.
41. Ahmed, *Cultural Politics of Emotion*, ibid.
42. Loveday Alexander has described the ending of Acts in Rome as a kind of anitclimax as well. Not only is Rome hardly the "ends of the earth," which is where it is predicted Paul's mission will lead him, but in the final scene Paul does not convince all of his hearers. Alexander suggests Acts ends in Jewish communal disharmony and conflict (*Acts in Its Ancient Literary Context*, 213-15).

reminding its readers to give away their possessions to those in need (6:29-30, 12:33, 18:18-25) and invite outsiders to dinner and humble themselves, even if only to make themselves more righteous (14:7-14).[43] The Gospel of Luke envisions solidarity as privilege engaging in moderate, if utopian, self-critique, and stooping to charitably raise up the lowly.[44] But the experience of solidarity through Acts is less warm, or less liberally optimistic. Suddenly "solidarity" is cast as unsatisfying, alarmingly precarious, and shot through with physical threat. As a diasporic story, Acts charts the meager and finite agencies, strange bedfellows and, most poignantly, the incessant journeying from romance to disillusionment that comprise imperial and colonial life.[45]

Acts begins with an ambiguous promise that foreshadows the complications of the rest of the story:

> So when they had come together, they asked him, "Lord, is this the time when you will restore the kingdom to Israel?" He replied, "It is not for you to know the times or seasons which the Father has set by his own authority. But you will receive power when the holy spirit has come upon you; and you will be my witness in Jerusalem, in all Judea and Samaria, and to the ends of the earth" (Acts 1:6-8).

---

43. Cf. 3:10-14; 12:33; 14:13-14; 16:19-31; 19:1-10.
44. There has been much, if conflicted, scholarship on Luke's perspective on wealth and poverty. Though many have seen Luke as critical of wealth with its constant attention to the poor and its reversals of fortune (1:52-53; 6:20, 24, e.g.) (cf. James Metzger, *Consumption and Wealth in Luke's Travel Narrative* [Leiden: Brill, 2007]), it seems that Luke's critique comes from a remarkably well-off position. But critique of the rich does not necessarily contradict the view that Luke's apparent audience is a well-off community or that his work is an elite literary composition, as Wolfgang Stegeman and Luise Schottroff have found (*Jesus and the Hope of the Poor*, trans. Matthew J. O'Connell [Eugene, Ore: Wipf and Stock, 2009]). They suggest that Luke follows the Cynic critique of wealth, but makes few actual demands on its readers: "poverty is a literary ideal in Luke" (80).
45. The broad arc of Luke-Acts is a journey from romance to disenchantment, but within are many micro-stages of villainy, heroism, success, entrapment, and failure. Paul, for example, begins as a persecutor, is later treated as a hero, gets arrested multiple times, escapes prison, is considered at one point to be a god, and in the end is a mildly successful preacher in prison.

Not only does Jesus dodge the question, but the story of Acts hardly concludes at the ends of the earth. It rather ends in the center of the known world.[46] In any case, after fixing a hitch in their image as symbolically loyal and complete (Judas is replaced by Matthias in 1:26), and following Pentecost, the disciples set off to spread the word of "the Way": the hope for Israel's salvation through the savior, Jesus. The message of Israel's salvation is, of course, a deeply national message about political sovereignty. I wish to underscore its political dimensions here because it intervenes in the elision of the sociopolitical that happens when this language is treated as "religious," meaning personal or pietistic. It also highlights the diasporic thrust of Acts: one of its most primary questions is "how and when will we be complete again?" While Acts contains traces of strong desires for completeness—a completeness made possible through Jesus and the twelve—at the same time, the hopes for completeness in Acts are continually debilitated, reignited, and complicated, again and again.

"The Way" in Acts manages, then, to be not only an imagination of an ideal route of diasporic togetherness, but also the passage to a kind of "monstrous family of reluctant belonging," to quote Jacqueline Rose. In monstrous belonging, togetherness is formed not out of volition or even fondness, but out of the tense, ongoing, and irrevocable entanglements brought into being through violence and its many potent afterlives—a kind of belonging that might knit conflicting groups, victims and perpetrators, and even their kin in uncomfortable and unconscious binds.[47] So too in Paul's travels, "the Way" is defined not only by the unity and faithfulness of its followers,[48] but also by coalitions that are brief and dubious, often formed under strained political, economic, and social circumstances.

---

46. Alexander, *Acts in Its Ancient Literary Setting*, 214.
47. Jacqueline Rose, *States of Fantasy* (Oxford: Clarendon Press, 1996), 30-31. On this concept of the diasporic monstrous family, see also Grace Cho, "Diaspora of Camptown: The Forgotten War's Monstrous Family," *Women's Studies Quarterly* 31, no. 1-2 (2006): 309-31.

While the question of Acts' genre is both an unresolved and theoretically complicated one,[49] Acts' resonance with the Greco-Roman epic tradition generally, and the *Aeneid* specifically, hints at some of the national and imperial affectivity of Acts.[50] While so many have read the *Aeneid* as a legitimating epic, others have seen it as a work of nostalgic patriotism or even one of national disenchantment.[51] As Wendell Clausen writes, attesting to the troubled poignancy of the *Aeneid*:

> . . . there is another reason why the *Aeneid* moves us: its larger structure enlists our sympathies on the side of loneliness, suffering, defeat. It is the paradox of the *Aeneid*, the surprise of its greatness, that a poem which

---

48. One of Acts' primary emendations of history is its elision of the differences between Paul and the Jerusalem "pillars" that Paul describes in Galatians 2. So, in Acts, we find that all the apostles are "of one mind" (Acts 15:25), showing that unity of "the Way" is an important issue for Acts.
49. The most popular theses regarding the genre of Acts include Acts as history, with various inflections and subtypes (cf. note 3 above), Acts as biography (cf. Charles Talbert, *Literary Patterns, Theological Themes, and the Genre of Luke-Acts* [Missoula, Mont.: Scholar's Press, 1974]), Acts as apologetic text (which also has many subtypes, cf. Phillip Esler *Community and Gospel in Luke-Acts* [Cambridge: Cambridge University Press, 1987], 205-19; as well as Lieu, who characterizes Acts as an "apologetic history" [*Christian Identity*, 90-94]), and Acts as novel (cf. Richard Pervo, *Profit with Delight: The Literary Genre of the Acts of the Apostles* [Minneapolis: Fortress Press, 1987]). Though, as Virginia Burrus argues, " . . . '[G]enre' itself was a moving target during the early imperial period, which witnessed a veritable explosion in the production of prose narrative, a practice of writing that not only defied traditional generic classification but also seemed intentionally to subvert the distinction between history and fiction, truth and lies." See Burrus, "The Gospel of Luke and the Acts of the Apostles," in *A Postcolonial Commentary on the New Testament Writings*, ed. Fernando Segovia and R. S. Surigrtharajah (Bloomsbury: T & T Clark, 2009), 145.
50. Marianne Palmer Bonz, *The Past as Legacy: Luke-Acts and Ancient Epic* (Minneapolis: Fortress Press, 2000). I do not necessarily stand by Bonz's classification of Acts as epic in the same vein as the *Aeneid*, but I find myself convinced of their resonances, and, as I explain here, I find those resonances to produce an interesting take on Acts' colonial affectivity. Bonz is not the only or first scholar to associate Acts with the epic tradition. See, e.g., Dennis MacDonald, *Does the New Testament Imitate Homer? Four Cases from the Acts of the Apostles* (New Haven: Yale University Press, 2003). McDonald takes up relationships between Acts and the Greek epic.
51. For a more ambivalent approach to the *Aeneid*, see Rhona Beare, "Invidious Success: Some Thoughts on the Aeneid XII," *Proceedings of the Virgillian Society* 64 (1963-64): 26; and James O'Hara, *Death and the Optimistic Prophecy in Virgil's Aeneid* (Princeton: Princeton University Press, 1990). For a summary and discussion of the debate on the *Aeneid*'s sincerity, disillusionment, irony, and more (though perhaps not in those terms), see Bonz, *Past as Legacy*, 195-202.

celebrates the achievement of a national hero and the founding of Rome itself should be such a long history of defeat and loss. Aeneas finally wins (for such is his fate), but he wins at a terrible cost. He sees every human attachment broken, except that to his son, who is destined to succeed him and possess the fateful fields of Italy—a cold comfort.[52]

The *Aeneid* hails Rome, of course, but it does so in a decidedly minor key.

While there are no direct parallels between the *Aeneid* and Luke-Acts, the stories share strikingly similar dramatic plot reversals, appeals to divine guidance and sanction, and, as Marianne Bonz puts it, an "interpenetrating of the mundane and supramundane worlds" through prophecy and visions.[53] That is to say, if Luke-Acts borrows from the *Aeneid,* it does so thematically and impressionistically, at the very least sharing in its grand perspective and mythic, dramatic aura. However, on Clausen's affectively sensitive reading, the *Aeneid* also braids idealism and melancholy, cosmic waxing, and personal and social pain into a reflection on the junction of national (or rather republican) sentimentality and imperial ascendency.

Reading the *Aeneid* and Luke-Acts as unambiguously victorious expressions of course produces the predominant picture of Acts as a story of successful Christian mission.[54] But it would seem this

---

52. Clausen, "An Interpretation of the Aeneid," *Harvard Studies in Classical Philology* 68 (1964): 143. With respect to the hero of Virgil's epic, Clausen also notes that "Aeneas thinks only of the past, of those who fell under Troy's high wall, and wishes he too had died there. Aeneas is more burdened by memory than any other ancient hero; he is unlike Achilles or the typical hero of Greek tragedy, largely careless of the past and only gradually coming to an understanding of the true present. Virgil's Aeneas is not Homer's, a commonplace hero save for his goddess mother. He does bear some resemblance to Odysseus, a suffering voyager who remembers the past; but Aeneas is no adventurer, and has none of Odysseus' resilience or lightheartedness. Aeneas most resembles Hector and Sarpedon, and it can be no accident that their names occur in his opening speech; for they, almost alone of Homer's heroes, strike that note of melancholy resignation so characteristic of Virgil's Aeneas" (140).
53. Bonz, *Past as Legacy*, 190.
54. Cf. Bonz's reading: "This last point—that Rome's eternal rule has been granted in accordance with divine will only if one accepts the divine legitimacy of Virgil's Jupiter—brings one directly to a consideration of the motives behind the composition of *Luke-Acts* in narrative epic style. If

reading of Acts is more historical retrojection than narrative, given not only Paul's unresolved plot finale full of disappointment, but also that the term "Christian" has little import in the story.⁵⁵ Rather than straightforwardly categorizing Luke-Acts as epic, and reading the *Aeneid* as only a legitimating and foundational myth for Rome, it seems both texts share a touching and even subtle reflection on the tensive and fluctuating pulls of grand national pasts and disenchanted imperial presents; wishful social wholeness and the sense of having had, as Clausen puts it, "every human attachment broken." The epic quality of embellished self-importance also importantly consoles, or even denies, Israel's wavering sense of relevance. Acts' epic and distanced vision, it's "bird's eye view," is therefore not only an assumption of imperial(izing) vision—vision that obsessively locates, charts, and objectifies,⁵⁶ it also perhaps relieves the feeling of being all too lost in the middle of a complicated, unpredictable, and hard to chart social landscape.

* * * *

imitation is indeed a genuine form of flattery, then one must acknowledge a definite admiration for Rome on the part of Luke. Nevertheless, *Luke-Acts* presents a rival vision of empire, with a rival deity issuing an alternative plan for universal human salvation" (*Past as Legacy*, 182). Certainly in more recent history, Luke-Acts has been put to use in "successful" Christian missions. See, e.g., John T. Townsend, "Missionary Journeys in *Acts* and European Missionary Societies," *AThR* 86, no. 2 (1986): 99-104.

55. As Loveday Alexander writes of Acts' ending, "In this sense, too, the movement of Acts is downward and outward, constantly further away from the mountain of revelation where Jesus speaks clearly and is visible (until the intervention of the cloud) to the disciples' eyes (Acts 1:9). It is, as so often in biblical narrative, a movement from clarity to unclarity, from a moment of public vision to an ongoing journey into darkness. Here, too, the epilogue to Acts functions as a bridge back into the mundane realities of the readers' world: no angels, no heavenly voice, just the ongoing task of teaching and proclamation, and the tragedy of eyes and ears that fail to perceive the salvation sent by God (Acts 28:26-27)" (*Acts in Its Ancient Literary Setting*, 228-29). Alexander continues: "The 'tragedy' is about something else for me, however—not the failure of the message of salvation to be received, but rather the failure of unity and completion that the message of salvation hopes to enact" (229).

56. See Moore, *Mark and Luke in Poststructuralist Perspective*, 130. See also Laura Nasrallah's treatment of Acts' "whole world" geographical perspective in "The Acts of the Apostles, Greek Cities and Hadrian's Panhellion," *JBL* 127, no. 3 (2008), 533-66.

It has been historically difficult to locate Acts on the very grid it seems to construct. Where, precisely, do we find it *on* the trajectory from Jerusalem to Rome? Acts scholarship in recent years is particularly polarized, either positioning of Acts as (roughly) pro-imperial and anti-Jewish; or, on the other hand, locating it solidly in Israel's traditions, and more resistant (or at least less friendly) to Rome than has been assumed.[57] More than any kind of resolution to this question, I am interested in what is at stake in this collective pingponging. At present, long after Acts and in the wake of other empires, a global and multi-ethnic Christian constituency tries to reckon not only with its own vastness, but also with its unfortunate coalitions with various political powers, its own increasingly flagging relevance, and with questions of how this tenuous collective has come to be composed in the first place. For this "monstrous family of reluctant belonging,"[58] any visionary language and idealized self-understanding is beset not only by the fact that this very collective has been concocted through long and twisted histories of occupation, coercion, and enslavement, but also by, more specifically, the realities of Western imperialism and the Holocaust. Thus the specters of Rome and Israel do not just denote historical entities, but all that

---

57. Richard Pervo and Shelly Matthews fall firmly in the first camp, Moreland and the contributors to the *Luke-Acts and Empire* volume in the other. Joseph Tyson and Virginia Burrus, complicating these poles, find Luke-Acts profoundly mixed—even exemplary in its ambivalence—towards Israel and Rome. See Tyson, *Images of Judaism in Luke-Acts* (Columbia: University of South Carolina Press, 2010); and Burrus, "Gospel of Luke." Even when work on Luke-Acts does not explicitly take up one of these positions, volumes tend to be organized around either the question of Luke's Greco-Roman or its Jewish/anti-Jewish context. Cf. Penner and Vander Stichele, eds., *Contextualizing Acts: Lukan Narrative and Greco-Roman Discourse* (Atlanta: Society of Biblical Literature, 2003). Jack T. Sanders, *The Jews in Luke-Acts* (Minneapolis: Fortress Press,1987); and Jacob Jervell, *Luke and the People of God: A New Look at Luke-Acts* (Eugene, OR: Wipf and Stock, 2002). This pattern seems to be *the* way of organizing discussions of Acts, although it is not unique to Luke-Acts.
58. I want to suggest that this "monstrous family of belonging," drawing from the concept itself, is not limited to those who identify as Christians, but includes those who are connected to Christianity in non-identitarian ways. See my earlier discussion of Daniel Boyarin and Christianity in chapter 1.

we hope, fear, despise, or mourn about ourselves as an imperially assembled collective.[59] In the contemporary United States, for example, public self-understanding paints itself as either Israel or Rome at various times, on occasion simultaneously, motioning towards magnificence and progress, chosenness and moral righteousness—but also subtly identifying, in the vein of the *Aeneid*, with both the imperial victor and the casualties of its own Pyrrhic victory.[60]

That is to say that, although played out almost entirely in ideological language and historical frameworks, the "how Jewish" and "how imperial" question of Acts as an apparently exemplary instance or signal moment of Christian identity is always a question asked with particular affective force. Plagued with transgenerational memories of and consumptions with violence,[61] the question contains

---

59. Of course Israel and Rome were also symbolic entities for Luke-Acts. See, e.g., Conzelmann's discussion of Luke's geography as having largely a symbolic value (*The Theology of St. Luke* [Minneapolis: Fortress Press, 1982]. Others have tracked, in different ways, the heaviness of colonialism, imperialism and the Holocaust on New Testament work, though the focus is almost universally on ideological stakes and interpretational or historical results. For a small sampling of texts, mainly ones that are especially impressive or memorable to me, see the essays in Musa Dube and Jeffrey Staley, eds., *John and Postcolonialism: Travel, Space and Power* (New York: Sheffield Academic Press, 2002). Joseph Tyson's first and last chapters in *Luke, Judaism and the Scholars: A Critical Approach to Luke-Acts* (Columbia: University of South Carolina Press, 1999) narrate some of the effects of the Holocaust on New Testament scholarship's thinking about the relationships between ancient Jews and Christians. See also Richard Horsley's introduction to *In the Shadow of Empire*, 1-8; and Stephen Moore's *Empire and Apocalypse: Postcolonialism in the New Testament* (Sheffield, England: Sheffield Phoenix Press, 2006), which integrates reflections on European and American imperialism into its analysis. Cf. Brigitte Kahl's autobiographical interlude in *Galatians Re-Imagined: Reading with the Eyes of the Vanquished* (Minneapolis: Fortress Press, 2010) and Wes Howard-Brook and Anthony Gwyther, *Unveiling Empire: Reading Revelation Then and Now* (Maryknoll: Orbis, 1999), both of which I discuss at more length in the final chapter.
60. I am indebted to Hal Taussig's analysis of the Achilles/Penthesileia relief at Aphrodisias for this observation. See Taussig, "Melancholy, Colonialism, and Complicity: Complicating Counterimperial Readings of Aphrodisias' Sebasteion," in *Text, Image and Christians in the Graeco-Roman World: A Festschrift in Honor of David Balch*, ed. Aliou C. Niang and Carolyn Osiek (Eugene, Ore: Pickwick Publications, 2012), 280-95.
61. Again, I want to reiterate the non-conscious, affective aspects of this haunting: "visceral memories."

crosscurrents of emotion that range from lingering guilt to adamant disgust, from longings for a momentousness that is not quite so nefarious, to sadness for what could have been. And while I do not want to take any of the straightforward significance and necessity out of the ethical stakes of this question, it is no less ethically necessary, I think, to notice the proximity of such ethical pleading to frustrated embarrassment, anger, and/or a sense of paralysis over a terrifying history.

Much more will be said about the affective saturation and slipperiness of Rome as a site of historical work in the last chapter. For the moment, though, I want to suggest that we might consider trading the language of "inside vs. outside" and "for vs. against"—or even their more poststructuralist incarnations of "hybridity" and "ambivalence," which keep a binary structure, if a more complex one[62]—for darker ecologies of violence and more richly distinguished landscapes of social involvement. Acts may not be the charter document (ideal or otherwise) for Christianity that we think it is,[63] but, as a reflection on the sharper edges of diasporic and imperial belonging, it still plots a familiar course.[64] The cycles of romance and almost cynical disenchantment, the designs for integrated wholeness and the sorrow over collapsed potential, as well as the residue of stubbornly defiant self-importance, are both Acts' and our own.

---

62. Massumi, *Parables for the Virtual: Movement, Affect, Sensation* (Durham: Duke University Press, 2002), 69.
63. Indeed Lieu notes Luke-Acts' immediate impact and importance was "slight," and there are very few clear allusions to Acts until the latter half of the second century (*Christian Identity*, 93-94).
64. Acts has already inspired some diasporic reflections: for instance, the edited volume, *They Were All Together in One Place? Towards Minority Biblical Criticism*, ed. Randall Bailey, Tat-Siong Benny Liew, and Fernando Segovia (Atlanta: Society of Biblical Literature, 2009). See the introduction in which the editors describe their playful use of and inversion of Pentecost to include more tension and less homogeneity. I would say their reading, then, is actually right on the pulse of Acts' own tensions and heterogeneity. Similarly, see Tat-Siong Benny Liew's chapter "Overlapping (His)Stories: Reading Acts in Chinese America," in *What Is Asian American Biblical Hermeneutics?*, 57-74.

In the next three chapters, I re-read the Secret Revelation of John, Hebrews, the Gospel of John, and the Gospel of Truth for their own traces of diasporic loss, relating them to aspects of other literature of this approximate period. Similarly sidestepping the most familiar categories for understanding and locating these texts, I suggest that categories such as "Gnostic" and "Christian," as well as the most common interpretive questions asked of these texts, obscure other social and theological questions. Each of these texts, too, exhibit and address colonial hauntedness and uncertain belonging, attempting in delicate and inventive ways to heal those pains.

4

Expanding the Diasporic Imagination: The Secret Revelation of John

Now it happened one day when John the brother of James, the sons of Zebedee, was going up to the temple, a Pharisee named Arimanios approached him. And he said to him, "Where is your teacher, the one whom you used to follow?"

He said to him, "He returned to the place from which he came."

The Pharisee said to me, "This Nazorene deceived you (pl.) with error. [He filled [your (pl.) ears with lies], and he shut [your hearts]. He turned you (pl.) away from the traditions of your fathers."

When I heard these things, I turned from the temple to the mountain, which was a place of desert. And I grieved greatly in my heart ... (Secret Revelation of John 2.1-7).

So begins one of the most elaborately mythological stories in the Nag Hammadi codices. John is on his way to the temple and finds himself caught in the question, posed as an accusation, of what constitutes true tradition. In grief over the accusation, he turns away from the temple and goes to a desert mountain where he pains over matters of origins and authority:

> How was the Savior appointed? Why was he sent into the world by his father who sent him? Who is his father? And of what sort is that aeon to which we will go? He told us that the aeon is modeled on that indestructible aeon, but he did not teach us about what sort the latter is. Just then, while I was thinking these things, behold the heavens opened, and the whole creation below the heaven was illuminated . . . (SRevJohn 3.1-2).[1]

The vision that follows is a story of two deeply contrasting worlds, and describes human beings as unaware of where and to whom they truly belong. It portrays human nature as caught in the crossed forces of various gods, veering between goodness and corruption.

Despite the fact that nearly all of the attention the Secret Revelation of John attracts centers on its vivid and dramatic cosmological scheme, the text's inaugural scene evokes rather humdrum conflicts around tradition and belonging. This strained conversation between Israelites, taking place in the vicinity of a now-wrecked Israelite institution no less, subtly establishes the text as a diasporic reflection full of tension, sorrow, and uncertainty. But while the text begins with an anecdote describing the contentiousness and uncertainty of Israelite belonging, as the story proceeds not only does this sense of uncertainty about belonging quickly fade, but another, intertwined

---

1. I am using Karen King's translation of the Secret Revelation of John from her monograph on the text, and thus also her versification numbering. There are actually four extant copies of Secret Revelation of John, which, as King points out, attests to its ancient popularity. King offers full translations of two versions, one from the Nag Hammadi Codex II and the other from the Berlin Codex. Codex II represents a longer version of the text than the Berlin Codex. I will be primarily drawing from her translation of the Berlin Codex version, and will note where I quote the longer version in Codex II. Following King, square brackets in the text [. . .] indicate a lacuna in the text or that the text has been reconstructed. Words in parenthesis (. . .) have been added to keep the language clear and fluid. See Karen L. King, *The Secret Revelation of John* (Cambridge: Harvard University Press, 2006).

mode of belonging, comes under scrutiny: belonging to the world (*cosmos*) of the Roman imperium.

Scholarship on this text has largely classed it as a "Gnostic" text, suggesting both that it does not properly belong to either Israel/Judaism or Christianity,[2] and that it evades nitty-gritty social dilemmas in favor of more rarefied or ethereal ones.[3] Karen King, on the other hand, has shown the historically and epistemologically

---

2. Most of the entire history of traditional scholarship on Gnosticism has been fixated on the question of how Jewish/how Christian "Gnosticism" and/or Nag Hammadi texts might be. To briefly summarize the spectrum of arguments and exemplary texts which represent them, I note the following: some have framed the question as the "Jewish roots of Gnosticism," but have nonetheless found Gnosticism and the texts said to comprise it as always already heretical within Jewish tradition, or as having rebelled or otherwise turned against it. See, e.g., Alan Segal, *Two Powers in Heaven: Early Rabbinic Reports about Christianity and Gnosticism* (Leiden: Brill, 2002); and Birger Pearson, *Gnosticism, Judaism and Egyptian Christianity* (Minneapolis: Augsburg Fortress Press, 1990). Hans Jonas does not quite suggest Jewish origins but nonetheless finds a kind of formative antagonism to Jewish traditions. See Hans Jonas, "Response to G. Quispel's *Gnosticism and the New Testament*," in *The Bible in Modern Scholarship*, ed. Philip J. Hyatt (Nashville, TN: Abingdon Press, 1965), 279-293. Others, such as Gerard Luttikhuizen suggest that the apparent critique of Jewish scripture in the Secret Revelation of John is evidence of Gnosticism's involvement in "intra-Christian" debates, though he still finds the origins of Gnosticism elsewhere than either Christianity or Jewish tradition. See Gerard Luttikhuizen, *Gnostic Revisions of Genesis Stories and Early Jesus Stories* (Leiden: Brill, 2006). Gilles Quispel has contrasted the Secret Revelation of John to "Christian/Valentinian Gnostic" texts, moving it as far away from Christianity as possible. See his "Valentinian Gnosis and the Apocryphon of John," in *The Rediscovery of Gnosticism: Proceedings of the International Conference on Gnosticism at Yale, New Haven, Connecticut, March 28-31, 1978, vol. 1*, SHR XLI, ed. Bentley Layton (Leiden: Brill, 1980), 118-27.

3. "The Gnostic redeemer myth" was produced primarily by the history-of-religions scholars (Richard Reitzenstein, Wilhelm Bousset, and Rudolf Bultmann, e.g.), who were seeking to find the origins and background for Christian mythic elements. This myth, a story that involves a redemptive messenger descending to earth to save imprisoned souls and return them to where they truly belong, does not directly derive from any single text, but was created from a mash-up of literary sources. It not only became a "staple of two-page summaries of Gnosticism," but in its specificities contains all the hallmarks of the Gnostic stereotypes of a world-hating, esoteric, elitist, pessimistic, and mythic religious phenomenon. See King's extended description in chapter four of *What is Gnosticism?* (Cambridge: Harvard University Press, 2003), 71-109, particularly her succinct summary which includes this statement: "We might also note the irony that contemporary scholars have often explicitly characterized this myth as 'artificial,' but they have seen this artificiality as the product, not of twentieth-century methods of historical reconstruction, but of the 'half-educated' minds of ancient 'Gnostics.' In this case I would say that historians have been guilty of precisely what they accused the Gnostics of: the creation of *Kunstmythen*. The fact that current scholarship has thoroughly undermined any foundation for this artificial construction has not stopped it from continuing to exert considerable influence" (109).

suspect nature of the category of Gnosticism and introduced another approach to the Secret Revelation of John. She suggests that clean and clear distinctions between cosmic/mythological language and social concerns are hard to sustain from a historical perspective. They miss the very thrust of a text that puts the cosmic perspective and foundational assumptions of creation motifs to work with oblique imperial references for a comprehensive critique of the lived world.[4]

King re-reads the Secret Revelation to John as a text within Christian tradition, and likewise notices how it negotiates a relationship with the ideals of the Roman Republic and the cruel realities of the Roman Empire (among other things). She describes its use of creation motifs and figures (from both Genesis and Plato's *Timaeus*) as generating a devastating critique of imperial rulers and the lived world, as well as a utopian (if compromised and assimilated)

---

4. King's reading of the Secret Revelation of John as an eviscerating critique of the injustice and brutality of imperial rule flies in the face of traditional scholarship on Gnosticism and Gnostic mythology, which casts the text as anti-political. Cf. chapter 5 in King, Secret Revelation of John in which she discusses the ancient context for not just a cosmo-social reading of texts, but also for how political critique often occurred in more oblique, "disguised" registers. Giving a broad range of examples from Justin to apocalyptic discourses, Stoic philosophers, and the Roman *imperium*'s own legitimizing rhetoric, King illustrates the deep, mutual involvements of philosophy, cosmology, and (shall we say) social theory. King follows Dale Martin, Elaine Pagels and Elisabeth Schüssler Fiorenza, who have drawn similar conclusions about the way cosmic language also had social relations embedded in it. Cf. Dale Martin, *The Corinthian Body* (New Haven: Yale University Press, 1995); Elaine Pagels, *Adam, Eve and the Serpent* (New York: Random House, 1988); and Elisabeth Schüssler Fiorenza, "The Followers of the Lamb: Visionary Rhetoric and Social-Political Situation," *Semeia* 36 (1986): 123-46. The only two other addresses to possible socio-political implications of figures and themes in Secret Revelation of John would be Ioan Culianu "The Angels of the Nations and the Origins of Gnostic Dualism," in *Studies in Gnosticism and Hellenistic Religions: Presented to Gilles Quispel on the Occasion of His 65th Birthday*, ed. R van den Broek and M.J. Vermaseren (Leiden: Brill, 1981), 78-91; and Elaine Pagels, "Christian Apologists and 'The Fall of the Angels': An Attack on Roman Imperial Power?," *HTR* 78 (1985): 301-25 and "The Demiurge and His Archons—A Gnostic View of the Bishop and Presbyters?" *Harvard Theological Review* 69 (1976), 301-324. The imperial investment in mythological and cosmological language to naturalize and articulate its rule has appeared in other empire-critical work within the field of New Testament, as well. Cf. Brigitte Kahl's *Galatians Re-imagined*, Davina Lopez *Apostle to the Conquered*. Likewise, the relationship of the political to the cosmic has been addressed in more historical-contextual studies such as Michael Peppard's *The Son of God in the Ancient World: Divine Sonship in its Social and Political Context* (New York: Oxford University Press, 2011).

vision of justice, goodness, and "true humanity." The Secret Revelation of John is a vision of idealized counter-belonging. But while King places the text firmly in a Christian school setting, and sees it as largely critical of Jewish traditions in its reading of Genesis,[5] there are significant textual nuances that upset such a characterization for the text. Even aside from the diasporic anecdote framing the story, it also seems that the Secret Revelation of John is reading Genesis through Second Isaiah, sharing Second Isaiah's sense of traumatic upheaval and homelessness, and borrowing Isaiah's imagination of a lofted divinity around which a diasporic population can coalesce.

Scholars of the supposed phenomenon of Gnosticism have long suggested that the Secret Revelation of John seeks out utopian freedom and true belonging that is counter to the "world." However, scholars imagined this freedom and belonging as the disconnected desires of an exotic fringe group rather than relatively mundane longings of an embattled collective. If we take the opening scene of the text seriously (and avoid Gnostic stereotypes), though, the Secret Revelation of John becomes a totalizing vision borne out of Israelite diasporic grief and homelessness. Even more than a searing political critique, it is a vision in which colonial excesses of pain and violence, mixed senses of loyalty, and the complications of diasporic return fuel the promise of a pure and perfect elsewhere—a homeland.

*   *   *   *

John's vision begins with a single figure who appears in three forms—a child, an old man, and a woman:

---

5. Though King does point out that the Secret Revelation of John uses Jewish scripture to critique scripture (*Secret Revelation of John*, 258-59). King, in her introduction for her hypothesis about the possible social location of the text, argues it is composed in a Christian school in Alexandria, followed by strong circulation in Egypt. King broadly suggests the second century as a date for the text (1-24). It seems that Irenaeus is already familiar with the text, however, so that would put it at or before the middle of the second century.

[He sa]id [to me] "John, wh[y] are you doubting and [fearful]? For you are not stranger [to this woman]. Do not be faint[hearted]! I am the one who is with [you (pl.) al]ways. I am the [Father]. I am the Mother. [I] am [the S]on. I am the one who exists forever, undefil[ed and un]mixed" (SRevJohn 3.9-13).[6]

Already this figure is defined by its unity and purity. But its unity and purity are somewhat fragile: "[Although I was watch]ing him, I did not [understand th]is wonder, whether it is a [likeness] having numerous forms [in the l]ight . . . or if it is one [likeness th]at has three aspects" (3.8).[7] This figure says he has come to teach John "what exists and what has come into being and what must come into being (3.14-15)" and "about the immovable generation of the perfect human" (3.16),[8] saying:

> The Unity is a monarchy with nothing ruling over it. It is the God and Father of the All, the holy, the invisible, who exists over the All,

---

6. This passage is an adjusted translation of King's, differing from the one in her monograph. In her monograph on the Secret Revelation of John, she translates and fills the lacuna with the following: "For you are not a stranger [to this likeness] . . . " However, in her essay on sex and gender in the Secret Revelation of John, she offers a full argument for translating "woman" instead of "likeness," including the identification of Christ with the Mother and with Pronoia. See Karen King, "Reading Sex and Gender in the Secret Revelation of John," *JECS* 19, no. 4 (2011): 519-38 (527 n.30).

7. Codex II is more assertive on this, assuring that "These (semblances) before me were not multiple beings but there was only a (single) [li]keness [having] many forms in the lig[ht]."

8. Secret Revelation of John 3.16 is from Codex II. I use Codex II here because of its evocation of "immovable generation," which for me has distinct diasporic resonances. The Berlin Codex version, however, also makes use of the phrase "immovable generation" in 23.3 and 27.5. In his book, *The Immovable Race: Gnostic Designation and the Theme of Stability in Late Antiquity* (Leiden: Brill, 1985), Michael Williams has set out the Septuagint uses of *asaleutos/akinetos*, the Greek translation of the Coptic word *atkim*, both meaning "immovable." Yahweh is described as immovable or unshakeable, and described as causing other things to shake, whether in a divine theophany or otherwise (cf. Williams's introduction, 1-7). While Williams suggests that "immovable race" (or "immovable generation," in King's translation) has the sound of an "oppressed and persecuted group" and has resonances with the "biblical theme of the people protected by Yahweh from being shaken or moved by enemy or catastrophe" (p. 12; cf. also 141-152), he nonetheless pursues exclusively mythical and Gnostic-stereotypical interpretations of this theme in the Secret Revelation of John. He likewise sees the text as only ironically pursuing this theme, due to its apparently negative take on the creator god of Genesis. He also separates the Greek and Israelite meanings of "immovability," whereas it seems to me that in Israelite diasporic culture these resonances might be rather productive and meaningful.

the one who [. . .] incorruption, existing as pure light, into which it is not possible for any light of the eye to gaze. It is the Spirit. It is not appropriate to think about It as god or that It is something similar. For It surpasses divinity. It is a dominion having nothing to rule over it (SRevJohn 4.2-6).

The figure, who turns out to be the Savior,[9] goes on to chronicle the monarchic Unity as both defying all description and (with some contradiction to its indescribability) the foundation and essence of all that is good.[10] It is illimitable, unsearchable, ineffable, unnameable; it is neither corporeal nor incorporeal. But it is also "knowledge-giving understanding" and "life-giving life" (4.37) and the head of all the aeons/ages (5.4).[11] Ever elusive but emphatically present, the beginning of everything and beyond divinity, this superlative oneness is not sustainable. Not only does this oneness almost immediately beget an entire population of other divinities, but it turns out the purity and harmony of this heavenly realm hinged on female compliance (an iffy proposition indeed). One of the divine figures— wisdom/Sophia—decides she wants to produce a "likeness

---

9. King assumes this figure is the Savior, and, by the end of John's vision, this figure is indeed called Christ/Savior. However, I find the elusive, associate quality of the figures important. Figures change name and shape throughout the text, which is characteristic of revelatory literature. By the end, the Savior is Pronoia (cf. Codex II, 26.26), and possibly Sophia, too, as figures fold into and diverge from one another, both preserving and upsetting the sense of divine unity. King disagrees, and finds them to be "distinct hypostases," although she notes that "both play roles as creator and revealer, and they share similar epithets, so that Autogenes-Christ is also a kind of wisdom figure" *(Secret Revelation of John*, 229).
10. Cf. King, *Secret Revelation of John*, 86, for a discussion of this seeming contradiction and its similarities to Middle Platonist philosophizing.
11. The text goes on: "For It is eternal. It does not need anything. For It cannot be made perfect as though It were deficient and only required perfecting. Rather It is always totally perfect. It is light. It cannot be limited because there is nothing before It to limit It. It is inscrutable for there is no one before It to scrutinize It. It is immeasurable because there is no other to measure It as though (anything) exists before It . . . . For It is neither corporeal nor incorporeal. It is neither large nor small. It is not a quantity. It is not a creature. Neither is it possible for anyone to know It. It is not something pertaining to the All which exists, rather It is a thing which is better than these—not as being superior (to other as though It is comparable to them) but as that which belongs to Itself" (SRevJohn 4.10-15, 24-29).

out of herself," and without permission, gives birth to Yaldabaoth, whose birth "rips the seamless fabric of divine Being."[12]

Yaldabaoth is not like his mother. He has some of his mother's power and spark, and though he becomes the chief ruler and creator of humanity and its world, he is ignorant about the world above him. "I am a jealous God; without me there is nothing" (14.2) he declares, echoing Exodus 20:3. The text is quick to undercut him, commenting that by announcing this he was "indicating to the angels who are below him that another God does exist. For if there were no other (god) over him, of whom would he be jealous?" (14.4). With this declaration it seems that the Secret Revelation of John has explicitly called out and lampooned the creator god of Genesis.[13] Indeed, Yaldabaoth is not just ignorant and jealous, he is violent, cruel, and relatively incompetent. He attempts to create humankind in the image of the perfect (hu)man, a divine image he spies as a reflection in water, but what he produces is a kind of "grotesque mimicry" of it. Adam is a lifeless mass lacking *pneuma*, and can only be enlivened with true divine intervention.[14]

> And they created the whole body, which was joined together by the multitude of angels. And it remained inactive a long time because neither the seven authorities nor the angels who had forged [the links of the chain] were able to awake it. And (the Mother) wanted to retrieve

---

12. King, *Secret Revelation of John*, 91. I am not attending to the gendered dynamics of the Secret Revelation of John's vision here, but there is certainly a lot to explore, not the least of which is how female figures take central roles in both the divine rupture and the saving of humanity, as well as how the creation of Eve differs from Genesis in that she does not derive from Adam's rib. Cf. King, "Reading Sex and Gender in the Secret Revelation of John"; Ingvid Gilhus, "Male and Female Symbolism in the Gnostic Apocryphon of John," *Temenos* 19 (1983): 33-43. Also important is Virginia Burrus, *Saving Shame: Martyrs, Saints and Other Abject Subjects* (Philadelphia: University of Pennsylvania Press, 2008), 57-64; and Benjamin Dunning, *Specters of Paul: Sexual Difference in Early Christian Thought* (Philadelphia: University of Pennsylvania Press, 2011), 75-96, though here in the context of comparison to On the Origin of the World.
13. Cf. King, *Secret Revelation of John*, 170.
14. Ibid., 100; Codex II's description is more vivid: "The body moved and gained strength, and it was luminous" (18.11).

the power which she had give to the ruler from (her) audacity. She went in innocence and entreated the Father of the All, whose mercy is great, and the luminous God. Following a holy design, he sent Autogenes and his four lights in the shape of angels of the Chief Ruler. They advised him with the goal of extracting the power of the Mother from within him. They said to him, "Blow into his face from the spirit which is in you and the object will arise." And he blew into it from his spirit, which is the power form the Mother, into the body. And [at that moment] he moved (SRevJohn 17.64-18.11).

Yaldabaoth is then of course jealous of the superiority of his creation, since he "had come into being through them all and they had given the powers that existed within them to the human . . ." (18.13-14). As King observes, Yaldabaoth is a stark contrast to the superlative divine being of the world above. She notes,

> Where the transcendent Deity is ineffable and unnameable, the creator God is named—he is called Yaldabaoth or Saklas. Where the transcendent Deity is the 'sole ruler,' Yaldabaoth is merely 'chief ruler' and his rule extends only over the authorities, power and angels he has created. . . . Where the transcendent Deity is knowledge and the source of knowledge, Yaldabaoth is ignorant and indeed arrogant in his ignorance. The character of Yaldabaoth's rule also stands in sharp contrast to that of the merciful providence of the transcendent Deity.[15]

The rest of the text is a tale of continual struggle between the forces and figures of the world above and the world below who, respectively, fight to save humanity by revealing to them their true nature, and deceive, imprison, and attempt to destroy humanity. In the Secret Revelation of John, Christ is not only the figure who provides and explicates John's vision. He is, by providing this knowledge, the means to humanity's salvation: "And it is to you (John) that I speak these things so that you might write them down

---

15. King, *The Secret Revelation of John*, 91-92.

and give them in secret to your fellow spirits. For this mystery belongs to the immovable generation" (27.3-4).

The Secret Revelation of John is a narrative elaboration of the two accounts of creation in Genesis. The divine realm and the lower world are parallel accounts of the two creation stories in Genesis, in which the initial creation story is an account of order, harmony, and justice, and the second is marred by disorder, death, and evil.[16] The Secret Revelation of John cites moments and figures in these creation accounts, fusing them with Jewish wisdom traditions and Platonist philosophy. In the vein of Philo's *On Creation*, the Secret Revelation of John reads Genesis as consonant with Plato's *Timaeus* and its philosophical afterlives, which posit the cosmos as a copy of its eternal, invisible form.[17]

However, while the visible world in the *Timaeus* is the way in which the invisible world is perceivable, for the Secret Revelation of John the created world is a debased mimetic copy of the world above it. As King carefully observes, "The emphasis in Plato's account, however, is on the goodness and perfection of the world, not on its defects. It is the best and most beautiful cosmos possible. *Timaeus'* demiurgic God does the best job he can as a good craftsman and is largely successful, producing an orderly world of beauty and justice."[18] Yaldabaoth, in his ruthlessness, foibles, and failures, is therefore quite different than the Platonic demiurge. The Secret Revelation of John, it seems, "relies heavily upon the framework of Platonic metaphysics while simultaneously criticizing it, primarily by exploiting the passages within Plato's dialogues that already portray

---

16. Ibid., 215-16. Though King also points out that not only the Genesis accounts, but the ontology of Platonizing philosophy as well gets extended narration in the Secret Revelation of John, "in its repetition of above and below, and by the drama of the moves and countermoves made to entrap or free humanity" (350-51, n. 24).
17. Ibid., 203-204.
18. Ibid., 196.

the inferiority, division, and disorderliness of the world below."[19] While King concludes that the Secret Revelation of John's critique of the creator god of Genesis is proof of its hostile attitude toward Jewish traditions (among others), it seems to me that it lampoons one divine figure of Genesis only to uphold the perfection of another.[20]

In any case, this mingling of textual sources and associations produce an "oppositional logic" in which the divine realm acts as a foil to highlight the atrociousness of the worldly (i.e., Roman imperial) rulers, who were not only as capricious, power hungry, and pompous as Yaldabaoth, but also styled themselves as gods.[21] However, the Secret Revelation of John is not a critique of all things Roman: the utopian imagination of the ideal world above is steeped in Roman values of universal truth, virtuous kingship and justice, making it a fully hybrid and ambivalent text.[22]

In part due to the legacies of Gnosticism as a category, reflections on divinity and oneness in the Secret Revelation of John have often taken on the form of diagnoses on how it differs from the proper monotheism of Judaism and Christianity.[23] The latter is an

---

19. Ibid., 198.
20. King sees "Christianity" as "the only tradition that escapes reproof" in the Secret Revelation of John (ibid., 16). I disagree in that I do not see the Secret Revelation of John as representing or assuming Christianity as a tradition. Its use of Genesis is both constructive and critical, especially since it so strongly affirms the divinity of the first creation account.
21. King writes, "The portrait of the transcendent Deity represents the utopian commitments of the Secret Revelation to John, while Yaldabaoth and his minions exemplify everything that is wrong. The breach between them marks the nearly unbridgeable gap between the imagination of how things were supposed to be and how they were experienced" (ibid.,158). On Yaldabaoth as a figure for Roman cruelty, see especially p.164.
22. Ibid., 160-63.
23. Cf. note 2 above. Segal, Quispel, Jonas, and Luttikhuizen all based a significant portion of their arguments on the notion that Gnosticism assumed two prime divine figures, one of which is evil, and thus represents a turn or provocation against Jewish tradition. This argument is closely related to the typology that presumes dualism to be a constitutive element of Gnosticism. It is important to note that the Secret Revelation of John never uses the word "demiurge" and the distinction between a divine creator/chief ruler of the lower world, or even a distinction between a world below and world above, is not clear or even present in much of Nag Hammadi literature. For a summary of the problems with dualism as a typological category for Nag Hammadi literature, see King, *What is Gnosticism?*, 192-201.

emphatically creedal approach to understanding notions of divinity, in which creed represents something like a decontextualization and abstraction of cosmology. But what we now call "monotheism," the singular height or universality of a particular god, was largely rhetorical in the ancient Mediterranean world.[24] Not unlike Stoic Zeus-monotheism, which placed Zeus in a heightened and exclusive power position, Jews regularly claimed an emphatic monotheism while simultaneously (and apparently without any sense of contradiction) accounting for, or even paying homage to, a whole host of divine entities—including but not limited to Moses, Enoch, Jesus, the Logos, or angels.[25] The monotheism/polytheism divide also has a sneaky way of preserving a theological uniqueness within ancient Judaism and Christianity.

Monotheism implies belief in one god, and while the contemporary notion of "belief" itself may be a misnomer for the relationship of loyalty and respect between humans and gods,[26] belief-based categories also do not get one very far as affective accounts of theological reflection. "Belief" ties affect to ontology, thus narrowing theology to the question of whether one *feels* that a particular divinity exists or not. The rhetoric of belief might even

---

24. By now a wide collection of scholars with varying investments have pointed out the difficulty of claiming a kind of unique and exclusive devotion to one god as a hallmark of Jewish or Christian practice/identity. Many of these scholars have suggested that "monotheism," defined as belief in the existence of only one god, is a misleading term for the ancient world. See particularly M. L. West, "Towards Monotheism," in *Pagan Monotheism in Late Antiquity*, ed. Polymnia Athanassiadi and Michael Frede (New York: Oxford University Press, 1999), 21-40; and Regina M. Schwartz, *The Curse of Cain: The Violent Legacy of Monotheism* (Chicago: Chicago University Press, 1997), 17. Perhaps the most succinct indictment is Paula Fredriksen, "Mandatory Retirement: Ideas in the Study of Christian Origins Whose Time Has Come to Go," *Studies in Religion* 35 (2006): 231-46. Cf. Michael Mach, "Concepts of Jewish Monotheism During the Hellenistic Period," in *The Jewish Roots of Christological Monotheism: Papers from the St. Andrews Conference on the Historical Origins of the Worship of Jesus*, eds. Carey C. Newman, James R. Davila, and Glays S. Lewis (Leiden: Brill, 1999), 21-42.
25. Larry Hurtado, *One Lord, One God: Early Christian Devotion and Ancient Jewish Monotheism* (Minneapolis: Augsburg Fortress Press, 1988).
26. Fredriksen, "Mandatory Retirement," 243.

funnel or disguise the particular affectivities that give theological reflection its color and shape. Zeus-monotheism, for instance, had a surprisingly earnest and textured social-affective life in its connection to the reinvigoration of cosmopolitanism in the late first and early second centuries. For both Epictetus and Seneca, for example, being a citizen of the cosmos was a universal status that was closely tied to a kind of humanism through the oneness and height of God (Zeus).[27] But this universal status was also tied to displacement. Both Seneca and Epictetus were exiles under Rome, and while Epictetus's notion of world-citizenship is evoked more generally as a comfort in circumstances of bodily peril,[28] Seneca's *Consolation to Helvia* expressly links being a citizen of the cosmos with Seneca's own pain in dislocation.[29] As he writes to his mother to comfort her on his banishment, he gives an extended description of the variety of people in the city (*Helv.* 6). He goes on to speak of how the "nature of the celestial is always mobile," in the way planets always move, following with a long list of dispersed cultural populations and the many possible reasons for their resettlement: "What is the meaning of Greek cities in the heart of barbarian country? Why the Macedonian idiom among Indians and Persians? . . . Man the wanderer has made his way through pathless and unfamiliar regions" (*Helv.* 7). In the next section, Seneca couples expanded citizenship with exile, celestial movements with terrestrial displacement, and the

---

27. Epictetus, *Discourses* 1.9.1. See the discussion in A. A. Long, *Epictetus: A Stoic and Socratic Guide to Life* (New York: Oxford University Press, 2002), 150. Cf. Epictetus, *Discourses* 2.10.5-6 and 3.24,10-12.
28. Epictetus, *Discourses* 2.10.5-6 and 3.24,10-12.
29. Elaine Fantham even calls the *Consolation to Helvia* a "dialogue of displacement." "Dialogues of Displacement: Seneca's Consolations to Helvia and Polybius" in *Writing Exile: The Discourse of Displacement in Greco-Roman Antiquity and Beyond,* ed. Jan Felix Gaertner (Leiden: Brill, 2007), 173-192.

oneness of the world with an omnipotent god.³⁰ In the same vein, when comforting a friend in exile, Plutarch writes,

> Such is your present removal from what you take to be your native land. For by nature there is no such thing as a native land, any more than there is by nature a house or farm or forge or surgery . . . For man, as Plato says, is 'no earthly' or immovable 'plant' but a 'celestial' one . . . Thus Heracles spoke well when he said, 'an Argive I or Theban, for I boast no single city; There is no fort in Greece but is my country' whereas the saying of Socrates is still better, that he was no Athenian or Greek, but a 'Cosmian' (as one might say Rhodian or Corinthian) . . . This is the boundary of our native land, and here no one is either exile or foreigner or alien . . . (Plutarch, *On Exile* 600 E-F)

For Seneca and Plutarch, cosmic citizenship abates the loss and grief of displacement by putting one "at home" in a world of other displaced people.³¹ God functions in this kind of cosmopolitanism as lofted and dislodged in a way that might seem at odds with ancient tendencies to localize deity, but that only goes to prove that god appears here less as divinity disarticulated from place than one

---

30. Seneca writes, "To compensate for mere change of place—disregarding other inconveniences involved in exile—Varro, the most scholarly of the Romans, held the fact that we enjoy the same order of nature wherever we go a sufficient recourse. Marcus Brutus thought the fact that exiles could carry their virtues with them a sufficient compensation . . . What we have lost is but a trifle, but wherever we stir the two resources which are the fairest of all attend us—nature, which is universal, and virtue, which is our own. Such was the design, believe me, of whatever force fashioned the universe, whether an omnipotent god or impersonal Reason . . . Briskly, and therefore, with head held high, let us stride with dauntless step wherever circumstances carry us, let us traverse any lands whatever. Within the world there can be no exile, for nothing within the world is alien to man" (Seneca, *Helv.* 8; Moses Hadas, trans., *The Stoic Philosophy of Seneca: Essays and Letters* [New York: W. W. Norton, 1958]).
31. While Seneca is exiled from Rome, Roman conquest is also what makes such an expanded citizenship—this being in the company of other exiles—possible. His citizenship is a contradictory condition highlighted by Aristides when he notes not only that "all everywhere are equally subjects" under Rome, but also that the empire has "divided people into Romans and non-Romans" (Aelius Aristides, *Roman Oration* 30, 63). One might think of cosmic citizenship under Rome through Benedict Anderson's claim about the construct of the nation that "is imagined as a *community,* because, regardless of the actual inequality and exploitation that may prevail in each, the nation is always conceived as a deep, horizontal comradeship." See Benedict Anderson, *Imagined Communities* (New York: Verso, 1983), 7. The conception of oneness thus often hides inequity and fracture while seeming to alleviate it.

which *functions like place*: divinity produces its own kind of locality. Similarly, universalism appears as a solution, if a troublesome one, to the complications of place/displacement—a notion that weighs particularly heavily on Hebrews and the Gospel of John, as I will suggest. God functions as an ideal fantasy and resolution to dislocation but also acts as, in psychoanalytic terms, the very container that makes possible a messy and unresolved expression of lostness.[32] Yet cosmopolitanism does not simply project an obvious or natural belonging "upwards." It actually generates belonging through senses or expressions of homelessness, a belonging that, notably, crosses localizing identity categories.

Although in an earlier era, the newly elevated and emphatically singular expressions of divinity in Second Isaiah are similarly tightly knotted to the social pains of Israelite diaspora in the sixth century BCE.[33] While the expression of divinity in Second Isaiah tends to be treated as a special achievement or inevitable intellectual development,[34] Mark Smith describes the language of Second Isaiah as both profound and defiant, addressing both the loss of land and king in the wake of the Babylonian exile: Yahweh is "exalted" as Israel is "demoted." He notes,

> Yahweh becomes more than the god above all other gods: the existence of other gods is denied and two images central to Second Isaiah's

---

32. In psychoanalytic terms, the analyst or the space of analysis acts as the "container"—meaning it holds expressions that might be difficult or unacceptable to articulate elsewhere. Jessica Benjamin in fact makes some smart parallels between the analyst and divine figures. She plays out the implications for analysts, but not for divinity. Jessica Benjamin, *Like Subjects, Love Objects: Essays on Recognition and Sexual Difference* (New Haven: Yale University Press, 1995), 143-174. I have borrowed from and expanded on Benjamin on this front, however, in another place: "Divinity as Excess," paper presented at the annual meeting of the Society of Biblical Literature, San Francisco, November 2011.
33. W. G. Davies notes that "the term *bara*, to create, is not used of Yahweh before the Exile." See his *The Gospel and the Land: Early Christianity and Jewish Territorial Doctrine* (Berkeley: University of California Press, 1974), 12-13.
34. As Laurel Schneider notes in *Beyond Monotheism: A Theology of Multiplicity* (New York: Routledge, 2008), 27.

presentation of Yahweh, the warrior king and creator, are melded and scored in the text to counter the peceived reality of other deities and therefore the putative stupidity of cultic devotion to their images . . . Yahweh is not just the god of Israel (both as land and people) but of all lands and nations.[35]

Thus Isaiah's monotheistic statements house not only polemical but colonial potencies, ones that reflect a certain cultural fragility and defensiveness. As Laurel Schneider suggests, "With the physical center of worship gone, the political and religious leaders in captivity far away, and the conquering powers ever present, such polemic makes sense as part of an attempt to keep the exiles, and perhaps particularly their children, from giving up and taking on the identity of their captors."[36]

Reading Second Isaiah from this perspective amplifies the diasporic pangs and longings in the Secret Revelation of John, which imagines the divine realm as a "monarchy with nothing above it," and whose cosmic claims are preceded by an intra-group argument on the way to the temple (an institution which, by the time the text is written, no longer exists). Reflecting or perhaps interpreting Second Isaiah, the Secret Revelation of John too melds notions of God as king and creator. Isaiah contrasts God's creative work with the ineffective work of the maker of idols,[37] and this is the very same dynamic between the ideal realm's "Father-Mother of the All" (a double reference to creative work) and Yaldabaoth's creation of the lifeless human being. In Second Isaiah, as in the Secret Revelation of John, figures arrogantly and stupidly take up divine language, the first being the craftsman/maker of idols who, in Isaiah 41:7, declares of

---

35. Smith, *The Origins of Biblical Monotheism: Israel's Polytheistic Background and the Ugaritic Texts* (New York: Oxford University Press, 2001), 179.
36. Schneider, *Beyond Monotheism*, 33.
37. Smith, *The Origins of Biblical Monotheism*, 180-87. So, for example, in Isaiah 46:3-7, God is associated with birthing and bearing—emphasizing God's ability to give life while idols *remain inanimate*.

his work: "it is good." The second instance is even more directly cited by the Secret Revelation of John: in Isaiah 47:8, Babylon, quite stunningly, says "I am, and there is no other."[38]

In Isaiah 42:5-8 there is an emphasis on the giving of *pneuma* or spirit to those who walk on the earth (cf. Isa. 42:1).

> Thus says the Lord God
> Who created heaven and established it,
> Who bolstered the earth and the things that are in it,
> and who gave break to the people upon it,
> and spirit to those who tread on it,
>
> I, the Lord, God, have called you in righteousness,
> And I will take hold of your hand and strengthen you;
> I have give you as a covenant to a race,
> As a light to nations,
> to open the eyes of the blind,
> to bring out from bonds those who are bound,
> and from the prison house those who sit in darkness.
> I am the Lord God; this is my name;
> My glory I will not give to another,
> nor my excellences to the graven images.

In this passage and throughout Second Isaiah these themes of true and false creation are combined with another motif that similarly appears in the Secret Revelation of John: metaphors of blindness. In Second Isaiah, God opens the eyes of the blind or leads the blind; God leads those in darkness into the light (42:7, 16); Israel is described as blind (42:18-19; 43:8-9; and those who make idols are blind (44:18). Blindness is equated with not knowing the truth,

---

38. "*Ego eimi kai ouk estin hetera*," a phrase uttered by Babylon, is repeated three times in this oracle (v. 8, and twice in v. 10). God speaks this phrase or similar iterations in Isaiah 43:11, 44:6, 45:5-6, 45:18, 46:9, among other places. This emphasis on the feeble work of the maker of idols which basically is a poor imitation of God's making and forming work is highlighted in the LXX with the use of the Greek words *poieō*, *plassō*, and *plasmata* (see 43:7 vs. 44:9-11). These are the terms used in Genesis 1 and 2 to refer to God's creative work, but both God and the craftsman perform these verbs here.

with being "bound," and with worship of idols. Similarly, in the Secret Revelation of John, Yaldabaoth is called "Sammael"—god of the blind, in Aramaic—and his deceptive minions function to keep humanity bound, cast into darkness (24.8), and to make "the whole creation blind so that they might not know the God who is above them all" (24.14).

Given that the Secret Revelation of John is fusing the creation stories of Genesis with Platonist philosophy, inflecting them with Roman republican values, and feeding all this through the theopolitical and rhetorical moves of Second Isaiah, it is no wonder that the Secret Revelation of John bespeaks so much conflictedness about belonging, a conflictedness that resides not only in its aggressively dualist metaphysics, but also in its deeply affective anthropology. While the worldly rulers create the human body, or rather the "soul-body" of humanity,[39] this bodily self is, in King's words, "quite real and has quite real effects."[40] It is the "site of revelation and the purveyor of true knowledge," as well as "the revelation of the image of God in the world."[41] Consonant with other ancient imaginations of the person as a microcosm (taken literally—a little cosmos), to be human in the Secret Revelation of John is to reflect the structure and content of "the all." So, as King notes, "the body's double genealogy

---

39. King's description of the Secret Revelation of John's take on the body/subjectivity, which I reference here, in addition to intervening in the caricatures of the text as understanding the body to be evil or a deception, has a special poignancy. But it also seems that "the body" may be a kind of Cartesian misnomer for a text that engages so many tensive and diverse dimensions of subjectivity, any number of which might be said to have "body." As Dale Martin has noticed, "the body" as a singular, material element in contrast with the non-substantial or immaterial spirit or soul, is a Cartesian dualism, not a Platonic one. Indeed, Platonic subjectivity, and one might say ancient subjectivity at large, is multiple; not to mention that different aspects of Platonic subjectivity (including the soul) can be said to "have body" (*Corinthian Body*, 3-37). The only immaterial aspect of subjectivity would be "mind," which is a strongly participatory and intersubjective reality, anyway. So not only are caricatures of the Secret Revelation of John poor readings of the text, they trade multiplex ancient subjectivity for a simpler (binary) modern one.

40. King, *Secret Revelation of John*, 123.

41. Ibid., 124.

represents the dual nature of reality above and below. The body is both at once spiritual and material, divine and fallen, immortal and mortal, perfect and flawed, pure and alloyed."[42] How poignant this description is, particularly when understood as recounting a lived, sensed reality, rather than simply an abstract anthropological schema. Read affectively, the Secret Revelation of John's human prototype and its "double genealogy" express, in part, the push and shove of imperial and national belonging, its confusions and simultaneous possessions sorted out into a moralizing framework. The double genealogy in the Secret Revelation of John illustrates, again, how diasporic belonging is not just in tension with imperial/colonial belonging, but fully dependent on it.[43]

Indeed the text's utopian counter-belonging and woeful double-genealogy echoes diasporic imaginations in more recent history. In the 1940's, the Akali Dal, the primary Sikh political party in the Punjab region of British India, invented the notion of Khalistan (meaning "land of the pure"), a wished-for Sikh homeland, during the political negotiations constructing Pakistan and India. Brian Keith Axel notes that while Khalistan never came to be geographically, it was an imagination that took on new significance at the height of Sikh conflicts with the Indian government decades later, in the 1980's and 1990's. During this later period, when large numbers of Sikh men were picked up, unlawfully imprisoned, tortured, and killed, Khalistan became something different than a wished-for geographic locale. It rather became a global reality of

---

42. Ibid., 124.
43. Brian Keith Axel's re-reading as diasporic belonging as productive of homeland, rather than a function of shared or original homeland, stresses this point: "Most commonly, the 'identity' of a diaspora is understood to be impinged upon, determined, demonized, or encompassed by the external force of a nation-state. In other words, the diaspora and the nation-state are seen to be isolable entities. In contrast with this position, my discussion of the case of the Sikh diaspora demonstrates that the two are complexly related." See Axel, "The Diasporic Imaginary," *Public Culture* 14, no. 2 (2002): 411-28 (426).

identification, "one among many points of orientation, or organization, for a globally dispersed people."[44] Axel describes the way state-inflicted violence and torture of Sikhs was a crucial component of the formation of Sikh diasporic belonging. The circulation and display of graphic images of the tortured or dead bodies of Sikh martyrs produced the Sikh subject "through gruesome spectacle . . . the authority of this spectacle, moreover, is elaborated through reference to a monstrous, inhuman Other: the Indian nation state."[45]

The tortured Sikh body importantly belongs both to the Indian state and Khalistan. The victim of torture is both disciplined citizen and abjected other of the state, as well as the "abject subject" through which Khalistan re-emerges (as if dormant) in one and the same move.[46] In fact, Axel writes, "the diaspora and the modern nation-state have become intertwined in dialectical relationship . . . This dialectic underscores the fragile—yet enduring—ground of the nation form itself, even as it animates the desires of diaspora to enter into representation."[47]

---

44. Axel, Ibid., 412-13.
45. Ibid., 415.
46. Axel writes, "Torture enacts a drama of contestation between the 'real' people of India and the people of an 'illusory' Khalistan. Such divisions of peoplehood notwithstanding, the performative act of torture produces its object, the body, as both Indian and Sikh, as both citizen and traitor, and both as belonging to the state and something that exceeds the state. Conjoined to Punjab, the 'disturbed area' and the 'sensitive border state,' the tortured male Sikh body has become a sign of the fragility of the national territory" (ibid., 420).
47. Ibid., 426. Axel also tracks the gendered and sexualized implications of torture, a set of considerations I wish I had the space to apply here, especially since the text is so interested in revalencing how gender and sexual reproduction function within creation. Axel also employs the Lacanian notion of *le corps morcele* (the body in bits and pieces). For Lacan, this fragmented body presents a "time before" against which the wholeness of the nation is constructed. "Countering this national fantasy," Axel writes, "the sight of the tortured body within Khalistani practices of subject formation provides the opportunity to elaborate repeatedly a time before the apotheosis of the Indian nation-state, before contemporary violence, and before a history of movement and mobility that scattered the members of an integral Sikh quam—a desire of the total body politic" (425).

The Indian nation-state and Yaldabaoth share shades and echoes as monstrous others against which true, utopian belonging can materialize. That utopian belonging is, in the case of both Khalistan and the ideal realm of the Secret Revelation of John, inscribed with purity.[48] Not unlike the Sikh martyrs, Christ, famous for his torture by the state if nothing else, becomes the emissary and paradigmatic citizen of the ideal realm in the Secret Revelation of John.[49] Amplifying the tension between (co-implicated) forms of belonging, however, Christ is "self-generated" (*autogenes*), defensively emphasizing that he is not made by Yaldabaoth, even while Christ's very figuration is inherited from—one might even say "derivative of," to underscore the irony—cosmic figurations of Augustus. Christ in the Secret Revelation of John is the savior of humankind, bringer of peace, and one through whom the world is created, calling to mind the Priene inscription which notably includes the figure of Pronoia (Providence), also a key figure in the Secret Revelation of John. From the Priene inscription:

> Since Providence [*Pronoia*], which has ordered all things and is deeply interested in our life, has set in most perfect order by giving us Augustus, whom she filled with virtue that he might benefit humankind, sending him as a savior, both for us and for our descendants, that he might end war and arrange all things, and since he, Caesar, by his appearance (excelled even our anticipations), surpassing all previous benefactors, and not even leaving to posterity any hope of surpassing what he has done, and since the birthday of the god Augustus was the beginning of the good tidings for the world that came by reason of him.[50]

---

48. The ideal realm and its divine figure are often described as undefiled, unmixed, incorrupt, etc. (cf. 3.13; 4.3; 4.20; 5.25; 6.7).
49. That Christ is tortured by the state is not mentioned in this text—which is not to say that it is not important. It may either be assumed, or strategically "forgotten" since it may interfere too much with the divine realm's perfection.
50. Reproduced from Craig Evans, "Mark's Incipit and the Priene Calendar Inscription: From Jewish Gospel to Greco-Roman Gospel" *Journal of Greco-Roman Christianity and Judaism* 1 (2000): 67–81. While not in King's monograph on the Secret Revelation of John, this ancient parallel also goes to prove that King's reading of the text is right on the money.

While Axel still focuses more on representation and the construction of subjects than affect (despite the fact that he considers affect a dominant factor in the diasporic imaginary),[51] a more affect-centered understanding of both Khalistan and the ideal realm of the Secret Revelation of John might discern ongoing emotional echo effects between imaginations of ostensibly opposing social/political entities. Belonging to the "homeland" intensifies belonging to its antagonistic or colonizing entity (as it does in 1 Peter). In the Secret Revelation of John, the more humanity becomes aware of its relationship to light, the more mired in matter and darkness it becomes. The lifeless lumps that are Yaldabaoth's creation, invigorated by and imbued with divine substance, illustrate how senses of deadness and aliveness, subjugation and freedom, actually heighten and interact with one another, despite the fact that they are usually figured as mutually exclusive experiences.

In general, the Secret Revelation of John has what would seem to be a rather contradictory relationship to affect. For one, motifs of forgetfulness, being "asleep," and references to numbness/deadness or enclosure (i.e., being "closed off") abound.[52] But it is in this state of sleep, amnesia, and being closed off that humanity is strangely most given over to affectivity: desire, pain, fear, shame.[53] In another

---

51. Axel elaborates on his use of the term diasporic imaginary: "*Imaginary* here is not an adjective that describes or qualifies the diaspora, its 'people,' or 'community' as illusory or as a mere figment of some misguided imagination. Rather, the *diasporic imaginary*—used as a noun—indicates a precise and powerful kind of identification that is very real. As a corrective to the primacy that diaspora studies has awarded to constructions of place, the diasporic imaginary shifts the emphasis to temporality and corporeality— their centrality to relations of recognition and their negotiation through discourses of purity and origin. Neither drawing from a commonsensical notion of illusions and mirages nor engaging in a recuperation of Benedict Anderson's (1991) 'imagination,' I am rather looking toward the analytic of subjectification. Although my use of the term *imaginary* owes much to the work of Jacques Lacan, the sort of analysis of diasporas I am proposing may be best served by here staging a productive debate with psychoanalysis. (Ibid., 423-24).
52. Cf. SRevJohn 18.1-2; 19.12; 21.4-6; 22.31; 23.7-8, 27; 25.12-13, 20; 25.14 (Codex II).
53. Cf. SRevJohn 17.48-58 (Codex II); 20.1-27; 22.10-15; 22.22-23; 24.13 (Codex II).

apparent paradox, the passages that describe these experiences of non-feeling are some of the most affecting. In the Secret Revelation of John 23.4-12, for example, the Savior describes that things will be different for the immovable generation on whom the spirit of life descends:

> Those upon whom the Spirit of the Life descends, having been yoked with the power, they will be saved and become perfect. And they will be worthy to enter these realms of the great Lights. For they will be worthy to be purified there from all evil and the enticements of wickedness. For they do not give themselves to anything else except this incorruptible congregation and they attend to it without anger or envy or fear or desire or overindulgence. They are not restrained by any of these nor by anything else in them except only the flesh to which they are subject while they are waiting fervently for (the time) when they will be brought forth and those who receive (them) will admit them into the honor of the imperishable eternal life and the calling, enduring all things, bearing all things so that they might complete the contest and inherit eternal life.

On the one hand, this position regarding affect is pretty straightforwardly Stoic: knowledge brings one control over "the passions." But to end there would be to miss all the subtle and more conflicted affective wisps and turns that crop up in the story, as well as to underestimate any possible affective complexity in Stoic thought. In another point in the story, as the human person is assembled piece by piece, element by element, by the powers attending Yaldabaoth, the Secret Revelation of John rather frankly declares that the passions are both virtues as well as vices, although "insight into their true character is Anaro, who is the head of the material soul" (17.58-59). Neither does the text repudiate "bad" emotions (the emotional experiences named are predominantly "negative" ones—pride, shame, fear, anxiety, jealousy, etc.), even as it suggests emotional experiences are something other than true reality.[54]

The text is absorbed with difficult experiences and encounters—not just diasporic grief or senses of disillusionment and isolation, but also rape, abuse and imprisonment—pressing one to ask whether less Stoic attitude toward "the passions" might be more tenderly approached as mitigating an affectivity that is otherwise unbearable to take. The addressees figured in the text are an "immovable" race both in their newly anchored belonging in the ideal realm and in their (apparent) refusal to be overcome by certain kinds of feeling. The carefully titrated emotional responsiveness breaks down, however, in the following passage when the Savior/Pronoia (Providence) describes travelling down to save humanity from its imprisonment:

> Still, for a third time, I who am the light that exists in the light and the remembrance of Pronoia, I traveled in order to enter into the midst of the darkness and the inside of Hades. I filled my countenance with the light of the consummation of their aeon. And I entered the midst of their prison, which is the prison of the body. And I said, "Whoever hears, arise from lethargic sleep!" And he wept, shedding tears; heavy tears he wiped from himself. And he said, "Who is it that calls my name and from where does this hope come to me who am dwelling in the fetters of the prison?" (SRevJohn 26.18-25).[55]

Arising from sleep and knowing where and to whom one truly belongs, while ending one's pained experience of grief and distress, is accompanied by an emotional release of "heavy tears" and a felt sense of hope—hardly the reasoned mastery of overwhelming affectivity that it would seem to be. Again, even "bad" emotions in all their

---

54. The text contains here what Christopher Gill has described as "two salient features of a passion in Stoic thought, namely that it is both an expression of reason and, at the same time, one that is mistaken, excessive, and forceful or violent . . . " See Christopher Gill, *The Structured Self in Hellenistic and Roman Thought* (Oxford: Oxford University Press, 2006), 221. Gill is extrapolating particularly from Plutarch's somewhat polemical description of the contradictions of Stoic thought in the *Moralia*, which I typically find problematic. Here, however, the contradictions of Stoic thought around "passions" (what we might call negative emotions, but have a distinct relationship to immoderation or excess) are precisely what are interesting to me.
55. This text appears only in Codex II

excesses have a conflicted place in the story. As Virginia Burrus observes, Sophia's shame about generating a likeness out of herself and creating Yaldabaoth later blooms into her repentance, thus initiating humanity's salvation and "nudging demiurgic mimicry in the direction of a true mimesis."[56]

In fact, for all of the Secret Revelation of John's dramatic plot turns and intensely polarized characterizations—what would seem to be an aggressive storytelling style—it throbs with vulnerability. In fact, I want to avoid understanding aggression and vulnerability (like senses of aliveness and deadness, freedom and entrapment) as binary phenomena, or poles on a scale of pathology. As consistently coinciding conditions or feelings, aggression and vulnerability appear in especially thorny combinations around sites of trauma. In *An Archive of Feelings*, Ann Cvetkovich frames and considers in an explicitly depathologizing manner the way trauma lives on in sexual lives and self-presentation (ostensibly more private and more public contexts). She takes a queer approach to trauma, which centralizes queer experiences as paradigmatic and allows for a more expansive and less event-centered conceptualization of trauma, making room for ongoing and mundane, though still formative, losses (having been homophobically shamed, e.g.).[57] In a chapter entitled "Trauma and

---

56. Burrus, *Saving Shame*, 59. Burrus notes that Adam's shame also initiates his redemption. By eating the fruit of the tree, he simultaneously gains the knowledge of his shame and the knowledge of his salvation (60). Burrus argues for the "ultimately productive" character of shame in Secret Revelation of John, but I would cast this (what?) as a contradictory and ambivalent.
57. Ann Cvetkovich, *An Archive of Feelings: Trauma, Sexuality, and Lesbian Public Cultures* (Durham: Duke University Press, 2003), 1-14. There has been a lot of recent theoretical work deconstructing the event-based narratives of traumatic shattering. Adam Phillips, for instance, one of the more insistent voices with this viewpoint, writes that "trauma has become one of the last essences that even the most radical anti-essentialists won't do away with because not believing in trauma can sound very much like not believing in suffering. The notion of trauma helps us to go on believing that lives turn on significant events, and that we need to be able to recognize them as such. We have the ability to do the trick of turning good and bad luck into meaning and substance, cause and effect, beginnings middles, and ends . . . Trauma theory puts

Touch," she focuses on butch-femme sexualities and presentations in relation to trauma. She suggests that the toughness or untouchability of butches should not be thought of as refusal to feel, and femme vulnerability should not be imagined as passivity/victimhood.[58] Exploring butch-femme cultural sources such as the novel *Stone Butch Blues*, Cvetkovich finds how these narrations of lived experience enrich and complicate common and more general psychological tropes for understanding trauma and its felt effects. Highlighting both the agency and activity in responsive receptivity and the constructive accommodation that is public hardness, Cvetkovich rather finds vulnerability and control to be constitutive of both butch and femme styles of relation. She summarizes:

> Butch dykes reconfigure the meanings of being hard or numb, showing both its necessity and difficulty, giving dignity to the moments when it is not possible to be vulnerable and also revealing the many ways in which vulnerability can be performed. Femmes also provide a range of ways of being open without being passive or stigmatized, rewriting the meanings of vulnerability and receptivity. Just as a wider range of possibilities for emotional response and its complexity makes it possible to expand understandings of gender, so too does it help in recognizing the many ways in which people live and respond to trauma without pathologizing them as abnormal.[59]

So much more can and will be said about Cvetkovich's book (see chapter 6 on the Gospel of Truth), but for the moment I want to highlight how this queer approach to trauma and trauma's effects/affects can amplify the Secret Revelation of John as a response to the various social pains I have described. On the one hand it is blustery and extravagant in its storytelling, unrelenting in its moral vision, and

---

a plot, if not a plan, back into modern lives . . . " See Adam Phillips, *Side Effects* (New York: Harper Perennial, 2006), 265-66.
58. Cvetkovich, *Archive of Feelings*, 44-45.
59. Ibid., 67.

heavily indicting of those it critiques. Its dichotomizing perception is, one might say, a kind of toughness. And yet, the liberatory rhetoric the book engages to produce this vision is saturated with feeling. The ideal realm is both untouchable in its height and perfection, and yet also the magnet for so much pain. In this way, its investment in a pure and ideal realm, however philosophically troubling it may be or guileless it may seem, softens its dichotomizing vision while still being part of it.[60] Nostalgia may be one, if not the easiest, way to describe or understand the Secret Revelation of John's ideal realm of perfection (life "before the fall") to which humanity seeks return, but that ease, and my own analytical over-reliance on that conceptuality, leaves me a bit suspicious. Rather, I wonder if the text's doubling down on a kind of belonging that remains in the imagination as, against all odds and even after perverse disaster, an unfractured consummation of light, might appear instead as a forceful refusal and, simultaneously and rather remarkably, a kind of active openness to further disappointment.[61]

Quite unlike Acts in which the senses of social belonging cycle from diasporic romantic ideals to colonial disappointment, epic expectation to melancholic anticlimax, the pieces of the Secret Revelation of John's story never quite fit together. The Secret Revelation of John, by virtue of speaking in the register of cosmic creation, sees pain and corruption as inevitable from the start while still vigorously defending the very space that will unravel, freighting it with nothing less than ultimate truth. It highlights how utopian imaginations and liberatory rhetoric often sidestep engagements with their own limits in favor of producing fragile and euphoric expressions of assurance and possibility, expressions that may not only

---

60. Similarly, Burrus sees the divine realm as incorporating vulnerability. Burrus, *Saving Shame*, 62.
61. My reading of Cvetkovich here alongside the Secret Revelation of John (and then again for the Gospel of Truth) provides one example of how queer analytics might be resourced in ways other than appealing to a transgressive Christian subject or political positioning.

be a kind of salve for brittle, injured skin, but gather and assemble constituencies in the meantime.

There is a lot that the scholarly discourse on Gnosticism got wrong: not only is Gnosticism not a category that ancient people would recognize, but it has primarily been a dumping ground for texts or ideas considered not properly Christian or Jewish. Pushback on this has placed texts formerly classed as Gnostic, including the Secret Revelation of John, within the bounds and context of Jewish and Christian attempts at identity construction, a tactic that still inches towards the question of "how Jewish" or "how Christian" is the text.[62]

As in the cases of Acts, 1 Peter, and Ignatius's letters, it is not clear that this framework is the best way to understand the Secret Revelation of John's rhetoric and affectivity around belonging. On the one hand, the text begins with Israelite diasporic conflict, and then uses Israelite texts to structure its ensuing story. On the other hand, categorizing it as a "construction of Jewish identity" misses so much of the text's own longings. While Jerusalem and its temple frame the story of the Secret Revelation of John, it is not clear that the implicit reference the trauma of their destruction is limited to that singular event itself. To borrow Cvetkovich's (and others') expanded understanding of trauma, it may be that the destruction of the temple and Jerusalem stand in for the more generalized traumas of Israelite diaspora—even colonial/imperial violence and diasporic conflict overall. Or perhaps all of these are possible readings. The

---

62. Not simply King, but also Michael Williams, *Rethinking "Gnosticism": An Argument for Dismantling a Dubious Category* (Princeton: Princeton University Press, 1996), Burrus, *Saving Shame*, and Dunning, *Specters of Paul*, place the Secret Revelation of John within a contested and/or variegated Christianity. Neither Williams nor David Brakke (*The Gnostics: Myth, Ritual and Diversity in Early Christianity* [Cambridge: Harvard University Press, 2012]) fully integrate the Secret Revelation of John into the social scene of "early Christianity," since Williams still places it within the typological distinction of "biblical demiurgical" traditions, and Brakke still assumes "Gnostic" as a usable category.

categorizing of the text as Jewish/Israelite misses the way it gathers alienated, lost, or otherwise un-homed others, who might or might not think of themselves as part of Israelite diaspora. And does it matter whether they do or not, really?

Unlike 1 Peter, the *telos* of the Secret Revelation of John is not Israel. The Secret Revelation of John begins with Israelite diasporic pain, but its universalism artfully avoids commitment to a single national entity. But just as Acts' vision of Pentecost is grounded in Israelite universalism, I want to emphasize that, while universalism is typically seen as a Christian move (I suppose because Christians in later history have been especially calculated and eager in deploying it), the Secret Revelation of John's universalism is resonant with both the cosmopolitanism of the first century and the longings of Second Isaiah. Universalism is a rhetorical gesture that, as Seneca, Plutarch, and Second Isaiah show, frequently appears as solace and an incomplete solution for the forceful obligations of place and the indelible touch of violence.

Identity or identity construction as an optic has, among other things, pushed the field to reckon with the thoroughly contested nature of belonging, and the simultaneously vociferous and shaky nature of self-articulation. But it also conscripts readers into woodenly analytical rhetorical diagnostics. Affective and diaspora theories invite more texturally and experientially rich readings, providing an important set of complications regarding belonging and the nation. Probably because for so long Christianity has articulated itself as a trans- or non-national diaspora, the ancient nation of Israel remains an undifferentiated node of belonging in the analysis of what we have called "early Christian" texts; thus the primacy of for-or-against, or inside-or-outside, conceptualities. But binary terms mitigate conflicted, multifaceted, or simply not-overtly-measurable relationships to Israel (or the Roman Empire, for that matter). It is not even clear to me that, as in the case of Acts' swinging from enchantment to disenchantment, a single, characterizable relationship to an entity as thickly threaded as Israel or as enormous and disparate as the Roman *imperium* is always present. Nations, like other entities, live on in innumerable ways long after they die or collapse politically. Depending on what you perceive to be the lifeblood of that nation, it may not even be dead to you. But again, deadness and aliveness are not mutually exclusive qualities. As we shall see in the case of Hebrews, it is all too often the case that the husk of the nation you aspire to leave behind still ends up as the beating heart of your aspirations.

5

Above It All: The Affective Life of Transcendence

God is not tied to place, and those who worship God must worship him as he truly is, without regard to place. (Gospel of John 4:24)

You have not come to something that can be touched, a blazing fire, and darkness, and gloom, and a tempest, and the sounds of a trumpet, and a voice whose words made the hearers beg that not another word would be spoken to them . . . But you have come to Mount Zion and to the city of the living God, the heavenly Jerusalem, and to the innumerable angels in festal gathering . . . Therefore since we are receiving a kingdom that cannot be shaken, let us give thanks . . . (Hebrews 12:18-19, 22, 28)

Beyonding is a rhetoric people use when they have a desire not to be stuck. (Lauren Berlant, "Starved," in Halley and Parker, *After Sex?*, 80)

Sharing a penchant for cosmic universals as well as a reputation for poetry, the Gospel of John and the Letter to the Hebrews are nothing if not lofty. Eschewing place itself as meaningful, but still finding temple and city to be meaningful metaphors, these two texts seem to glide above it all with the help of florid figuration.[1] These texts alternately draw in and repel their readers with their lyricism and designs on transcendence, the latter of which reflects, at least to postmodern and postcolonial eyes, an ominous and familiar form of imperializing. Hebrews is suspicious for its "timeless and geographically vague guise,"[2] which has allowed it to levitate above history in most scholarship, floating "unanchored in time and place."[3] The Gospel of John evokes special discomfort and ire for its embedding of hot rhetoric around "Jews" into its superlative, delocalized claims.[4] Indeed many interpreters of both Hebrews and the Gospel of John read their language of superlatives and universals as supersessionist at base, pitting an inclusive and all-encompassing "Christianity" and Christians against a particularizing and provincial "Judaism."

While I am no fan of superlative rhetoric and hazy universals myself, I do think there is more to say about these texts' interest in being or getting "beyond." Indeed, without Christian identity as a viable category for either of the texts, the unfastened vagueness of universals and the designs on getting above it all may have a different feel, and may suggest other social subtexts. Transcendence, hardly a unique hallmark of Christian theologizing or simple recapitulation of imperial ideology, regularly arises as an attempt to blunt the force of intractable social entanglements, thus also archiving forms of diasporic affectivity. Such pining for heavenly, unshakeable cities and delocalized entities may arise out of diasporic forces and feelings

---

1. Harold Attridge opens his commentary on Hebrews with this exaltation: "The document known as the Epistle to the Hebrews is the most elegant and sophisticated, and perhaps the most enigmatic, text of first-century Christianity . . . Its argumentation is subtle; its language refined; its imagery rich and evocative." See his *The Epistle to the Hebrews: A Commentary on the Epistle to the Hebrews,* Hermenia Commentary Series (Minneapolis: Fortress Press, 1989), 1.
2. Christina Petterson, "The Land is Mine: Place and Dislocation in the Letter to the Hebrews," *Sino-Christian Studies* 4 (2007): 69-93 (71).
3. Ellen Bradshaw Aitken, "Reading Hebrews in Flavian Rome," *USQR* 59, no. 3-4 (2005): 82-85.
4. Adele Reinhartz, *Befriending the Beloved Disciple: A Jewish Reading of the Gospel of John* (New York: Continuum, 2001), 11-16.

that give the notion of place of origin increasing currency while simultaneously disjoining one from it. Without denying the interpretational risks and ideological consequences of the placid language of "beyond" in these texts, the sense that Hebrews is "unanchored," for example, may perhaps instead suggest twin (diasporic) senses of being both aloft and stuck.

In fact, in these texts, transcendence never manages to get off the ground the way one expects. Evocations of the one, the true, or the beyond almost instantly devolve into the mess of place or get snagged in the gnarls of the particular, whether through the ghostly referents of those localized metaphors they employ or other loose ends left dangling in the text. Mining some of these moments for their diasporic references and resonances provokes broader reconsiderations of the social investments and landscapes inherent to the Gospel of John and Hebrews respectively, and also begs us to reconsider the terms on which we imagine transcendence itself—one of the most dearly beloved Western/Christian yearnings and stubbornly persistent epistemological concepts.

* * * *

Like the Secret Revelation of John, the Letter to the Hebrews has most often been read as remote from the grainy texture of social life. In the case of Hebrews, however, the result has been doctrinal and systematic readings rather than Gnosticizing ones.[5] While many scholars have noticed the diasporic thrust and themes of dislocation in

---

5. As Ellen Aitken notices, Hebrews has primarily produced theological, sacramental, ethical, structural, and source-critical readings with little interest in what social and political dynamics other than Christian persecution might infuse it (Aitken, "Reading Hebrews," 82). Aitken addresses this problem by giving Hebrews a more concretized historical context—Flavian Rome—so as to set its language and ideology in oppositional relationship to imperial rhetoric of triumph. See her extended article, "Portraying the Temple in Stone and Text: The Arch of Titus and the Epistle to the Hebrews," *Sewanee Theological Review* 45, no. 2 (2002): 131-51.

the letter, as in the case of 1 Peter, the language of being foreigners or living in foreign lands that defines the text has mainly been scrutinized for its implications regarding Christian self-understanding and rhetorical self-presentation.[6] But again: what if Israelite diasporic themes and the language of displacement in Hebrews are used quite simply because Hebrews is an Israelite diasporic expression of and redress for feeling lost?

Doctrinal and systematic theological readings lean heavily on the text's emphasis on faith, and the focus on faith in the letter is also part of what would seem to position it as "Christian." But while "faith" is an important term and topic in Hebrews, its resonances are much wider, and probably more disconcerting, than any creedal imagination of faith as personal belief in Jesus.[7] In fact, Jesus never appears as an object of *pistis*, but rather appears as one among many models of fidelity to Israel's god.[8] This detail—Jesus as model of

---

6. See, for example, Ernst Käsemann, *The Wandering People of God: An Investigation into the Letter to the Hebrews*, trans. Roy A. Harrisville and Irving L. Sandberg (Minneapolis: Augsburg Press, 1984), as well as W. G. Johnsson, "The Pilgrimage Motif in the Book of Hebrews," *JBL* 97, no. 2 (1978): 239-51; Jeremy Punt, "Hebrews," in *A Postcolonial Commentary on the New Testament Writings*, ed. Fernando Segovia and R. S. Sugirtharajah (Bloomsbury: T & T Clark, 2009), 338-368; and C. K. Barrett "The Eschatology of the Epistle to the Hebrews," in *The Background of the New Testament and Its Eschatology: Essays in Honor of C.H. Dodd*, ed. W. D. Davies and David Daube (Cambridge: Cambridge University Press, 1956), 363-93. Also see Benjamin Dunning, *Aliens and Sojourners: Self as Other in Early Christianity* (Philadelphia: University of Pennsylvania Press, 2009), 46-63.
7. On several occasions the text does refer to holding fast to a confession (3:1; 4:14; 10:23), but it is not at all clear that this is a confession with creedal content (contra Harold Attridge, *Epistle to the Hebrews*, 108). In 3:1, Jesus is the "apostle and high priest" of this confession, and in 10:23 the confession is simply a confession of hope.
8. Further, as Markus Bockmuehl notices, "aside from Jesus himself no exemplars of New Covenant faith are singled out anywhere in this letter—no apostle or prophet; no congregational leader past or present, no Epaphras, no Phoebe or Chloe, not even Timothy, despite his cameo appearance in 13:23. In other words, the writer appears convinced that the practice of New Covenant faith, even as defined in its pioneer and perfecter Jesus, is most impressively and adequately exemplified in the saints of the Old Covenant." See his "Abraham's Faith in Hebrews 11," in *The Epistle to the Hebrews and Christian Theology*, ed. Richard Bauckham, Daniel Driver, Trevor Hart and Nathan MacDonald, *The Epistle to the Hebrews and Christian Theology* (Cambridge: Wm. B. Eerdmans Publishing Company, 2009), 365.

faith—and its relationship to diasporic themes, however, produces a frightening, grisly, and sometimes nearly farcical counter to the elevated language and artful structure in Hebrews. The most sustained reflections on faith, for example, occur in Hebrews 3 and 11, and in both cases faith is linked to hardships in Israelite history. In Hebrews 3, faith is directly linked to Exodus and the wilderness:

> For we have become partners of Christ, if only we hold our first confidence firm to the end. As it is said, "Today, If you hear his voice, do not harden your hearts as in the rebellion." Now who were they who heard and yet were rebellious? Was it not all those who left Egypt under the leadership of Moses? But with whom was he angry forty years? Was it not those who sinned, whose bodies feel in the wilderness? And to whom did he swear that they would not enter his rest, if not those who were disobedient? So we see that they were unable to enter because of unbelief (Heb. 3:14-19).

In Hebrews 11, the faith of the patriarchs and other figures from Israelite history are evoked, and the sense of payoff for endurance is much more elusive, or even absent. The chapter begins, "Now faith is the assurance of things hoped for, the conviction of things not seen. By faith, our ancestors received approval" (11:1-2). But the very first example the text offers is already quite grim: "By faith Abel offered to God a more acceptable sacrifice than Cain's. Through this he received approval as righteous, God himself giving approval to his gifts" (11:4). The text is quick to notice of course that "he died," explaining "but through his faith he still speaks." The next examples narrated at length—including Noah, Enoch, Abraham, Sarah, Joseph, Moses—are a mixed bag of inspiration at best, since "all these died in faith without having received the promises" (11:13). They were, instead, "looking ahead to the reward" (11:26; cf. 11:13-14). While the entire chapter would seem to be an argument for what fidelity to Israel's god can yield, it teeters between rousing pep talk and a nihilistic sense of defeat. By the end of the chapter, it has turned into an extended meditation on just how bad these acclaimed Israelite models of fidelity had it, in the name of a vague and distant prize:

> And what more should I say? For time would fail me to tell of Gideon, Barak, Samson, Jepthah, of David and Samuel and the prophets—who through faith conquered kingdoms, administered justice, obtained promises, shut the mouths of lions, quenched raging fire, escaped the edge of the sword, won strength out of weakness, became mighty in war, put foreign armies to flight. Women received their dead by resurrection. Others were tortured, refusing to accept release, in order to obtain a better resurrection. Others suffered mocking and flogging, and even chains and imprisonment. They were stoned to death, they were sawn in two, they were killed by the sword; they went about in skins of sheep and goats, destitute, persecuted, tormented—of who the world was not worthy. They wandered in deserts and mountain, and in caves and holes in the ground. Yet all these, though they were commended for their faith, did not receive what was promised, since God had provided something better so that they would not, apart from us, be made perfect (Hebrews 11:32-40).

If the articulation of faith in Hebrews seems to have a lofty and poetic aura (cf. the eternally quotable "faith is the assurance of things hoped for, the conviction of things not seen" in 11:1), it often takes an equally steep nosedive into gloomy and gruesome mortal realities, a swing that feels less manic-depressive than somewhat resigned and, occasionally, tartly comic. Jesus is, of course, the model of faithfulness to beat all models, but one for which the height of his declared position and the scale of his torture produce bizarre and unsettling configurations. Most memorably, the priest above all other priests is himself the sacrificial animal victim (7:27, e.g.). Likewise, while "Moses was faithful in all God's house as a servant," Christ's faithfulness is that of a son's (3:5-6)[9]—it is a privilege and

---

9. There is interlinked symbolism here: God's house is a recognizable term for the temple sanctuary in the Hebrew Bible, and this connection is made explicit in Hebrews 10:19-25. Cf.

accomplishment repaid, it does not escape notice, with brutal violence: "Endure trials for the sake of discipline. God is treating you as children; for what child is there whom a parent does not discipline? If you do not have that discipline in which all children share, then you are illegitimate and not his children" (12:7-8). Is that a threat or a promise?

Anguish is an index of entitlement, the text opines, even while it sketches how the rewards for enduring it are alarmingly elusive. Hebrews' readers, for all their troubles (which are bad and getting worse, it appears in 12:4), are promised an entry into the "rest" (*katapausis*), but it is a concept whose mixed referents mean it appears neither here nor there, exactly.[10] Because rest implies not only land, but a philosophical description of a condition, Sabbath, and the temple sanctuary as well, it is ambiguously temporal and spatial.[11] Even temporally, "rest" is variously a present condition like the new

---

Jared Calaway, "Heavenly Sabbath, Heavenly Sanctuary: The Transformation of Priestly Sacred Space and Sacred Time in the 'Songs of the Sabbath Sacrifice' and the Epistle to the Hebrews" (Ph.D. diss., Columbia University, 2010), 270.

10. For one summary of the neither here nor there problem of the rest in Hebrews, see Harold Attridge, "Let Us Strive to Enter That Rest: The Logic of Hebrews 4:1-11," *HTR* 73, no. 1-2 (1980): 279-88.

11. Craig Koester has noted that, because you can enter the rest, it has a spatial dimension, and therefore Sabbath and sanctuary and land all converge. See Craig Koester, *Hebrews: A New Translation with Introduction and Commentary*, The Anchor Bible (New York: Random House, 2001), 257-58, 268. But the most extensive discussion of the question of "rest" regarding space/place and time is Jared Calaway's dissertation, "Heavenly Sabbath, Heavenly Sanctuary," which focuses on rest in Hebrews and the *Songs of Sabbath Sacrifice* as both temporal and spatial, and particularly on its resonances with both Sabbath and temple sanctuary. As Calaway writes, "[w]hile previous scholarship focuses upon the broad contours of spatial cosmology and temporal eschatology in terms of two realms (earthly and heavenly) and two ages (past and future) . . . these same aspects play out with regard to the Sabbath and the sanctuary. Both 3:7-4:11 and 9:1-14 overlap spatial and temporal registers: rest starts out as spatial only to become temporal, while the Tabernacle both represents space of the tent and time of the current age and the age to come. Moreover, the language of copies, shadows, etc., heightens the spatiotemporal interrelationships: the earthly sanctuary may be an antitype of the heavenly type, but temporally also shadows of good things to come (or that have come)" (272-73). Calaway also places these moves within a diasporic context: "The mobility of the sacred shrine, which allowed God's presence to be present anywhere, and the heightening of the holiness of the Sabbath to the level of the sanctuary, which allowed God's holiness previously associated with the sacred enclosure alone to be experienced by any covenanted person every week, had their

covenant (4:3), established at creation (4:4, 9), only recently established (9:15), an open promise (4:1), and a condition that is not yet achieved (4:11).[12] The unclear time and place of rest, however, makes it ripe for affective and diasporic readings. As Christina Petterson stresses, however much Hebrews wants its notion of rest to be a condition (and conditional, cf. 3:6), one attainable outside the bounds of history, it draws much of its meaning from diaspora geographical politics in the Exodus tradition: "[I]n order for the symbolic space of heaven to have a meaning, its literal counterpart must be in operation. The camp must be there for the reader to go out of its gates . . . And suddenly the land takes on a rather menacing presence."[13]

The notion of the land's ghostly and menacing presence is not only evocative, but part of a larger set of gnarls in Hebrews that continually tie its heavenly, invisible, or eternal aspirations to the very objects, places, and realities they would seem to overshadow. Hebrews offers constant confusions and complications to any dualist or otherwise loosely Platonic metaphysics, most terrifyingly in the surprising and conceptually difficult image of Jesus' flesh as the curtain to the heavenly temple (10:19-20).[14] Jesus not only stands for

---

greatest poignancy in the temple-less situation. The Sabbath, thereby, became the temporal access to the sanctuary's holiness" (163).

12. This neither here nor there quality is so often noticed by scholars, but results mostly in resolving it through conclusions about the text's realized eschatology or apocalyptic undercurrents. See, for example, A. T. Lincoln, "Sabbath, Rest, and Eschatology in the New Testament," in *From Sabbath to Lord's Day: A Biblical, Historical, and Theological Investigation*, ed. D. A. Carson (Eugene, Ore.: Wipf and Stock, 2000), 211; Barrett "Eschatology of the Epistle to the Hebrews"; and George W. MacRae, "Heavenly Temple and Eschatology in the Letter to the Hebrews," *Semeia* 12 (1978): 179-99.
13. Petterson, "The Land is Mine," 84. Petterson, however, claims that Hebrews finally wants to maintain a difference between space and place, even though divorcing them is impossible.
14. A. J. M. Wedderburn, "Sawing Off Branches: Theologizing Dangerously *Ad Hebraeos*," *JTS* 56, no. 2 (2005): 393-414. Determining Hebrews to be "incoherent," Wedderburn waxes most, indeed for pages and pages, on the image of Jesus' flesh as the curtain to the heavenly temple (Heb. 10:19-20). Wedderburn writes, "[t]he screen marked a divide that should have been insurmountable, but here was one that passed over that chasm, and if he did so as a being of

the divide to the inner sanctuary, but passes over the divide, bringing his blood with him.[15]

While it turns out that Hebrews cannot quite get out of its binds, its struggle with the question of place in particular might be read as at once an attempted escape from the mundane specificity of Israelite homeland *and* a newly asserted attachment to it. The present-tense is a giveaway that rest in Hebrews is, not unlike Khalistan or knowing one's true origin in the Secret Revelation of John, a condition that functions like place, providing "ground" for diaspora belonging when it has been thwarted elsewhere. The frictive combination of conditionality and universality in descriptions of the rest, as well as the crossing of the registers of time and place, constitute a scrambling to anchor belonging somewhere, somehow.

The relationship between rest and faith is also curiously circular: *pistis* is what guarantees entry into the rest (3:19; 4:5-6), and, at the same time, the promise of the rest is what inspires *pistis* (4:10-11). That the means and the end are practically indistinguishable is, too, a diasporic and affective signal: *pistis*, wielded for a range of related meanings from endurance to confidence to loyalty,[16] is the affective glue that holds such an uncertain and imperiled sociality together. It likewise manages to give continuity to figures and moments whose other bases of connection (land, genealogy) are overextended or impossibly complicated in the colonial clutter. Additionally, the

---

flesh and blood then the basic principles of Platonic ontology were irretrievably undermined" (401).
15. Wedderburn continues: "If, on the other hand, he entered heaven without his flesh, are we to say he left his blood behind as well? Yet then the analogy with the rites of the Day of Atonement and the sprinkling of the sanctuary on that occasion would be weakened, despite the need for the heavenly sanctuary to be cleansed 'with better sacrifices' than those for the earthly one (9:23)" ("Sawing Off Branches," 401).
16. While Hebrews 11 begins by defining faith in terms of confidence (11:1), so much of the rest of chapter's focus on faith seems to be more along the lines of "endurance" (since so many of the models of faith are victims of intense hardship). Likewise, in Hebrews 6:12 and 6:15, faith appears in close proximity to patience. However, Moses and Christ as servant and son, respectively, of God's house are described as "faithful," which suggests loyalty (3:3-6).

slippery presentness of "rest," and *pistis* as a circular investment in it, suggests that what the promise of rest offers is not only a ground for sociality but an in-the-moment sense of height and escape—although one that only and repeatedly points back to the force of what binds. Getting above it all is a mode of endurance, a promise whose effect is in the promising.

Hebrews's designs on getting above and beyond not only figure as ways of *getting through*, but also display a complicated dynamics of attachment and detachment, the temple being perhaps the most distinct example. How much could Hebrews really be nullifying the high priesthood, the sacrificial system, and the physical temple if it spends the better part of five chapters—close to half of the entire text—writing about them?[17] Like a blind date talking incessantly about *how completely over* his ex he is, Hebrews fixes itself most energetically on exactly what it has ostensibly erased. If Hebrews negates the importance of the cultic system, as it is often read, its own metaphors and representations have no significance.[18] A. J. M. Wedderburn finds Hebrews nearly non-sensical because of this contradiction, and Richard Hays reads this apparent logical problem as a kind of theological poetry whereby the text enacts its own theology of self-annihilation.[19] But other scholars such as Kenneth Schenck address Hebrews's cultic contradictions from a social perspective. Inspired by the sentiment, "[w]e have no lasting city here," Schenck characterizes Hebrews as a response to the destruction of Jerusalem and the temple in the Roman-Jewish war.[20] He writes,

---

17. Likewise, the heavenly temple, or temple-structured heaven, and heavenly Jerusalem were common Israelite diasporic reflections, as seen in Philo, Josephus, 1 Enoch, and Qumran literature. Cf. MacRae, "Heavenly Temple and Eschatology." These reflections are closely related to the growing variety and influence of Rabbinic practices and thought in this period, which also de-emphasized the importance of the physical temple.
18. Hays, "We Have No Lasting City Here," in Bauckham, et al, *The Epistle to the Hebrews and Christian Theology*, 168.
19. Ibid., 168-73.

"[t]he key is to recognize that Hebrews is a consolation *in the absence of* a temple rather than a polemic *against* a cultus that continued to operate even as the author made his argument."[21] Intervening in the supersessionist reputation of Hebrews, Schenck describes the upward gestures of Hebrews in language consonant with Greco-Roman cosmopolitanism: "Hebrews reminds its audience that they need not be concerned about Jerusalem's destruction, for they are after all citizens of heaven rather than earth."[22] The levitation above history, time, and land so forcefully imagined in Hebrews is, in other words, a more palatable expression of feeling untethered.

As I emphasized in the last chapter in relation to the Secret Revelation of John, though, it may not necessarily be the temple's destruction itself that catalyzed the sentiments in Hebrews. As much as that represents a remarkable event with numerous and serious reverberations for first-century people associated with Israel, the temple might simply have been an extreme example of many imperial and colonial co-optations and dispersals already imbuing Israelite diasporic experiences. Or it could be that the temple was always already "lost" for some who felt themselves to be part of Israel but separated from one of its most evocative social symbols and its related practices. This separation might be a function either of physical distance or of disillusionment in the wake of the temple's Roman entanglements and corruption, but the latter possibility fits rather

---

20. Schenck dates Hebrews to the mid-70's ("The Levitical Cultus and the Partitioning of the Ways in Hebrews," paper presented at the annual meeting of the Society of Biblical Literature, San Diego, 2007), Calaway follows (cf. Calaway, "Heavenly Sabbath, Heavenly Sanctuary," 270-78). What city is being referred to here? Schenck and Calaway suggest Jerusalem, but Jason Whitlark has suggested this (what?) is a (counter-imperial) reference to Rome as "the eternal city." See Jason Whitlark, "Here We Do Not Have a City That Remains": A Figured Critique of Roman Imperial Propoganda in Hebrews 13:14, *JBL* 131:1 (2012): 161-171. Others have simply assumed that the phrase is a general statement of having no city on earth. Cf. Helmut Koester, "Outside the Camp," *HTR* 55 (1962): 299-315, 303.
21. Schenck, "Levitical Cultus."
22. Ibid.

snugly within Hebrews's designs. The distant, powerful figure (and highly contested position) of the high priest, for example, who was sometimes directly appointed by the Romans (as in the case of Pompey and Hyrkanos), is re-imagined as a consoling and humble/humiliated figure: "Since, then, we have a great high priest who has passed through the heavens, Jesus, the son of God, let us hold fast to our confession. For we do not have a high priest who is unable to sympathize with our weakness, but we have one who in every respect has been tested as we are, yet without sin" (Heb. 4:14-15).[23] The contestations and corruptions of the mortal high priesthood are eliminated, but the figure itself persists perfected in a deified and (conveniently?) dead figure who cannot disappoint.

Imagining Hebrews within a "lost" Israel lends a depth to the text that is otherwise forfeited when its transcendent imagination is taken too seriously on its own terms. It is not that the stakes are not high when it comes to the language of being above and beyond—it is not only a hallmark of Western imperialism, but also of misogyny and scientific objectivism, to name a few other damaging versions. But perhaps one important way to relativize the pompousness and power of the language of transcendence is to read it for its melancholy, or even simply its quirky impossibilities, alongside its aspirations. While transcendent imaginations have colluded with all kinds of malevolent forces, they can also exhibit softer edges. Or, to put it more pointedly, not all transcendent imaginations are the same, and anecdotal and affective differentiation between them is no less important for drawing out their political ramifications than for noticing they are there in the first place.[24]

---

23. Christ is not "self-appointed" but rather appointed by "the one who said to him 'You are my son'" (Heb. 5:5). This reference is perhaps a shot at a history of people who purchased the high priesthood, such as Jason and Menelaus.

A similar set of tensions regarding transcendence has trailed the Gospel of John. Several debates center around the Gospel of John and the ideological content of its longings for cosmic transcendence, often associating the Gospel of John's superlative rhetoric and universalizing ambitions with an especially fierce instance of Christian anti-Judaism and/or its alignment with empire.[25] One of the most crucial literary pivots for the latter is John 4:1-42, in which Jesus encounters the Samaritan at the well. Musa Dube observes how imperial social dynamics suffuse Jesus' interaction with the Samaritan woman. She spells out the implications of Jesus' foray into Samaritan territory, the Samaritans' proclamation at the end of the passage of Jesus as savior of the world, and the scripting and negation of the woman that occur in between, noticing that this passage evokes centuries of tension between Jews and Samaritans (or Samaritan Jews and Samaritans).[26] She writes that, through its very characterizations, this passage underwrites colonial/imperial ideologies of occupation:

> [T]he Samaritan woman is characterized as an ignorant native (v. 10) and in need of help (v. 10). She is constructed as morally/religiously lacking, that is, she has five husbands, and the one she has is not her own, (vv. 17-18), and she does not know what she worships (v. 22). On the contrary, Jesus, a superior traveller, is knowledgeable (vv. 10, 22); powerful (vv. 14, 25, 42); sees everything about her past (vv. 17-18, 29); knows and offers answers for her society (vv. 21-26); and teaches her and her people (vv. 21-23).[27]

---

24. I want to clarify here that a sympathetic reading does not mean rationalizing. Sympathetic readings, readings that pay attention to affective contexts, instead allow for more relational complexity rather than less when it comes to power, pain, and violence.
25. Though there have been plenty of treatments of the Gospel of John as anti-imperial and/or liberatory. Cf. Lance Byron Richey, *Imperial Ideology and the Gospel of John* CBQMS 43 (Washington, D.C.: The Catholic Biblical Association of America, 2007); and David Rensberger, *Johannine Faith and Liberating Community* (Philadelphia: Westminster Press, 1988).
26. Dube, "Reading for Decolonization: (John 4:1-42)" *Semeia* 75 (1996): 37-59, 46.
27. Ibid., 51.

Dube also problematizes Jesus' negation of Mt. Gerazim and the Jerusalem temple in favor of a placeless God. The Gospel of John caps the scene with Jesus saying: "God is spirit, and those who worship him must worship him in spirit and truth," (v. 24), and as Dube notes,

> The seemingly inclusive replacement maintains the religious/racial superiority of Jesus (v. 22), a characterization that clearly shows that imperialism's universal standards never intend to create relationship of equals but to win devotees. Therefore, the transcendence of both Jewish and Samaritan cultural spaces by the realm of Spirit and truth (vv. 23-24), is, in fact, an installation of the superiority of Christianity ... [28]

It seems to me, however, that Dube, as intensely sensitive to the text's stinging colonial and imperial dynamics as she is, relies on mixed assumptions about the ancient sociality that the text represents. On the one hand, she places the text in the middle of a set of Jewish social negotiation—suggestively using the words "national" and "intergroup." On the other, Dube evokes "Christianity" as a distinct phenomenon that the Johannine community is seeking to install.[29]

Dube also claims the loss of the temple as a defining moment for the Gospel of John, suggesting that the episode with the Samaritan woman might register a more intricate and ambivalent set of relationships. In fact, not one but *two* lost temples haunt the scene, since Mt. Gerizim's significance is punctured by the destruction of its

---

28. Ibid., 52.
29. Her terms come under particular duress in the following passage: "Both Pharisees and Christian Jews are trying to define Jewish identity during the Roman occupation of Palestine; in particular, after the destruction of their religious symbols, Jerusalem and the Temple ... It seems safe to say that Jesus' disciples are losing (6:66; 12:42-43), not making many disciples (4:1), and hence they are turning to proselytize the Samaritans. Ironically, the alternative vision of the Johannine community embraces an ideology of expansion, despite the fact that they are themselves victims of imperial expansion and struggling for their liberation (Dube, "Reading for Decolonization," 47). Jesus' and his disciples' activity, as painted by the Gospel of John, is described by Dube as "proselytizing" a universalizing "religion," although they are "trying to define Jewish identity."

temple in the second century B.C.E.[30] Gerizim's temple, a Samaritan site of worship derided by Jews, is indeed a source of the contentiousness that suffuses the scene in the Gospel of John, but one accompanied by a whole host of colonial issues involving ethnic purity.[31] One could hardly question the ethnically and geographically charged arrogance of the passage, as well as the enlisting of the woman as a gendered figuration of a people. But the Samaritan woman is not quite an oppositional figure to Jesus: after all, she appeals to their shared ancestry, a point that the narrative does not otherwise contradict.

Other possible meanings issue from the detail of the woman's five husbands, though; the detail is not necessarily a slander of her morality. Second Kings 17 mentions five nations which have settled in Samaria, and Josephus associated the Samaritans with foreign lineage and unfixed loyalties,[32] supporting the possibility that what the "Samaritan" stands for is not Jesus' opposite, but more generally Israelite cultural ambivalence.[33] Later, when Jesus is accused of being a Samaritan and being possessed by a demon, he only answers that he does not have a demon. Jesus' silence on the question is provocative, and might be suggestive of a wisp of connectedness, or even a whole subtext of diasporic mess, between him and the Samaritan woman. Joined not only through distant ancestry, but through Roman imperial possession and the difficult absences of their respective worship sites, Jesus and the Samaritan woman represent in the text

---

30. According to Josephus, Hyrcanus destroys it (*Antiquities* 13.9.1).
31. Once the capital of the Northern Kingdom, but largely de-populated by the Assyrians (cf. 2 Kings 17:6), Samaria held a dubious, but distinct, relationship to Israel as part of its history and self-understanding. Samaritans represented a thoroughly impure and denigrated parcel of Israelite belonging, which the story of the good Samaritan in Luke 10:25-37 relies upon for its irony.
32. Rome, then, is the man the woman is said to live with now. Craig Koester, "Savior of the World," *JBL* 109, no. 4 (1990): 665-80 (675-76).
33. Sung Uk Lim, "Speak My Name: Anti-colonial Mimicry and the Samaritan Woman in John 4:1-42," *USQR* 62, no. 3-4 (2010): 35-51 (45).

a moment of reckoning with Israel's strange and tangled colonial history.[34] It is not a coincidence then that God's blank ubiquity is proclaimed in this scene in which the places evoked are confused, contested, and in ruin. As with the living water that Jesus offers the Samaritan woman, when need and social entanglements become too overwhelming, the Gospel of John fires the old silver bullet of indistinction. God's "placelessness" is a desperate, if troubling, attempt at holding together a splintered sociality.[35]

This move to the one, the true, and the unrivaled when things get too sticky is subtly echoed in the other elements in the scene, and other places in the gospel at large. Jesus tells the woman to call her husband, and she claims that she has no husband. Jesus congratulates her for telling the truth because, "[i]n fact, you've had five husbands, and the man you are now living with is not your husband" (4:18). Her complicated involvements are solved in the narrative by negation. Scholars have long noticed that the famous "words of institution" which occur at the last supper scene in the Synoptic Gospels appear not at the last supper in the Gospel of John, but in a mass feeding in John 6, which has the effect of broadening

---

34. Jeffrey Staley has similarly suggested a sympathetic position regarding the Gospel of John's appeals to placelessness. While Jesus' words to the Samaritan woman may very well reek of colonizing impulses, Staley writes, "[o]n the other hand, Jesus' statement ' . . . neither on this mountain nor in Jerusalem . . . ' can sometimes have a totally different meaning when spoken by one victim of oppression to another. And both Jesus and the Samaritan woman fit this description. Both have fallen under Roman domination, that ruthless imperialistic regime which will not stop its quest for power until the entire Mediterranean region is under its sway. And just as the Samaritan temple had once been destroyed, so also will the Jerusalem temple one day be destroyed (Jn 11:48). Furthermore, although Jesus' own words suggest that he displaces the displaced, Jerusalem temple (Jn 2:19-22), he also will be destroyed, displaced by the same *pax romana* (19:10)." See Jeffrey Staley, "'Dis Place, Man':A Postcolonial Critique of the Vine (the Mountain and the Temple) in the Gospel of John," in *John and Postcolonialism: Travel, Space and Power* (New York: Sheffield Academic Press, 2002), ed. Musa Dube and Jeffrey Staley, 46. Staley, however, uses the term "liberating" to describe this way of hearing Jesus' words. The term "liberation" seems to contradict his reading, though, which points less to freedom than to painful intractabilities.
35. I emphasize "troubling" because I do not think that the diasporic and affective context makes universalism a better enterprise, just a more understandable one.

the significance of Jesus' body (or in this case, "flesh") as bread.³⁶ In a later explanation to the quarreling Jews, Jesus explains that the bread he gives is the "life of the world" (6:51), denying the simpler and smaller formulation of "for you" directed at twelve students. Perhaps the last supper scene is too chaotic, what with its betrayals, disagreements, and misunderstandings, to suggest that Jesus' body might have been broken for such a dissatisfying group. Again, the Gospel projects upwards and outwards when most bogged down in the mess.

Indeed the Gospel of John's blanketing and often dismissive deployment of "the Jews"/*hoi ioudaioi* may represent a similar tactic of universalizing and negation when things get too tricky. Scholarship has worked and worried over the Gospel of John's nasty castigations of "the Jews" (a phrase which appears more in the Gospel of John than the other three Gospels together), collectively wondering what to make of this rhetoric in the face of the clear enmeshment of the Gospel in Jewish scripture and symbols. Some have argued that translating *hoi ioudaioi* as "the Jews" instead of the more literal "the Judeans" removes the geographic specificity from the rhetoric, thus forcing it out of its context of intra-group disputes and implying an entire people. On the other hand, as Adele Reinhartz suggests, the Gospel of John stretches *hoi ioudaioi* from its geographical implications to include a broader population than simply those specifically located in Judea (John 6:41, e.g.), and the text likewise extends critiques of the Pharisees to *hoi ioudaioi* at large (cf. John 9:15-16, 18). While she admits that the Gospel assumes Jesus and his disciples to be Jews, she points out that they are never directly

---

36. Cf. John 6:48-51: "I am the bread of life. Your ancestors ate the manna in the desert, but they still died. This is the bread that comes down from heaven, anyone who eats it never dies. I am the life-giving bread that came down from heaven. Anyone who eats this bread will live forever. And the bread that I will give for the world's life is my mortal flesh."

referred to as Jews, with one exception—Jesus' encounter with the Samaritan woman—and so the generalized and hostile implications of the translation "the Jews" is warranted.[37]

Reinhartz's resolution to the problem deserves special attention because her explorations of the Gospel in *Befriending the Beloved Disciple* attend to her affectively uneven and conflicted relationship to the text. Her own relationship to the Gospel of John is one that is, by her account, comprised of admiration, exasperation, curiosity, companionship, aversion, and even defiance—one that refuses reduction (Reinhartz reveals herself to be a Jewish New Testament scholar, as well as a child of Holocaust survivors).[38] Her reading of the problem of *hoi ioudiaoi*, however, does not allow space for a similarly rich affectivity in the Gospel, as she compresses the text's affectivity around Israel and its collectivities to hostility.[39] The Gospel of John's use of *hoi ioudaioi* may be no less turbulent. Not only does seventy uses of the term *hoi ioudaioi*, whatever its meanings, suggest a serious preoccupation, but the exception which Reinhartz names—the meeting between Jesus and the Samaritan woman—is, it seems, no small or simple usage. In the one scene in which Jesus is directly named as *ioudaios*, he encounters the tensive colonial history haunting that belonging, the inexorable binds of homeland even, and especially, in the face of its wreckage.

---

37. Adele Reinhartz, "Judaism in the Gospel of John," *Interpretation* 63, no. 4 (2009): 382-93 (383-384).
38. Adele Reinhartz, *Befriending the Beloved Disciple*, 11-16.
39. Reinhartz challenges arguments that the Gospel of John's rhetoric represents an "intra-Jewish feud," not because they are wrong per se, but because they underestimate the emotional pull and thus viral potential of the negative rhetoric in the text against "the Jews" (*Befriending the Beloved Disciple*, 77-78). Though Reinhartz is obviously correct about some of the historical effects of this rhetoric, I do think it is worth surfacing the complex affectivity of the Gospel of John on this point, just as any kind of historicizing and complication of a text's conditions/context/circumstances can have an effect on contemporary receptions of that text. As Reinhartz also points out by her own reading, the affective relationship one has with a text is anything but predictable.

Within these contexts of diasporic enmeshment, the image of Jesus as the temple in the Gospel of John reads not like Christian replacement theology, but rather as an answer to the loss of and mixed feelings around a central site of cultural practice and worship. In the Gospel of John, not only does Jesus challenge the money changers at the temple as he does in the Gospel of Mark, but the narrator follows the line, "[d]estroy this temple and I'll raise it in three days," with an aside that "he was speaking of the temple of his body" (2:19-21), leaving no room for ambiguity. This association of Jesus with the temple and its practices is also embedded in the continued elaboration of the image of Jesus as "the lamb." The Gospel of John, like Hebrews, represents Jesus as the one and the true, both temple and sacrifice, and a superlative figure of cosmic importance to quell the acutely felt quandaries of place and amorphousness of diasporic life.

In her essay "Voices from the Teum: Synesthetic Trauma and the Ghosts of the Korean Diaspora," Grace Cho chronicles some specific circumstances for the quandaries of place and amorphousness of diasporic life. She gives a fragmentary narration of the 1945 sinking of the *Ukishima Maru*, a ship leaving Japan for Korea, filled with thousands of newly freed Korean slaves.[40] It is still unclear how many people died on the ship and what caused the explosion. The Japanese government claimed the ship hit a mine planted by U.S. Forces, but survivors reported seeing Japanese sailors abandoning the ship before the explosion, claiming the ship was blown up to destroy witnesses of Japanese brutality. Using the archives of the melodramatic filmic account of the disaster in the movie *Soul's Protest*, narrative from the film *History and Memory*, as well as newspapers and legal claims from both Korean survivors and the Japanese

---

40. Grace Cho, "Voices from the Teum," in *The Affective Turn: Theorizing the Social*, ed. Patricia Ticineto Clough and Jean Halley (Durham: Duke University Press, 2007), 151-169.

government, Cho tries to account for her own feelings about the mysterious past of her mother who was freed from Japan in 1945 at the age of four, just after the sinking of the *Ukishima Maru*. In one place in her chronological reconstruction, she writes:

> **1945**: Returned to Korea, shortly after liberation. "Returned," let us say, even though she had never been there before. The exact date of the return is undocumented. Maybe it was in September, shortly after liberation. "Liberation," let us say, even though she would find no freedom in her homeland either. "Homeland," let us say, even though she had never lived there. Returned to her homeland in 1945 shortly after liberation, maybe in September.[41]

Cho's halting description illustrates the complexity and tortured subtext of diasporic narratives of emancipation. While Cho's mother survives her own trip "back" to Korea, she, like the victims of the *Ukishima Maru*, never makes it to freedom. Home is neither in Japan nor in Korea; though she belongs painfully to both, Cho suggests. The vision of the ship forever floating in the space between Japan and Korea acts as a powerful metaphor for diasporic experience:

> The image of the sailing ship packed with slaves, suggests, as Hortense Spillers has pointed out, a suspension in the "oceanic," in what Sigmund Freud described as "limitlessness . . . a bond with the universe," or, in other words, a feeling reminiscent of a pre-oedipal state in which the baby does not sense its separation from the mother and the breast and the milk . . . In the context of the [African] slave vessel, the oceanic feeling associated with a oneness with the universe/mother is displaced by an oceanic of "undifferentiated identity removed from indigenous land and culture." These captives were "culturally unmade" beings whose destinies were "exposed . . . to an unknown course." The vessel's movement toward an unknown destination implies not only the vulnerability and the erasure, or unmaking, of the subject but also a moment of radical possibility. In *Soul's Protest*, the circling of the ship and its seemingly endless movement toward a never arrived-at

---

41. Cho, "Voices from the Teum," 162.

destination suggests that time itself is suspended, unaccounted for—*an unguarded moment*...⁴²

Cho notes that the difference between Spiller's analysis of enslaved Africans and the *Ukishima Maru* is that the slaves were not being taken to an unknown land, but returning to a place that was "once known but only existed phantasmatically," and was "always already fragmented," comprising thick layers of cultural tumult.⁴³ Not only is the suspension in the oceanic poignant for Hebrews's sense of "rest" being neither "here" nor "there" exactly, or ambiguously a time/place/condition. But the cosmic oceanic and the question of an already-fragmented relation with one's supposed homeland resonates with the Gospel of John in its negation of place as a viable form of belonging. The blank "nowhere" of beyond can recapitulate an experience of cultural indistinction, but it can also ease (through flattening) a whole history of repeated cultural disjoints, turning it into a sense of "radical possibility."

Given the stickiness of place (it sticks with you, even as you are unfastened from it), it is no wonder that the kind of belonging imagined in the Gospel of John is one that hinges on a disidentification with "the world" and a kind of alienated identification with Christ.⁴⁴ This is a belonging animated by displacement, but moored in a singularly transcendent origin, putting it in precisely the same kind of conceptual territory (pun intended) as Hebrews and the Secret Revelation of John.⁴⁵ All three texts feature

---

42. Ibid., 160.
43. Ibid., 160-61.
44. Vincent Wimbush, "'Not of This World': Early Christianities as Rhetorical and Social Formation," in *Reimagining Christian Origins: A Colloquium Honoring Burton L. Mack*, ed. E. Castelli and H. Taussig (Valley Forge, Pa: Trinity Press International, 1996), 23–36.
45. Karen King's work on the Secret Revelation of John has suggested that these and other close resemblances between the Gospel of John and the Secret Revelation of John might be understood as the Secret Revelation of John "filling in the gaps" in the Gospel, "offering a fuller narrative of the Divine Realm, the creation of the world and humanity, the condition

juxtapositions such as stability and movement, flux and timelessness, the one and the many, light and dark, the true and the illusory—juxtapositions that attempt to sort out the confusing vicissitudes of colonial and imperial life.[46] They chronicle an affective circuit of diasporic grief: instability, change, and fracture heighten desires for their opposites, while oneness, stability, and truth cast the losses of the felt present in stark, somber, and more understandable terms.

In Hebrews, the Secret Revelation of John, and the Gospel of John, the juxtapositions of light vs. dark, true vs. illusory, one vs. many, create a sense of drama. But at least as dramatic is the way such juxtapositions buckle under their own weight, and do so with very distinct effects in each text. For the Secret Revelation of John, the excessive perfection of the heavenly realm simply cannot bear itself. Or rather it was too enamoured with itself: Sophia, deep in self-contemplation, wills a likeness of herself that becomes Yaldabaoth, suggesting that excessive perfection bubbles over into the less divine excesses of power, arrogance, and sex (SRevJohn 10.1-6). Thus, grotesque mimicry, flesh, and violence are meticulously kept outside of the heavenly realm in the Secret Revelation of John. If binary figurations are an acknowledgement and frustrated redress to the

---

of humanity in the world, and salvation" See Karen King, *The Secret Revelation of John* (Cambridge: Harvard University Press, 2006), 238.

46. As both Vincent Wimbush and Warren Carter have suggested. Wimbush made one of the earliest suggestions to read the Gospel of John's dualistic language of this world/another world as a rhetorical and social response to imperialism ("'Not of This World'"), but Carter outlines in more specific terms what is at stake emotionally in such language: "The stark dualism suggests that the gospel is addressing readers who are not especially clear on their identity and who live in ethical and social circumstances that are confusing and somewhat ambiguous" (*John: Storyteller, Interpreter, Evangelist* [Peabody, Mass.: Hendrickson, 2006], 88). Both Wimbush and Carter suggest such dualist language indicates a kind of resistance and position such resistant social figuration as or within a Christian identity. I am more cautious, however, about reproducing the binarizing strategy of these texts through such figurations as resistance and anti-society. Carter specifically uses the word "anitsociety," but Wimbush is more careful to note that such resistant, otherworldly rhetoric is often hyperbolic, while still socially productive (Carter, *John*, 86; and Wimbush, "'Not of This World'," 34).

complexities of the world, it may be, then, that the confusing combinations of beauty, goodness, and pain in the lived world are sorted out and resolved in the Secret Revelation of John, to some degree, into two worlds at odds with one another.

In Hebrews and the Gospel of John, by contrast, a kind of perverse fleshiness infuses their loftiest concepts. Both Hebrews and the Gospel of John even place flesh—soft, solid skin and muscle—at the center of their transcendent imaginations. Despite Hebrews's airy and remote reputation, by placing Jesus' death in the context of an extended meditation on the temple and associating it with sacrifice Hebrews provokes, if by subtext, an imagination of his death at least as graphic as any direct description offered in the Gospels. The description of Jesus' flesh as curtain surprises in part because it gets tossed out almost offhandedly in a puzzlingly assumptive form.[47] But even as metaphor, Jesus-as-curtain immediately inspires a practically cartoonish image in the mind's eye. If Hebrews repeatedly associates Jesus with the most macabre of images, the Gospel of John nearly matches Hebrews by making sure its audience hears all the indelicate resonances of consuming Jesus' body as bread: "Very truly, if you don't eat the flesh of the Son of Man and drink his blood, you have no life in you. Those who eat my flesh and drink my blood have eternal life, and I will raise them up on the last day; for my flesh is true food and my blood is true drink. Those who eat my flesh and drink my blood abide in me, and I in them" (John 6:53-56).

Jesus likewise authenticates his resurrection with two rather fleshy moments: Thomas puts his hand in Jesus' wound (20:27), and Jesus eats with the disciples (21:15). The tortured, susceptible, and supple dimensions of Jesus' bodily experience are evoked through the

---

47. In Hebrews 10:19-20, the fleshly curtain is not introduced as particularly noteworthy. The NRSV even reads the flesh-curtain as parenthetical: "Therefore my friends, since we have confidence to enter the sanctuary by the blood of Jesus, by the new and living way that he opened for us through the curtain, (that is, through his flesh) . . . "

Gospel's gloried end, disarming some of his steely cosmic power. Though perhaps with less dark comedy than Hebrews, the Gospel of John, too, curiously replaces the contingencies of place and belonging with the contingencies of the flesh.

* * * *

In trying to make non-ironic sense of this knitting together of transcendence with the chaotic, unromantic realities of "bodily life" (otherwise known as life), I find myself recalling a dream I had while in the early stages of planning this book, one in which this book figured. In the dream, however, this book was not a book but little scraps of paper with handwriting on them, stuck on the underside of tables at the institution in which I was living and working. At that time, the institution had felt to me like it was falling apart, even dying or dead, and it had been the source of more injury to me and some close to me than I wish to recount (although it may have been, by other accounts, just as sturdy and imperfect as ever). But in the dream, the feeling of the place was warm and wild, as when I first moved there. Sun and the sound of traffic surged through classroom windows. In the dream, I was wandering around carrying another book I had written, one on the Gospel of Mark and loss. It was not a book either, however. It was an organ, round and wet, that I was carrying around in a plastic bag.

There is much that I could say about this dream, but it may be more effective and affecting to under-read it here, and to offer it as an open-ended and commiserating complement to Hebrews and the Gospel of John. But I will say the following: in the middle of that drama of institutional loss and my disabled sense of home—of feeling simultaneously chained to and cut loose from the place—I often told myself, and was told by countless others, to "focus on the work" and "just finish up and get out." I had no problem doing just that, taking off into periods of intensely personally rewarding flights of historical and theoretical fancy. My own creativity was my sense of escape, and yet there it was in the dream, in slips and slivers, fixed to the underside of the very place of which I was writing my way out. The organ was, while a graphic and strange representation, simultaneously frightening and consoling. Both mine and outside of me, the organ was my aliveness, my creativity, my sense of exposure, and my sadness all spun into one. Binding my flight to my flesh, although against my conscious inclinations, turned out to be a profoundly satisfying way to consider the enormous risks and gifts of creativity in particular, and living in general. What is more, the risks and gifts are often inextricable.

Contemporary Christian theology has, especially in the last decade, struggled with transcendence, primarily its philosophical, gendered, and colonial implications. Part of this struggle has been whether or not to retain transcendence as a conceptuality at all, and, if so, how to imagine it.[48] Perhaps the better question is not whether transcendence should be considered fundamentally flawed or if it is even worth keeping around, especially since I find myself both opposed to it as a concept and, as my dream reminds me, periodically trying to achieve it. Perhaps the more prescient question is: what are the specific pains, the terrifying realities of limits, the desperate if imprecise wishes for possibilities, that foster and fuel desires for "getting beyond"? This question has a special significance since the

---

48. Cf. the various critiques, as well as minor and major resuscitations, of transcendence as a concept in Grace M. Janzten, *Becoming Divine: Toward a Feminist Philosophy of Religion* (Bloomington: Indiana University Press, 1999); Mayra Rivera, *The Touch of Transcendence: A Postcolonial Theology of God* (Louisville: Westminster John Knox Press, 2007); and John D. Caputo and Michael J. Scanlon, eds., *Transcendence and Beyond: A Postmodern Inquiry* (Bloomington: Indiana University Press, 2007). It should be noted that feminist theologians such as Mary Daly and Rosemary Radford Ruether noticed the gendered dimensions of divine transcendence decades earlier than this.

language of beyond may itself be an attempt to circumvent difficult confrontation with those feelings.

Removing transcendence from its social/affective complexities—here, its diasporic chafe and ache—not only shuts down the possibility that such an imagination might be a useful (though not faultless) response. It additionally naturalizes transcendence as a baseline or defining feature of Christian thought, rather than a thoroughly unexceptional rhetorical/emotional management of specific limits. It may very well be that it is this elision, this *removal* of cosmic aspirations and universalism from their pained circumstances, rather than transcendence itself, that gives flight to the notion of a Christian identity.

6

Pleasure, Pain, and Forgetting in the Gospel of Truth

And there was empty ignorance as if they were sleeping and found themselves in disturbing dreams—running some place or powerless while pursued, coming to blows or themselves beaten, falling from heights or flying through air without wings. Or sometimes as if people are trying to kill them or they are killing their neighbors, smeared with blood. Until the time, after having all these dreams, they awaken. Those in the midst of all this confusion see nothing for these things are nothing. Such are those who cast ignorance from themselves like sleep. They do not consider it anything or its works as real things, but leave them behind like a dream in the night. (Gospel of Truth 14.12-15.2)[1]

Because trauma can be unspeakable and unrepresentable and because it is marked by forgetting and dissociation, it often seems to leave behind no records at all. (Cvetkovich, *An Archive of Feelings*, 7)

---

1. I am using Celene Lillie's translation of the Gospel of Truth in *A New New Testament: A Bible for the 21st Century Combining Traditional and Newly Discovered Texts*, ed. Hal Taussig (New York: Houghton Mifflin Harcourt, 2013), 230-241, as well as her versification and numbering.

The Gospel of Truth is, if nothing else, a text about enjoyment. It cocoons its reader in the sensuous realities of the Father, its vivid imagery appealing to a full spectrum of sense experience. The Father's sweetness appears as the fruit of guiltless enjoyment, fruit that when eaten "did not cause destruction" (4.6); his fullness is imagined as a warm swell of fragrance (19.4-14); and unity feels like a deep kiss: "For everyone loves truth, because truth is the Father's mouth; his tongue is the holy spirit. Whoever clings to the Father's mouth and by his tongue will receive the holy spirit" (13.3-4). So much of the body is implicated in the revelation of the son: according to the Gospel of Truth, seeing and hearing the son also means getting to taste, smell, and touch him (16.2). Access to the superlative reality of the Father is imagined through "other-worldly" moments of this-world enjoyment.

The pleasurable and erotic force of the Gospel of Truth is so palpable that it infuses the secondary literature on the text, although most scholars leave the almost embarrassingly graphic imaginations of fullness alone. Rather, the Gospel of Truth has come to be characterized as a singularly seductive text through associations with poststructuralist theories of language that emphasize desire and lack and a kind of eroticized surfeit of meaning,[2] or with an alluring interplay between the known and the strange, disclosure and secrecy.[3] The Gospel of Truth is seen as sexy, then, less for its interest

---

2. See, for example, Joel Fineman's Lacanian reading of the Gospel of Truth, which draws grand conclusions about "Gnostic" interpretation from the text, finding in the text a hot linguistic rebelliousness: "Gnosticism will always retain its propensity to violate a text, to force and twist it, as its opponents continually complained . . . the force of Gnostic exegesis derives from the scandal that its readings deliberately intend and provoke." Joel Fineman, "Gnosis and the Piety of Metaphor: The Gospel of Truth," in *The Rediscovery of Gnosticism: Proceedings of the International Conference on Gnosticism at Yale, New Haven, Connecticut, March 28-31, 1978*, vol. 1, ed. Bentley Layton (SHR XLI. Leiden: E.J. Brill, 1980), 289-312, 309. Similarly, Patricia Cox Miller finds the Gospel of Truth exhibiting a "Gnostic" approach to canon that treats texts not as closed, but as beguilingly open and endlessly fecund. "The 'living book of the living' is a continuous process of discovering that the book is a lure," she writes (480). "Words with an Alien Voice: Gnostics, Scripture, Canon," *VC* 42, no. 4 (1988): 327-38.

in the sensual than for its coy dynamics of exposure and promiscuity of meaning.

Yet such readings of Gospel of Truth as seductive, rebellious, provocative, and open align all too easily with gendered figurations of licentious, if tempting, "heretical" others.[4] Such readings of the Gospel of Truth as seductive also, as I have argued elsewhere, bear a certain uncomfortable resemblance to imaginations of "the Orient," therefore following a long history of sculpting the supposed phenomenon of Gnosticism and the texts presumed to be part of it with the romanticized and eroticized open horizon of "the East."[5] Such interpretations of the Gospel of Truth testify to the force of colonial histories undergirding our own search for meanings in and interpretation of ancient texts. But they also importantly chronicle

---

3. Harold Attridge, for example, has described it as an "exoteric" text, a text that combines "familiar" (i.e., what is now canonical) and "unfamiliar" material in such a fashion as to enticingly persuade its ancient readers into alternate interpretations of authoritative Christian materials. See his "The Gospel of Truth as an Exoteric Text," in *Nag Hammadi, Gnosticism and Early Christianity*, ed. Charles W. Hedrick and Robert Hodgson, Jr. (Peabody, Mass: Hendrickson Publishers, 1986), 239-55. Elliot Wolfson disagrees but finds the text no less flirtatious. Locating the text as a precursor to Jewish mysticism, he sees it as "thoroughly 'esoteric' in its parabolic deportment; indeed, the text displays an esotericism so abounding that it appears to be exoteric: the secret secrets itself in the concealment of disclosure wrought by the disclosure of its concealment." Elliot R. Wolfson, "Inscribed in the Book of the Living: Gospel of Truth and Jewish Christology," *JSJ* 38, no. 2 (2007): 234-71 (249).
4. In an essay entitled "The Heretical Woman as Symbol in Alexander, Athanasius, Epiphanius and Jerome," Virginia Burrus has shown how anxieties about social boundaries in heresiological writings played out in the form of representations of women and women's sexuality. "[T]he fourth-century figure of the heretical woman," she writes, "who is almost invariably identified as sexually promiscuous, expresses the threatening image of a community with uncontrolled boundaries." The idealized community was imagined as virgin and bride, under wraps and boundaries closed. The "bad church" was imagined as "bad girl," susceptible and alluring—which is also to say that "heresy," as these writers imagined it, had a distinct sex appeal. Burrus, "The Heretical Woman as Symbol in Alexander, Athanasius, Epiphanius and Jerome," *Harvard Theological Review* 84:3 (1993): 229-248, 232. Burrus concentrates on the anxious forces undergirding the figurations of heretical women. However, I have suggested that there is more, affectively, at play in such figurations, including disgust, excitement, or shame, for example. Maia Kotrosits, "Romance and Danger at Nag Hammadi," *The Bible and Critical Theory* 8, no. 1 (2012): 44-45.
5. Kotrosits, "Romance and Danger." I follow Karen King's work in *What is Gnosticism?* (Cambridge: Harvard University Press, 2005), 83-109.

the contemporary feelings of boredom and comfort so often associated with the Bible. The Gospel of Truth's attractiveness and threat becomes both foil and escape for contemporary readers for whom the canon has become rather unsexily domesticated.[6]

I want to take the romance out of the Gospel of Truth's interest in pleasure, and do so by putting it in express relationship with the violence and the terror in the text. Although scholarship has shown considerably less interest in the troubling passages in the Gospel of Truth—ones that reference murder, blood, pain, confusion, and being chased or lost—I would like to take these references to violence, confusion, fear, etc. as a *starting point* for making sense of the text. Rather than a negative imprint of the text's lustrous theology or traces of an abstract Gnostic world-denigration, these references to violence and turmoil might actually be central experiences underwriting the text.

Approaching the Gospel of Truth as a response to traumatic experience demands a rhetorical reading of the text, since the text repeatedly relegates these experiences to the spectral, understanding them as "insubstantial." The recourse to phantoms and nightmares (as seen in the epigraph, above), however, may itself be an expression of trauma's haunting and uncertain effects.[7] At the same time, this inversion is one of the text's modes of response in that it refigures trauma and its effects as less real through comparisons to and multi-sensory elaborations of the Father's billowing fullness.

There is encouragement for such a rhetorical reading not only in the text's strong contrast between realities, but in its vacillation on whether or not the Father's fullness has actually arrived. The Gospel of Truth exists in a suspended present: despite the fact that

---

6. Again, see Kotrosits, "Romance and Danger," 45-48, where I lay out in more detail some possible psycho-social dynamics in the relationship between Nag Hammadi and the Bible.
7. In addition to the epigraph, see also Gospel of Truth 14.5-9.

the revelation of the son enables knowledge of, and therefore a return to, the Father's fullness, there is a more-than-faint sense of not yet: "This is the Word of the good news of the discovery of the fullness for those who await the salvation coming from above. Their hope, toward which they stretch, is stretching toward them—they whose image is light with no shadow in it (Gospel of Truth 20.1-2)." In other places in the Gospel of Truth, phrases such as "in time, oneness will make the places full" (11.1) and "if indeed these things have happened to us" (11.3) lend wariness to the text's more assertive declarations of reality that "he did away with torture and torment" (16.8). This sense of being in-between is especially resonant with diasporic displacement, and with the unsure time/place of "rest" in Hebrews. But this suspension and uncertainty is, as I will argue, also ripe for the affective redirection or reorganization that the text stages in other passages.

Through such affective redirections, the Gospel of Truth obscures the very traumas that underwrite it, and its concealments are a refusal to speak about what its audience already feels to be true. While the other texts discussed in this book contain more manifest diasporic hauntings and preoccupations with Israel, it is the very absence of references to national belonging in the Gospel of Truth that become the imprint of diasporic trauma. Indeed, the Gospel of Truth's absences and affective redirections may speak volumes about more than the Gospel of Truth; they may additionally recast some developments in the second century and, perhaps more crucially, suggest some conditions for the historical production of Christianity.

* * * *

Trauma and pleasure would seem to be distinct or even opposing experiences. Strands of queer theory that have rejected sex positivity, however, remind us that the domain of sex and pleasure bristle with less ideal or agreeable feelings and subtexts.[8] Illustrating the ways that discourses of trauma and sexuality "touch" one another, Ann Cvetkovich notes that the very term "penetration" carries associations with both pleasure and violence or trauma: "Trauma is present in the association of penetration with domination, the assumption that anal penetration constitutes not only emasculation but annihilation of the self, and the construction of rape as sexualized power. Such representations of penetration lend themselves to constructions of sexuality as fundamentally traumatic." In their shared recourse to tropes or images of penetration, "discourses of both trauma and sexuality invoke the powerful fears of vulnerability that being affected by sensations or being touched can arouse."[9] The butch-femme discourses considered in Cvetkovich's work, which may or may not directly describe the traumas affecting them, provoke us to rethink not only hardness or toughness as related in a constructive way to vulnerability and responsiveness as its own kind of agency. They also "depathologize the relationship between trauma and sexuality, [though] they don't necessarily refuse it," thereby "forging creative responses to the trauma of touch."[10]

---

8. Leo Bersani's essay "Is the Rectum a Grave?" has been pivotal in the rejection of sex-positivity in queer theorizing and gay and lesbian studies, and Ann Cvetkovich addresses that essay at length in her book. Bersani's essay theorizes from the Freudian death drive to affirm the self-shattering capacity of passive receptivity, i.e., "getting fucked." He and others such as Lee Edelman and Michael Warner have used this "negative" stance on sex to intervene, in part, in the normative associations of sex with life/reproduction. See Leo Bersani, *Is the Rectum a Grave? And Other Essays* (Chicago: University of Chicago Press, 2010); as well as Ann Cvetkovich's discussion in *An Archive of Feelings: Trauma, Sexuality, and Lesbian Public Cultures* (Durham: Duke University Press, 2003), 61-63.
9. Cvetkovich, *Archive of Feelings*, 50-51. Elsewhere she clarifies that "[i]t is possible to ask how penetration comes to mean domination or trauma without presuming that these are natural connections, and how it can materialize not just gendered and sexualized forms of power, but hierarchies of race and nation as well" (37).
10. Ibid., 52.

Trauma has incredible interpersonal and social productivity, as well as a surprising affective richness, as Cvetkovich illustrates. In a chapter entitled "Sexual Trauma/Queer Memory," she explores lesbian narratives for "perverse" forms of healing in the aftermath of incest and sexual abuse. She cites a "queer interdependence of that which harms and that which heals in order to embrace the unpredictable potential of traumatic experience."[11] These social and affective dynamics of trauma, pleasure, pain, and healing resonate with the Gospel of Truth, and offer a way to think socially about a text for which the primary imagined social context has been a battle between orthodoxy and heresy.[12]

The Gospel of Truth represents a circuit in which self-understanding as a child of the Father and an emotional re-valencing of difficult experience as beautiful and enjoyable underwrite each other. That is to say, belonging to the Father depends on an affective re-association of pain with pleasure. Nowhere is this circuit more conspicuous than in the descriptions of Jesus' death:

---

11. Ibid., 116-17.
12. One caveat to largely non-social interpretations of the Gospel of Truth is found in Anne McGuire's "Conversion and Gnosis in the Gospel of Truth," *NovT* 28, no. 4 (1986): 338-55. McGuire modestly reframes some predominant ideas about the text as a Gnostic conversion text, and in the meantime provides some helpful qualitative descriptions about the text's emotional life. She writes of the Gospel of Truth that "the author directs the reader to an understanding of Gnosis that links the individual's reception of Gnosis to a radical reorientation of emotional attitude toward existence, of theological conception, and of life in the world" (346). Although McGuire, like others, sees this reorientation as a "radical revision of Christian tradition," she mostly highlights the affective movements in the text—from anxiety to rest, emptiness to fullness, and alienation to oneness and restoration—and impressively manages to veer away from an individualist reading of them. She in fact sees the text as knitting the individual and the collective together through the emotional reorientation that its mythology engenders: "For within the symbolic world of the text, the individual act of response is part of the mythic process by which the Entirety returns to the Father. Individual conversions participate in the collective conversion or restoration of the Entirety. The myth of the Entirety's return thus invites the readers to identify as members of the Entirety, as it provides the interpretive key to the meaning of the individual's own experience" (349). I would like to gently over-read McGuire here and say that what she is getting at is precisely affect's intersubjective variability and social productivity—the social life of emotion.

> This is the good news of the one whom they seek, revealed to those filled through the mercies of the Father. Through the hidden mystery, Jesus Christ shone to the ones in the darkness of forgetfulness. He enlightened them and showed them a way. The way he taught them is truth. Because of this, Transgression was angry with him and pursued him. She was distressed by him and left barren. He was nailed to a tree and became fruit of the Father's knowledge. It did not cause destruction when it was eaten, but it caused those who ate it to come into being and find contentment within its discovery (Gospel of Truth 4.1-6).

In the passage above, the text evokes not one but two images of death, only to shift them in the direction of a satisfaction and generativity enjoyed collectively.[13] In fact, Jesus' crucifixion is mentioned directly twice, and each time the text re-describes it as an exquisite production that has relational and participatory implications:

> Like a will not yet opened, the fortune of the dead master's house is hidden; so too all things which were hidden while the Father of everything was invisible, but which come from within him, from who every way comes forth. Because of this, Jesus appeared and clothed himself in that book. He was nailed to a tree and published as the Father's edict on the cross. Oh, what a great teaching! He drew himself down from death, clothing himself in never ending life. He stripped off the perishable rags and put on imperishability, which no one can take from him (Gospel of Truth 6.7-12).

---

13. The association of Jesus' death with food and/or eating is not itself singular to this text, of course. One should contrast this image with Paul's insistence in Corinthians that the association of Jesus' body with the bread means that the meal is a rather sober affair. Cf. 1 Corinthians 5:6-8, in which Paul tells the Corinthians to act like unleavened bread; or 1 Corinthians 11:26-27, in which Paul reminds the Corinthians that eating and drinking "proclaims the Lord's death until he comes" and that eating and drinking in an "unworthy manner" is "answerable for the body and blood of the Lord." The sacrifice motifs in Hebrews and the Gospel of John, for example, tend to underscore the gruesome dimensions of the Jesus' death/food association—an association that probably arose rather organically if we keep the associational meal context as a primary one for understanding sociality and this literature we call "early Christian." Sacrificed meat was served at such meals, where the dead and the divine were memorialized.

In these passages the Gospel of Truth is perhaps suggesting, but never exactly mentions, resurrection. It does not need to: the death of Jesus was, for this text, always a vibrant event and need not be followed or confirmed by another (cf. 6.6). The crucifixion of Jesus—not his being raised from the dead—was the revelation, the publication of a mystery, the meaning of which was always already good. Yet even the imagistic morphing of the crucifixion cannot totally erase the visceral horror of such a drawn-out and grisly death. While in other passages the Gospel of Truth treats pain and violence as simply phantasmic, pleasure does not quite "defeat" death here. Especially in the image of Christ as fruit of the cross/tree, ready for exquisite consumption, but also in the comparison to inherited riches, pleasure and death are indistinguishable. Like the naming of terror and pain as illusions or nightmares, these juxtapositions are part of a larger set of affective reorientations in the text, ones that both tacitly admit trauma and attempt to experientially re-associate it.

In a close reading of Dorothy Allison's novel *Bastard Out of Carolina*, Cvetkovich offers not only an example of the queerness of trauma, but the queer vicissitudes of healing after sexual violence. Bone, the lead character of *Bastard Out of Carolina*, is a young girl raped and abused by her stepfather, but the focus of the story is the relationship between Bone and her mother, who cannot finally leave "Daddy Glen." Cvetkovich praises the affective and narrative intricacy of the story which chronicles, in addition to the abuse, a whole landscape of poverty and pain: "[F]ocusing on the mother-daughter relationship, Allison refuses easy dichotomies of victim and perpetrator and explores the complexities of emotional trauma. Transforming the melodramatic narrative structure that would locate the event of sexual abuse as the scene of violence, Allison weaves a much more complicated narrative of family and social structures, where loss and betrayal are not punctual events."[14]

For Cvetkovich, Allison's novel "powerfully examines the intimate connections between sexual trauma and sexual pleasure, and by implication the connections between incest and, if not lesbianism explicitly, then, perverse sexuality" (Allison is a lesbian and, at the end of the semi-autobiographical novel, Bone is revealed to be a lesbian). At one point in the novel, Bone begins to make the association between masturbation and the first incident of her abuse:

> Sex. Was that what Daddy Glen had been doing to me in the parking lot? Was it what I had started doing to myself whenever I was alone in the afternoons? I would imagine being tied up and put in a haystack while someone set the dry stale straw ablaze. I would picture it perfectly while rocking on my hand. The daydream was about struggling to get free while the fire burned hotter and closer. I am not sure if I came when the fire reached me or after I had imagined escaping it. But I came. I orgasmed on my hand to the dream of fire.[15]

Elaborating on the passage, Cvetkovich observes how Bone begins to associate masturbation and incest; the way the "excitement of struggling to get free from the fire climaxes in an ambiguous way":

> [S]he is unsure if escaping the fire or being reached by it coincides with the moment of orgasm, unsure if this is a fantasy about submitting to extinction or triumphing over its threat, particularly since both possibilities are pleasurable. The ambiguity of fantasy, its own kind of pleasure, is accompanied by the certainty of her body's pleasure in orgasm. Indeed, the "dream of fire" articulates the fusion of fear and pleasure, shame and anger, that fuels Bone's queer childhood sexuality.[16]

Cvetkovich argues against viewing these fantasies as masochistic or perverse (as they are often viewed), observing the ways they provide pleasure, agency, and comfort. Indeed her fantasies provide agency and comfort *through* her ability to give herself pleasure.[17]

---

14. Cvetkovich, *Archive of Feelings*, 102.
15. Quoted in Ibid., 102.
16. Ibid.

Cvetkovich thus carves a path for associations between trauma and sexuality that do not suppose queer sexualities to be *only or primarily* the result of trauma, and even see queer sexualities as part of intimate healing processes.[18] In another instance of Bone's fantasizing, more links between pain and sexuality appear, as Bone's masturbation coincides with a fantasy of her absent mother's comfort. Cvetkovich writes:

> The dream of fire, in fact, quite explicitly serves as a substitute for Bone's mother, daring to articulate the potentially incestuous connection between mother-daughter bonds and sexual desire . . . "I dreamed I was a baby again, five or younger, leaning against Mama's hip, her hand on my shoulders. She held me and I felt loved. She held me and I knew who I was. When I put my hand down between my legs, it was not a sin. It was like her murmur, like music, like a prayer in the dark" (253). When Bone wakes up and examines the fingers that have given her maternal comfort, she imagines the fire again, "purifying, raging, sweeping through Greenville and clearing the earth" (253). Out of this fantasy comes not only the triumph of vengeful anger but sexual pleasure . . . Bone uses the fantasy that comes from emotional need to counter it.[19]

I find Cvetkovich's work remarkable and even urgently important on its own terms. However, the story of Bone and Cvetkovich's sympathetic reading of it also reflect the Gospel of Truth's investments in pleasure—particularly its threading together of pleasure with pain, fright, or death in pivotal passages, but also its mixing of sensuous imagery into familial relationships. Aside from that mouthwatering fruit of the edible son and his consumptive interrelation to his siblings, the other children of the Father are "joined to the Father by his mouth; his tongue is the holy spirit" (13.3-4), and the unity between children and Father is otherwise

17. Ibid., 103.
18. Ibid., 90-91.
19. Ibid., 104.

expressed as a fragrance being inhaled (19.1-14), inviting possibly more subtle but no less distinctly sensual associations. Without meaning to suggest incest itself, I am interested in the ways the Gospel of Truth parallels the accounts of trauma/healing that Cvetkovich discusses by evoking pleasure at unpredictable, uncomfortable, or pained sites; and it does seem that, for the Gospel of Truth, family as a structure of belonging is one such uncomfortable or pained site.

Familial belonging is an ardent interest of the text. It is actually the only kind of belonging mentioned in the Gospel of Truth, and represents a set of relations that is not just intimate but emphatically gracious and good.[20] But the idealization of family relations makes the meaning and necessity of the death of the son a pretty sticky proposition, and the logic for it is not entirely clear in the text. In the first mention of Jesus' death, Transgression is "distressed by him" (4.4). It is because he "shone to the ones in the darkness of forgetfulness" (4.2), and "he enlightened them and showed them a way" (4.3) that Transgression "was angry with him and pursued him" (4.4). Yet the text curiously uses a passive construction to describe his death ("He was nailed to a tree"), concealing the agent.[21] A bit later, however, an unusual set of locutions offers more (if not entirely clear) detail:

---

20. The Gospel of Truth 8.8-12, for example, describes the model of a loving, wise, available Father: "He became a guide, at rest and at leisure. He came into their midst and spoke a teacher's words in places of learning. Those thinking themselves wise tested him, but he reproached them because they were empty and hate him for they were not truly wise. After all these, the little children came—those to whom knowledge of the Father belongs. When they had been strengthened, they learned about the Father's face. They knew and they were known, they were glorified and they glorified." Cf. Gospel of Truth 23.10-13, which features the security and "perfect power" of the Father, or the last two lines of the text, which promise: "He is good and his children are full and worthy of his name. For he is the Father and it is children like this that he loves" (Gospel of Truth 27.16-17).
21. In Coptic, the passive voice is expressed as the third person, so the literal rendering of the line is "they" nailed him to a tree. Since Transgression is given the feminine singular pronoun throughout, however, there is a disjoint or ambiguity in who, exactly, is to blame for Jesus' death.

> In their heart the living book of the living was revealed. It was written in the thought and mind of the Father and, since the beginning of all things, was in his incomprehensibility. This book was impossible to take because it was placed there for the one to take it to be killed. No one would have appeared from among those who trust in salvation if that book had not appeared. Because of this, the compassionate, faithful Jesus was patient. He accepted sufferings until he took up that book, since he knows his death is life for many (Gospel of Truth 6.1-6).

The perpetrator of Jesus' sufferings is notably left out here, too. The Father may not be directly involved in the death of the son, but certainly the death of the son was the price paid for the Father's availability. Suddenly the Father seems severe and withholding in this passage—incomprehensible and unavailable, or only available with dire consequences. The deep mark of the absence of the Father appears in another place, but is tied thoroughly into intimacy and pleasure: "The Father opens his bosom and his bosom is the holy spirit. He reveals his hidden self—his hidden self is his son—so that through the compassion of the Father the generations might know him and end their strenuous search for the Father, resting in him and knowing that this is rest (Gospel of Truth 10.7-8)."

The generations' strenuous searching for the Father casts a shadow on the Father's laying bare of his deepest self. That this deepest self is the crucified son additionally knots pain, absence, and intimacy to the Father, though not in any obvious way. In the section on the name of the Father, knowing and fullness are hopelessly tied to inaccessibility, unknowing, and absence. While several readers have found the Gospel of Truth to reflect Lacanian linguistic paradigms which place lack at their center,[22] in a more concretized or

---

22. Cf. Joel Fineman, "Gnosis and the Piety of Metaphor." Eliot Wolfson builds on Fineman's reading, writing, "Insofar as the name is the sign of that which cannot be signified except as the hidden signifier that is present through its absence displayed in the potentially inexhaustible chain of signification, it follows that 'the Son through whom knowledge of the Father is revealed is at the same time a representation of the very lack that the revelation is intended to

experiential reading, this passage instead appears as a halting attempt at trying to reconcile promise with abandonment, if in a heightened and abstracted mode.[23] Yet the Gospel of Truth ends by foreclosing any question about what experience of the Father predominates, describing his presence and approachability in eminently sensible terms: "They hold his head, which is rest for them, and they grasp him, approach him as if to receive kisses from his face" (26.6).

The text continues, leaving something yet hidden: "But they do not reveal this. For they did not exalt themselves or need the Father's glory. They did not think of him as small or bitter or wrathful. He is without evil, tranquil and sweet" (26.7-8). Shortly thereafter, the Father is also described as a Mother (27.2). This is not the first time "mother" has been interjected into the predominantly male familial framework (cf. 10.6), but in both cases it seems to be an afterthought, an added bonus to make sure that the family structure remains complete (or, perhaps, an additional way to endow the Father with everything, including motherhood).

I would like to return for a moment to the question of the son's closeness to the Father, a closeness now clearly characterized by loss on multiple levels. As I have suggested in other chapters, Jesus and his death, for all of its acclaimed singularity, is probably best understood as an emblematic and affectively dense site of meaning. In the wake of later Christian tradition's investment in trying to distinguish the capital "s" Son from the "children" of God, the constructive ambiguity of the earlier uses of the term "son of God" often disappears.[24] The Gospel of Truth, however, exhibits and preserves

---

redeem.' The 'semiotic reality' of the name, therefore, is perched between Father and Son, the fullness of lack and the lack of fullness, the presence of absence and the absence of presence . . ." ("Inscribed in the Book," 255).

23. Though we might say that Lacan, too, was reconciling promise and abandonment in a heightened and abstracted mode.

24. While "son of God" can clearly indicate a figure of unique and divine importance, it is also used in the Septuagint and other ancient Jewish literature to designate Israel as a people. A

this ambiguity. At the same time that the son retains a unique title as the "name of the Father," the text regularly refuses to distinguish between the son and the reader.[25] It does so not only with its persistent use of familial language—the ones "from above" are, like the son, also children of the Father—but with its open-ended use of pronouns.[26] In other words, Jesus, his pain, and his intimacy with the Father are associatively close to (if not representative of) those the text addresses.

In a way compatible with the Secret Revelation of John, Hebrews, and 1 Peter, Jesus emerges here as a magnet for diasporic affectivity and a conduit for belonging. As in so much other diasporic Israelite literature, figurations of Israel's god as the abusive or abandoning patriarch bump up uncomfortably against promises for restoration and assurance of privilege.[27] As a trope, the combination of crucifixion with the cosmic prestige of the son seems to become a heightened expression of those contradictions, as Hebrews illustrates so wildly.[28] Yet Hebrews still wavers between attraction to the

---

notable example being Wisdom of Solomon 18:13, as part of a rhetoric of belonging over against idolatrous Egyptians. Similarly, in Galatians 3:26, Paul writes, "For you are all sons of God through faith in Christ Jesus."
25. McGuire, "Conversion and Gnosis," 350.
26. Ibid.
27. See, for example, Hosea's metaphor of the abusive husband/"disloyal wife" for God's patriarchal abandonment and reconciliation, which is especially memorable and disturbing (cf. Hosea 2). The following quote from 2 Baruch in response to the destruction of the second Jerusalem temple also illustrates the tension of chosenness and abandonment in striking family terms: "Oh Lord, my Lord, have I therefore come into the world to see the evil things of my mother? No, my Lord. If I have found grace in your eyes, take away my spirit first that I may go to my fathers and I may not see the destruction of my mother. For from two sides I am hard pressed: I cannot resist you, but my soul also cannot behold the evil of my mother. But one thing I shall say in your presence, oh Lord. Now what will happen after these things? For if you destroy your city and deliver up your country to those who hate us, how will the name of Israel be remembered again? Or how shall we speak about your glorious deeds? Or to whom again will that which is in your Law be explained? Or will the universe return to its nature and the world go back to its original silence?" (2 Baruch 3:1-8).
28. As another example, in the Gospel of Mark's depiction of Jesus' death, the centurion proclaims Jesus as the son of God precisely at the moment of Jesus' cry of abandonment by God, poignantly combining privilege with abandonment (cf. Mark 15:34-39).

graphic particularities and placid escape. The Secret Revelation of John, on the other hand, bypasses the problem by removing responsibility for suffering from the true Father and god completely. The Gospel of Truth, in contrast to both Hebrews and the Secret Revelation of John, periodically demands that the trauma of abandonment and abuse be forgotten (or, rather, that true reality be "remembered"), though it also fuses that trauma to a sense of oneness and fullness.

Distinct from each of these texts, and not insignificantly, the Gospel of Truth manages to neglect the very category most taxed in the conditions of diaspora: the nation. The absence of any reference to national belonging (Judea, Israel, Jerusalem, Jews, temple, gentiles, circumcision, etc.) is especially conspicuous when comparing the Gospel of Truth to Colossians and Ephesians, for instance. These three texts share much in the way of vocabulary and concept: Colossians and Ephesians, like the Gospel of Truth, are dense with the language of fullness, perfection, bringing back/drawing towards, light and truth.[29] The famous Christ hymn of Colossians 1:15-20 claims that "in [Christ] all the fullness of God was pleased to dwell, and through him God was pleased to reconcile all things to himself,

---

29. There is much literature and speculation on the relationship between Colossians and Ephesians given their remarkable, and sometimes word for word, parallels. It has been suggested that Ephesians is dependent on Colossians, though more detailed and nuanced work on this would need to be done. For a detailed summary of the issues, see John B. Polhill, "The Relationship between Ephesians and Colossians," *RevExp* 70, no. 4 (1973): 439-50. For language resonances and parallels between Colossians, Ephesians, and the Gospel of Truth, see Colossians 1:13-15, 19-20; 2:9-10; and Ephesians 3:19; 4:10; 5:11-14. Ephesians also uses "riches" and "wealth" language that echoes its use of fullness. Cf. Colossians 2:2 and Ephesians 1:7, 18; 2:4; and 3:8. There is even a parallel with Gospel of Truth's uncertain present. For example, Sarah Tanzer has suggested an "already/not yet" reading of Ephesians: "The 'already' is most obvious in the unity made possible through the death of Jesus . . . the 'not yet' is most apparent in ' . . . the promised Holy Spirit, which is the *guarantee* of our inheritance *until* we acquire possession of it . . . ' (1:13-14)." What Tanzer opens up is the ambivalence of Ephesians—a slippage between present and future tenses. See Sarah J. Tanzer, "Ephesians," in *Searching the Scriptures: A Feminist Commentary*, Vol. 2, ed. Elisabeth Schüssler Fiorenza (New York: Crossroad, 1994), 327. All the parallels between the Gospel of Truth and Colossians and Ephesians are too many to list here. More will be said below about how I think about these texts together, however.

whether the things on earth or in heaven, by making peace through the blood of the cross" (1:19-20). Colossians and Ephesians both imagine Christ as a figure who holds the world together, rescues people from darkness, and removes alienation and blame (cf. Col. 1:21-23; 4:10-11; and Eph. 2:11-22), and both have a reticence around "negative" affects that resonates with the Gospel of Truth's affective redirections toward pleasure (cf. Eph. 2:14-16; 4:25-32). In Colossians and Ephesians, too, family gains heightened attention, not only in the standard form of household codes, but in the reference to God's "household" as a major structure for affiliation (Eph. 2:19; cf. Col. 3:18-4:1; Eph. 5:21-6:9).

One important distinction, however, is that in contrast to the Gospel of Truth, Colossians and Ephesians occasionally evoke this unity in assimilations of Pauline language around Jews and gentiles, showing investments in Israel and circumcision as designations of belonging (cf. Col. 2:11; Eph. 2:11-13).[30] This investment is tentative, however. The vision in both Colossians and Ephesians is largely directed "upward," not unlike Hebrews and the Secret Revelation of John. Though, to reiterate, it is not that this upward vision is an articulation of Christian identity in a cosmic supersession of an identification with Israel; rather it is a diasporic re-negotiation of belonging heavy with the losses surrounding the nation.

The Gospel of Truth's lack of language around the nation is no less heavy with the nation's loss. In a certain way, while paternal

---

30. The unity longed for and expressed in the Gospel of Truth has mostly been described as "monistic," and this monism has not generally been read for its possible social implications. In contrast, as I have suggested in previous chapters, particularly with regard to Stoic Zeus monotheism and cosmopolitanism, this kind of oneness can do particular kinds of social work. See William R. Schoedel, "Gnostic Monism and the Gospel of Truth," in *The Rediscovery of Gnosticism: Proceedings of the International Conference on Gnosticism at Yale, New Haven, Connecticut, March 28-31, 1978*, vol. 1, ed. Bentley Layton. (SHR XLI. Leiden: E.J. Brill, 1980), 379-90; and Bentley Layton, *The Gnostic Scriptures: A New Translation with Annotations and Introductions* (Garden City, NY: Doubleday, 1987), 250.

language has its own pains for those in diasporic Israel, the exclusive attachment to familial language in all three texts and the absence of other forms of belonging in the Gospel of Truth mark a related set of anxieties and sadnesses. Diasporic conditions often result in a kind of doubling-down on generational reproduction and conventional arrangements as a site for recovery of cultural loss. (Whether that staunches the wound, and at what cost, is perhaps the bigger question.) The family may also seem like the only "safe" abiding social structure when others have become irreparably complicated. That is to say that an articulation of familial belonging may be a "way of refusing the trauma of cultural dislocation through the fantasy of uninterrupted lineage," as Cvetkovich puts it, and, given the absence of nation as a category of belonging, it may be a way of deliberately forgetting such dislocation in the first place.[31]

Another move that these three texts share is a recurrent interest in interiorization. By "interiorization" I do not mean to suggest anything like a Freudian psyche or a Cartesian soul, or to say that these texts are or wish to be disentangled from social relations. But I do want to suggest that these texts' focus on states of being and sensing, on awareness and knowledge, on individualized understanding and affective reorientation do lay claim to an inner person, and do such as a result of pain or trauma.

Early in Cvetkovich's chapter on butch/femme sexualities, she discusses Freud's model for consciousness, an organism with a protective shield that is itself dead, but which as a membrane preserves the deeper parts of the organism from harm and overstimulation. Freud writes, "We describe as 'traumatic' any excitations from outside which are powerful enough to break through the

---

31. Cvetkovich, *Archive of Feelings*, 108. In chapter 4 of her book, Cvetkovich also addresses diaspora, particularly for its queer instances and variations, and she points to the long history of diasporic conditions and forced migration creating "sexual panics" (fears of intermarriage, the failure to sexually/culturally reproduce).

protective shield. It seems to me that the concept of trauma necessarily implies a connection of this kind with a breach in an otherwise efficacious barrier against stimuli."[32] Cvetkovich observes that "[e]ven this simple model of penetration is freighted with symbolic meaning as a painful experience, one that has not just physical but psychic dimensions," and describes the way she has been "mysteriously moved by Freud's image of the simple amoebalike organism having been 'so thoroughly baked through by stimulation' that is has developed a 'crust.'"[33] She puts Freud to work to notice, in an emphatically non-diagnostic way, how untouchable butches "might be said to possess a version of Freud's numb or toughened cortical shield," for example.[34]

It appears that trauma, or more generally an especially painful over-stimulation, often results in the construction of interiority, in these texts and elsewhere. Sara Ahmed, for instance, theorizes that affect is part of the very production of the surfaces and boundaries of bodies, objects, and collectives. She proposes a Marxist model of emotion, in which objects and relationships bear the traces of our contact with them, but the social processes that produce those emotions are effectively erased, so that objects seem to possess an inherent affective value.[35] Ahmed suggests that the sense that emotions are "inside" or arise from within oneself is itself an indication of the depth of their formative effects, but her description of pain illustrates more precisely how hurting or being hurt might relate to interiority:

> It may seem counterintuitive to say that pain is crucial to the formation of the body as a perceiving surface. For example, don't I already have a sense of where my body is *before* I feel it as 'being hurt'? . . . Of course,

---

32. Quoted in Cvetkovich, *Archive of Feelings*, 53.
33. Ibid., 55.
34. Ibid., 56.
35. Sara Ahmed, *The Cultural Politics of Emotion* (New York: Routledge, 2004), 11.

in some ways I do already have a sense of my body surface. After all, life experience involves multiple collisions with objects and others. It is through such collisions that I form a sense of myself as (more or less) apart from others, as well as a sense of the surfaces of my body . . . The intensity of pain sensations makes us aware of our bodily surfaces, and points to the dynamic nature of surfacing itself (turning in, turning away, moving towards, moving away).[36]

Ahmed further writes that it is "not incidental that the sensation of pain is often represented—both visually and in narrative—through 'the wound' (a bruised or cut skin surface). The wound functions as a trace of where the surface of another entity (however imaginary) has impressed upon the body, an impression that is felt and seen as the violence of negation."[37] It is with pain and the sense of being penetrated that the boundaries of the self, the construction of an inside and outside, most distinctly surface.

Interiorization occurs in various places throughout Colossians, Ephesians, and the Gospel of Truth, mostly in the form of attention to one's spiritual and/or affective disposition, as well as in the form of locutions like "in us" or "in our hearts."[38] But the dynamic surfacing of boundaries is perhaps most movingly and directly expressed in Ephesians when, after giving directives of obedience, the text instructs its readers to "put on the whole armor of God, so that you may stand against the wiles of the devil" (6:11). Here the text employs an individualized metaphor of protective outer hardness. In the rest of Ephesians, an almost guileless sense of goodness, aliveness,

---

36. Ibid., 26.
37. Ibid., 27.
38. The language around affective or spiritual disposition abounds in these texts. For a few examples, see Ephesians 4:17-32; Colossians 3:8-10; and Gospel of Truth 15.4-6. For examples of "in us" or "in our hearts," see Gospel of Truth 4.7; 6.1; 27.4; Col. 3:15-16; and, perhaps most explicitly, Eph. 3:16: "I pray that, according to the riches of his glory, he may grant that you may be strengthened in your inner being (*esō anthrōpon*) with power through his spirit . . . " This interiorization also occurs on the divine level in the recourse to the hidden self or aspects of God/the Father (Gospel of Truth 10.7-8; Col. 3:3).

fullness, and unity permeates the text. Even the household codes seem less malevolently bullying than deeply naïve in claiming that, for instance, master/slave relationships could contain anything like mutual subjugation (6:9). But in contrast to the rest of the letter, and particularly in tension with a demand that the recipients of the letter be gentler and more vulnerable with one another, there is a sudden recourse to external hardness: armor made from the very stuff that brought one vibrant fullness and unity in chapters 1–3 (faith, truth, and the gospel; cf. 6:10-17). A boundaried, internal self emerges just as the twisted, difficult realities of social relations ("And masters, do the same to them. Stop threatening them . . . " in 6:9) interrupt the letter's claims to lush, idyllic belonging.

Again, this is not to say that these three texts necessarily live in or produce a historical moment that assumes a certain structure of the person that includes an interior self, as much as they argue for a set of local instances of a construction of that inner or personal self. Such instances of innerness should not be seen as antithetical to the more overtly social (or cosmological) references in the text. They are rather an acknowledgement of the sting of the social, and a less-direct engagement with it. Without according interiorization any absolute virtues, such turns inward do allow for the sense of a protected space or self. Interiorization allows for the retention of a (cordoned off) softness and vulnerability in the face of conditions that harden or threaten to destroy the self. In Cvetkovich's reading of Freud's imagery, the creation of a shell or an outside/inside boundary allows one to admit to having been hurt: it simultaneously shuts out the world and enables a mitigated engagement with it.

The forceful forgetting of dislocation, the erasure of the haunting nation, interiorization, and oblique or covered allusions to social life constitute genuinely constructive responses to social trauma. Forgetting can be a powerful form of response to trauma or loss that threatens to define, destroy, or make passive those who have suffered it. As Jack Halberstam writes, while "forgetting can easily be used as a tool of dominant culture to push the past aside in order to maintain the fantasy and fiction of a just and tolerable present," it is "still worth assessing the power of forgetfulness in creating new futures not tied to old traditions."[39] Forgetting is, according to Halberstam, "a gatekeeping mechanism, a way of protecting the self from unbearable memories. And so shock and trauma, as so many scholars have noted, engender a form of forgetting, a cocooning of the self in order to allow the self to grow separate from the knowledge that might destroy it."[40]

But as constructive as these responses may be, they are not unambivalent. What happens, for instance, when such responses are distanced from their traumatized contexts? What happens when the very language and ways of being that offer comfort and oblique acknowledgement of pain to some find their way into the mouths, minds, and skin of others further from the damage? Indeed, the language of familial belonging, inheritance, secrecy, and revelation in the Gospel of Truth plunges one deeply into the dynamics of transgenerational haunting. In certain kinds of transgenerational haunting, the forgetting of trauma and the affective re-association of pain can do selective healing work for immediate survivors. But that forgetting is not total, and those survivors often end up transferring amorphous senses of loss, anxiety, and unease to related others for whom the specificities of that traumatic history—or that there even is a traumatic history at all—remain unknown.[41] As I suggested in

---

39. Judith Halberstam, *The Queer Art of Failure* (Durham: Duke University Press, 2011), 82-83.
40. Ibid., 84.
41. In "Voices from the Teum," Grace Cho also describes the vicissitudes of silence surrounding her mother's (and her own) history, as well as the diffuse mechanisms for meeting the felt imperative to witness and speak this trauma. She calls this "machinic vision," in which memories are assembled across bodies and collectives with different relationship to the trauma at hand. Cho draws from the psychoanalytic work of Nicolas Abraham and Maria Torok to describe

the first chapter, the film *Nostalgia for the Light* depicts how abstract, speculative, and even technical language has a more complicated relationship to pain and trauma than simply denying it. But such language does, it must be said, submerge or even partially obliterate its context, making it less visible (though maybe not necessarily less viscerally or unconsciously palpable) to more distant readers.

The question of the ambivalence of these responses to trauma and pain is not only theoretical or ethical. It is a rather pressing historical concern, too. The Gospel of Truth's erasure of nation as a social framework, its forgetting of pain, and its affective re-associations (abandonment with mystery, loss with fullness and riches, and alienation with belonging) may represent a kind of conceptual key for understanding the eventual production of not only a triumphal Christianity, but also of a sense of Christianity in the first place. The notion of Christianity as a distinct phenomenon in the first and second centuries, the apparent emergence of which coincides with various collapses and creative reorganizations of Israelite belonging, is only possible because of such erasure, forgetting, and recoding of painful diasporic experiences.

Another effect/affect of trauma and traumatized haunting is the fetishization of objects, language, symbols, and moments that contain the residue of loss or dislocation: a sweater, a letter, a story.[42] It is

---

the ways the unconscious is haunted by trauma, and ways that such trauma might be relieved. She notes that "there are two alternatives for relieving the unconscious from being haunted—to remain silent and allow the ghosts to wither away after several generations, or to speak and set the ghosts free" (Cho, "Voices from the Teum," 165). Although I am not convinced that such a model of catharsis is the best one, I agree with Cho's conclusion that what she calls "setting the ghosts free" has a performative and relational effect.

42. Cvetkovich, for instance, writes that "the fetishization of objects can be one way of negotiating the cultural dislocation produced by immigration. She elaborates through a striking example: "In *We Came All the Way from Cuba So You Could Dress Like This?* Achy Obejas tells the semiautobiographical story of coming by boat from Cuba to the United States in 1963. The narrative of her family's encounter with the INS as they apply for political asylum is interwoven with the subsequent history of the conflict between the narrator's lesbian life and her parent's ambition for her. But it's also a story about a sweater. Because 'there are things that can't be told . . . things like when we couldn't find an apartment . . . things like my doing very poorly on an

worth asking, for instance, how not only the elision of pain but the fetishization of the emblems which cover over or re-associate pain give way to ideologized theological readings and apparently de-socialized embattlements of heresiological literature. For instance, Daniel Boyarin's work on Justin Martyr charts something like the advent of ideologized theological readings within heresiological literature. In *Border Lines*, Boyarin describes heresiological literature as a covert construction of belonging under the auspices of the very ideological and theological differences it produces.[43] Focusing his study on the deployment of the Logos as a wedge for producing difference between, and thus inventing, Judaism and Christianity, Boyarin shows how Justin Martyr doubly constructs Jews and heretics in his *Dialogue with Trypho*, a work that Justin undertook not only to defend himself against "ditheism,"[44] but to answer the charge, ventriloquized through Trypho, that "[y]ou do not distinguish yourselves in any way from the gentiles."[45] Importantly, Boyarin notes that, although understandings of the Logos and Sophia as divine figures for veneration were relatively ubiquitous, and crossed ostensible boundaries between Christians and Jews, Justin is "establishing a binary opposition between the Christian and the Jew

---

IQ test because I didn't speak English, . . . like my father, finally realizing he wasn't going to go back to Cuba anytime soon, trying to hang himself with the light cord in the bathroom while my mother cleaned rooms at a nearby luxury hotel, but falling instead and breaking his arm,' and other painful memories that the narrator only lists but doesn't elaborate, she begins with a sweater. 'I'm wearing a green sweater. It's made of some synthetic material, and it's mine. I've been wearing it for two days straight and have no plans to take it off right now.' Years later, her mother sends her the same sweater wrapped around mementos of immigration—her Cuban passport, the asylum papers, family photos from Cuba." Cvetkovich concludes, "[t]he sweater that the young girl in the story was wearing when her family was processed by the INS is the material sign of her fear and apprehension, which might otherwise be invisible or forgotten. See *Archive of Feelings*, 118.

43. Boyarin, *Border Lines: The Partition of Judaeo-Christianity* (Philadelphia: University of Pennsylvania Press, 2004), introduction.
44. Ibid., 38.
45. *Dialogue with Trypho* 10.3, quoted in Boyarin, *Border Lines*, 38.

over the question of the Logos."⁴⁶ In doing so, Justin "*articulates Christian identity as theological.*"⁴⁷

Boyarin, then, more broadly argues that Christian and Jewish heresiological discourse (on *haireisis* and *minim*, respectively) arose concurrently in the late second century, suddenly lending "heresy" the inflection of otherness or deviance from a norm, defining belonging around doctrine ("orthodoxy").⁴⁸ Boyarin claims Jewish heresiological discourse to be a "response" to Christian heresiology, an argument that complements and supports his larger thesis that Christianity "invented" religion as a category disembedded from social life, and Judaism responded in kind, if only in part.⁴⁹ The prioritizing of Christianity, however, is questionable for several reasons, one of which being that, as Boyarin notes, Justin marks the first attribution of *haireisis* (as "heresy") to *Jewish* usage, suggesting that Justin's work was not entirely novel. Boyarin's prioritizing of Christianity relative to heresiology also presumes, against Boyarin's own project in this book, too much distinction at such an early stage.

In fact, Justin's *Dialogue with Trypho* is highly frictive in ways that enrich Boyarin's historical reorientation. For one, why does Justin put himself in dialogue (however fictive) with a Jew in the first place? Clearly, his vile differentiation from *ioudiasmos* already comes in the context of a reckoning with his sudden *connectivity* to Jewish scriptural traditions as a non-Jew, one who finds himself philosophically interested in "the prophets and Christ."⁵⁰ Justin's articulation of the content of a Christian orthodoxy would then seem to be tangled in a simultaneous affinity to Jewish traditions

---

46. Ibid., 39.
47. Ibid., 39. Emphasis mine.
48. Boyarin contrasts this development of "heresy" as deviance or non-orthodxy with its earlier uses in Josephus and Acts which understand hairesis as "choice of adherence" (ibid., 54-56).
49. See ibid., 8-9 for a summary, and chapters 7 and 8 for the full argument.
50. *Dialogue with Trypho*, 7-8. "The prophets," however, seems to include the entire Septuagint.

and sense of outsideness relative to emerging Jewish orthodoxy—a sense of outsideness, I would emphasize, that *takes place within its own discourse*.[51] His scriptural arguments proceed along these very lines, as well, notably exploiting the text of Second Isaiah to give the weight of Israelite history and righteousness to the very outsideness produced and inscribed within its own texts.[52] Justin is painfully and mercilessly mocking the very diasporic conditions that enable his own affinity to Jewish scriptural traditions. In doing so, he turns the diasporic discourse of a True Israel, not without its own arrogances, back on itself. As poisonous and deleterious in its effects as Justin's rhetoric is, this rhetoric nonetheless places his production of Christian identity as theological squarely within senses of diasporic conflictedness.

I offer this limited re-reading not as some kind of definitive reinterpretation of Justin, of course, but rather to loosen our tight grip on what we imagine the investments of Justin, and more generally the circumstances of heresiology, to be. Perhaps heresiology is a mode of both absorbing and amplifying the yearning for distinct belonging, as well as deflecting the diffusions and losses that constitute diaspora in the first place. In any case, heresiology involves an elision of the diasporic pain and traumatized social contexts from which its own terms—and its own founding interest in discourses of authenticity—are produced. This elision includes, strikingly, the traumatized contexts for the very terms "Christian" and *christianismos*: while Justin is fully aware of violence that accompanies "the name" (*1 Apol.* 4), his own theological assertions seek to detach that name from its associations with imperial violence

---

51. I actually think this is extremely close to Boyarin's argument, and takes more seriously his own general assumption that what we call Judaism and Christianity were hardly distinguishable entities in the second century, and had deep and surprising local entanglements through the sixth century.
52. Cf. Matthew W. Bates, "Justin Martyr's Logocentric Hermeutical Transformation of Isaiah's Vision of the Nations," *JTS* 60, no. 2 (2009): 538-55.

as well as, it should be noted, its direct social implications (*1 Apol.* 11).[53]

I am not suggesting that, because of their affective rerouting and indirect approaches to trauma, the Gospel of Truth, Colossians, and Ephesians are the touchstone texts that themselves kick off a chain of events resulting in heresiology or Christianity. I am arguing that they evince a set of strategies that create some of the most important conditions of possibility for the articulation of a Christianity by wiping out most, if not all, references to the nexus of social conditions that engender their aspirations.[54] Christianity's own triumphalism and self-understanding as an epic phenomenon, transcendent of the concerns of the (ghostly) nation, are not only palpable effects of diasporic traumas, but indicative of the healing and attempted erasure of those traumas as well.[55] I say "attempted" erasure because, as transgenerational haunting presupposes, total erasure is impossible. If the limns and specificities of trauma are gone, the *sense* of trauma remains long after. Indeed, such ancient diasporic traumas seem to mix and merge with other losses, living on even into the present, doing so, in part, through texts. Therefore, in my last chapter, I will theorize quite specifically about how readings of what has come to be termed "early Christian" literature bespeak an ongoing hauntedness, and, last but not least, I will suggest how writers of history and other readers of these texts might better engage such ghosts.

---

53. Justin makes sure to mention that Christians are neither interested in the present, nor in politics ("human kingdoms").
54. Cullen I. K. Story has suggested even stronger temporal and thematic connections between Justin and the Gospel of Truth, not only placing them in the same decade (150/160 CE), but finding consonances in their use of traditions and cosmic understanding of "truth." See his *The Nature of Truth and the "Gospel of Truth" and the Writings of Justin Martyr: A Study of the Pattern of Orthodoxy in the Middle of the Second Christian Century* (Leiden: Brill, 1970).
55. It may very well be that turns toward the figural, abstraction, and interiorization so characteristic of what we call "late antiquity" (or even the heightened abstraction of Jewish mysticism that the Gospel of Truth is said to portend) are a collective set of gestures that are inheritances of such coping strategies on a broader scale.

7

Returning to Rome

> The notion of a totalized system, of which everything is always already somehow a part, is not helpful (to say the least) in the effort to approach a weighted and reeling present. This is not to say the forces these systems [neoliberalism, advanced capitalism, globalism] try to name are not real and literally pressing. On the contrary, I am trying to bring them into view as a scene of immanent force, rather than leaving them looking like dead effects imposed on an innocent world.[1]

So begins Kathleen Stewart's book *Ordinary Affects*, which is comprised of a long series of prose pieces in the third person (though the voice is hers), pieces narrating everyday experiences such as a trip to Target, or seeing coal miners at a health clinic for poor people. Her goal in this memoir-esque book is to heighten the reader's attention to the sense-effects of living in a world supersaturated by capitalism and strung into troubling new configurations by globalization. While interested in affect, Stewart shies away from explicit theorizing in this book. Instead she lends the mundane affects/effects of life in

---

1. Kathleen Stewart, *Ordinary Affects* (Durham: Duke University Press, 2007), 1.

the contemporary United States an acute aliveness, a sinister energy powered by capitalism's electric current.

Stewart thus provokes me to reconsider what is typically understood to be political analysis. Like Sedgwick, she takes a break from the hermeneutics of suspicion, writing that her book is "[c]ommitted not to the demystification and uncovering of truths that support a well-known picture of the world, but rather to speculation, curiosity, and the concrete, it tries to provoke attention to the forces that come into view as habit or shock, resonance or impact."[2] While she clearly assumes a certain amount of what we might call "systems analysis," she proposes an alternative approach that is, for her, less flat and frozen: "To attend to ordinary affects," she writes, "is to trace how the potency of forces lies in their immanence to things that are both flighty and hardwired, shifty and unsteady but palpable too."[3] Stewart is not interested in "bottom-line" analyses, "evaluative critique," and diagnosing "underlying causes"—in other words, ideological approaches—which characterize so much of what is generally considered political analysis.[4] But the reading of everyday life that Stewart produces is one in which the reader makes sharpened contact with the socio-political force field. Her vignettes haunt the reader as she too, after reading, returns back to her "own" life walking around Target and so on.

I obviously admire Stewart's recourse to the personal/fictional, but I find that her book poses a number of questions, both for the discipline(s) of New Testament and Early Christianity, and for Stewart herself. While I find the blurring of personal and fictional theoretically attractive, I wonder what it is, affectively speaking, that moves her to use the third person. Is it the dissociative force of

2. Ibid.
3. Ibid., 3.
4. Ibid., 4.

capitalism itself? Does the distance of the third person allow her to engage the overwhelming intensity of her experience? What other things might be made of the space or relationship between the "I" and the "she" in her description of everyday life in the late-capitalist United States? Finally, what does Stewart's approach to politics and her challenge to typical understandings of "political readings" mean for a very different discipline's address to empire and power, and how might we rethink the politics of doing ancient history?

So much of this present book has been about imperial politics, and yet what I have not said directly yet is that taking affect into account complicates and enlarges our notions of what counts as a political reading. Because empire is one of the primary subjects of interest in this project, and because empire has become something of an interpretive hotspot over the last twenty years in the study of the New Testament and "early Christian" history, I wish in this chapter to narratively work out the implications of affect for the field's discussions of empire. Stewart's approach, one in which she speaks her experience through indirection, is indeed reflective of the field's analogizing of Rome with the United States. What are the affective implications of that circumlocution? How might our affective involvement with Rome become ground for theorizing approaches to reading and history that give credence to, rather than allay, the uncertain forces of our haunting?

* * * *

Empire, as a term of sudden and elevated significance for the North American scholarly study of the New Testament, cropped up in the early 1990's with the advent of postcolonial and empire biblical criticisms.[5] In the two decades since its emergence as interpretive

---

5. What tends to be referred to as "empire criticism," which largely designates socio-historical

hotspot, "empire" has generated a huge volume and range of critique and theologizing, such that the question is no longer whether the Roman Empire is a viable analytical category, but rather how the sprawl and machinery of empire is best understood and how it should figure in interpretation. With this fervor for empire has come an increasing sophistication in technical vocabulary and theoretical conceptualization for describing not only the broad economic and social structures/effects of Roman imperialism, but its consequences for subject- or identity-formation, its production of territory and peoples, the self-expression of Rome's power, mythology and cosmic destiny…the list goes on. Inevitably, tense disagreement continues to arise over each of these points, as well as whether the ancient Roman imperial and colonial context should be such a driving obsession in the discussion of the Bible as opposed more recent (more pressing?) biblical-imperial entanglements.[6]

and exegetical readings of ancient literature, arose in Pauline studies and in close association with the "new perspective" on Paul (cf. Robert Jewett, Richard Horsley, Dieter Georgi, Neil Elliott), though Elisabeth Schüssler Fiorenza's 1985 work on the Roman Empire and Revelation precedes the trend. The other significant component of the field that puts empire at the center of the conversation is postcolonial biblical criticism, which is less easy to encapsulate. Stephen Moore describes postcolonial criticism as a "critical sensibility acutely attuned to a range of interrelated historical and textual phenomena" (*Empire and Apocalypse: Postcolonialism in the New Testament* [Sheffield: Sheffield Phoenix Press, 2006], 7), and his own performance of postcolonial criticism is thoroughly poststructuralist. If postcolonial tends to imply engagements with the work of Gyatri Chakravorty Spivak, Homi Bhabha, and Edward Said, however, that conceptuality of "postcolonial" misses a huge portion of postcolonial work that is either more materialist in its bent, or less textually or epistemologically based. Some of the work in this latter category draws importantly from colonized and/or diasporic experiences, and places its emphasis on histories perhaps hidden by the field's obsession with ancient history. For several different geneaologies and descriptions of what is said to comprise empire and postcolonial biblical criticisms, see Stephen Moore, *Empire and Apocalypse*, 11-17; Brigitte Kahl, *Galatians Re-Imagined; Reading Through the Eyes of the Vanquished* (Minneapolis: Fortress Press, 2010), 5-6; David Rhoads, David Esterline, and Jae Won Lee, eds. *Luke-Acts and Empire: Essays in Honor of Robert L. Brawley* (Eugene, Ore.: Wipf and Stock, 2011), 1-2; and Fernando Segovia, "Introduction: Configurations, Approaches, Findings, Stances," in *A Postcolonial Commentary on the New Testament Writings* (New York: T&T Clark, 2009), 1-68.

6. Musa Dube's critique, for example, is that the dogged interest in ancient history extends a fetishization of European origins and conveniently "forgets" to discuss modern American and European imperialism. Her work, as well as that of R.S. Sugirtharajah and Fernando Segovia, have trained their vision on the colonial investments of the Bible and biblical interpretation in

As Stephen Moore and Yvonne Sherwood tease, "What defines the biblical studies discipline is less that it possesses method than that it is *obsessed with* method and as such *possessed by* method. Biblical scholarship seems to turn everything it touches into method . . ."[7] Their complaint that the field turns everything it touches into a kind of criticism seems especially shrewd here since what we have is no longer simply "empire criticism," as it has been called, but the incorporation of "empire" into every kind of traditional biblical criticism (the rhetoric of empire, imperial geography, Roman representations of gender, etc.) such that it is hard to tell whether empire or biblical criticism is more muscularly assimilative. Despite containing a variety of "methods," empire-critical and postcolonial approaches to empire nonetheless evince a significant inclination toward a single task: exposing the ideologies of texts and readers, thereby revealing as much of the total extent of imperial hegemony as possible. The most politicized wing of the field, in other words, finds itself strongly identified with what Stewart calls "evaluative critique" or "bottom-line" analysis and Sedgwick calls the "tactics of unveiling." How is it that ideological readings became practically synonymous with political readings and even with political engagement?[8]

---

the modern and postmodern world, including, importantly, biblical scholarship as a discipline. See Fernando F. Segovia, *De-colonizing Biblical Studies: A View from the Margins* (Maryknoll, N.Y.: Orbis, 2000); Rasiah S. Sugirtharajah, *Exploring Postcolonial Biblical Criticism: History, Method, Practice* (Malden, Mass.: Wiley-Blackwell, 2012), 94-141; and Musa Dube, *Postcolonial Feminist Interpretation of the Bible* (St. Louis, Mo.: Chalice Press, 2000).

7. Moore and Sherwood, *The Invention of the Biblical Scholar: A Critical Manifesto* (Minneapolis: Fortress Press, 2011), 33. They note that even "methodologically unpromising" concepts such as "intertextuality" have been wrenched from their iconoclastic primary texts into more predictable methodological deployments.

8. As I discussed in earlier chapters, Sedgwick's worry about the ascendency and prestige around modes of "tracing and exposure" is that such modes tend to take an objective positioning, not only laying claims about the truth of the world, but "disavowing [their] affective motive and force" (138). For Sedgwick, it is "a great loss when paranoid inquiry comes to seem entirely coextensive with critical theoretical inquiry rather than being viewed as one kind of cognitive/affective theoretical practice among other, alternative kinds." She doesn't suggest abandoning

But while ideological readings tend to be over-identified with political reading, their politics are far from uncomplicated, and there are other ways of reading politically. Indeed some of the most ideologically driven projects open up into affectively responsive and alternatively political readings, if only momentarily and at odds with their otherwise quite procedural analyses. I shall discuss two of them below.

"At this point a detour through my own life experience is in place," writes Brigitte Kahl in the introduction to her tome *Galatians Re-Imagined*.[9] She recounts growing up in post-World War II East Germany, being captivated by the reformation mythology of Martin Luther, as well as by a particular and hazy memory retold again and again by her mother.

> It was nothing more than a vague memory, a puzzled question that somehow never quite faded away. My mother had been an elementary student in the 1930's. Not long after Hitler seized power, she was invited to a birthday party where she was surprised to see the face of a classmate, a girl named Ruth, gazing through a fence from a neighboring garden. Had Ruth not been invited to the party? My mother did not understand why Ruth was on the other side of the fence and not at the party with all the rest of her classmates. Nor did she ask. Not long afterward, Ruth disappeared from the class altogether. Again, no one asked after her.
>
> But my mother carried the question with her for years as if something hidden, something unspeakable, was driving her. She would only hint darkly at that something as she retold the story over the years. It took me some time to understand what had probably happened to Ruth and that the question was not the stuff of childlike innocence as I had first heard it. We learned about the Holocaust at school and went as a class

---

the hermeneutics of suspicion, but since it "knows some things well and others poorly," she suggests engaging reparative, accretive, and pleasure-seeking impulses and practices alongside of it. Sedgwick, *Touching Feeling: Affect, Pedagogy, Performativity* (Durham: Duke University Press, 2003), 126, 130. Likewise, I do not wish to question the necessity of approaches that seek to uncover the depth and breadth of all kinds of social violence, only the way these approaches have defined political readings.

9. Kahl, *Galatians Reimagined*, 13.

to the Buchenwald concentration camp at Weimar, the town of Goethe and Schiller.[10]

Years later, her mother found out that Ruth was alive, even living blocks from where Kahl's own son was attending school. Kahl describes the evening her mother was reunited with Ruth. They exchanged stories and filled out scenes from their overlapping childhoods, and Kahl describes her mother's deep and overwhelming relief when Ruth says she cannot remember either the birthday party when they were twelve, or the fence.

> I regard that evening as one of the moments when I have come closest to the miraculous, healing presence of the *ruach* in my life, the mending power of the Spirit that transcends murderous boundaries and deadly wounds. It was not long after the World Trade Center towers had fallen and any dream of worldwide reconciliation that might have been nurtured after 1989 was suffocated in a nightmare of war and violence. Since that evening it has become more urgent for me to re-imagine my Lutheran heritage—and to revisit Paul's Galatia in search of his "true" story. Part of the energy in this scholarly exploration is a desire to find out whether, after all and against all odds, the dream of peacemaking and justice seeking between East and West, North and South, those inside and those outside the "fence,"—Jews and Christians, Christians and Muslims, poor and rich, civilization and nature—might have a chance with the apostle.[11]

With this evocative but brief, almost hesitant, two-page aside, Kahl gives a biographical link to the themes of war, otherness, boundary-crossing, fellowship, and displacement that suffuse her reading of Galatians.[12] In her book, Kahl tracks the history of the Galatians,

---

10. Ibid., 13-14.
11. Ibid., 14.
12. Kahl begins her acknowledgments with a similarly moving and lovely description of the circumstances for the genesis of the book that resonate strongly with the elements of the text and of history that she accents in her study. She also gestures to her own sense of hauntedness: "Many people have assisted me in the long gestation of this book, which was conceived on two continents, somewhere between the fall of the Berlin Wall and the attack on the World Trade Center in New York. It reflects two decades of migration from East to West, from Europe to

otherwise known to Classicists as the Gauls, as a conquered people in diaspora who loomed large in the imperial mythological imagination.[13] The bulk of the book concentrates on devising a comprehensive picture of Roman imperial social and ideological mechanisms such as the arena, that produce a "new creation" on the backs of monstrous others, through hierarchy, assimilation, and violence. In the last two chapters, this massive construction of Roman imperial ideological, social, and mythological world becomes the surprisingly subtle subtext for Paul's letter to the Galatians: Paul's monotheism opposes Caesar's, Paul's new creation through the cross counters the hierarchical unity of the arena, Paul's criticism of the law and its works is not a criticism of Torah or Jewish piety, but rather a takedown of the Roman system of euergetism.

A major hinge for Kahl's construction of the Roman imperial context and Galatians is a detailed reading of the Great Altar of Pergamon as a condensed articulation of the Roman world order. Depicting a primeval battle between the gods of Mount Olympus and monstrous giants/Titans, the Great Altar, according to Kahl, naturalizes Greek dominance against barbarian others, imagining conquest as a beautiful triumph of order and over chaos, civilization over savagery.[14] The Great Altar was not only "inherited" by the Romans when Pergamon and the Attalid kingdom were absorbed after 133 B.C.E.; it reflects all manner of Roman identification with Greek gods and greatness, as well as Rome's handy appropriation of Greek discourse about civilization.

The Great Altar is a monument housed in Berlin, itself entangled in histories of politics and power from the second century B.C.E.

---

the United States, from socialism to capitalism, from German to English, and it is heavy with history, both ancient and contemporary, secular as well as biblical" (Kahl, *Galatians Reimagined*, xiii).
13. Ibid., 31–76.
14. Ibid., 77–128.

(when it was built under the Attalid dynasty) up to the contemporary moment.[15] Excavated in the same year as the establishment of the German empire, and used as a prototype in Nazi architecture, the Altar not only crosses, but provides a *point of contact* between empires and eras.[16] Kahl notes its persuasive "emotional intensity," and she puts herself alongside Peter Weiss in a tradition of subversive readings of the Altar that change the valence of its ideological message.[17] But what Kahl emphasizes is the ideological transferability of the Altar, the dichotomizing "spatial semiotics" of the Great Altar that oppose the monstrous outsider to the righteous insider and accommodate different dominant self-imaginations in different times.[18] What I find more conspicuous about the Altar than its apparent ideological utility, however, is its bellows-like expansion and contraction of time and space, its blend and bleed of nations and their ghostly constituencies. Myself less inclined to structuralist readings, I wonder if the Altar might be just as well understood through Kahl's own pained involvement in it—an involvement hinted at in her autobiographical narration, but also clearly exceeding it. Kahl's and Weiss's counter-readings are not so much exceptions to the rule of ideology as witnesses to the unpredictable dynamism of "emotional intensity." Their readings witness to our lostness and affective captivity to pressures and potencies we can only barely name.

Roman arenas are "megachurches" of imperial religion. Ruth lives within miles of the World Trade Center site. Kahl produces a reflection on empire that is both lavish and wily in its open-ended, sliding referentiality (and suddenly I am remembering a picture,

---

15. For Kahl's history of the monument, see Ibid., 83-86, 118-21.
16. Ibid., 326 n73.
17. Ibid., 106.
18. Throughout her book Kahl emphasizes how various groups have been slotted in the place of the vilified "other" through such (mis)readings of the Pauline rhetoric of faith vs. works of law along ideological lines similar to the Great Altar (for Luther, for example, it was the Jews, the peasants, and the Moors who became the monstrous others).

projected on a large screen at her book party, in which she is standing in front of the Great Altar in Berlin). In Kahl's work, pain, humiliation, aggression, and hope for reconciliation resonate through time, texts, and monuments. Such affective resonance in her work attests to a generous and fluid historical imagination that appears to me (since I have been a student in many of her classes) many times cultivated, but also sometimes accidental and occasionally against the grain of her strivings; it both depends on and stands in deep tonal contrast to her encyclopedic historical work and meticulous exegetical technique.

There is too much to be said about Kahl's book (perhaps because as her former student, I am so familiar with its thesis). But though it has been praised for its comprehensiveness and ingenuity of method,[19] and criticized for its insistence and urgency of tone,[20] what stays with me most about it, at least as much as its picture of ancient history, is the way her language often vibrates with multiplicative meaning, generating an affective field thick and ready for association.

Kahl's book not only makes assertive claims about what empire is and does, but positions itself, usually through interpretation of an ancient text, as opposing or critical of empire, and Kahl's book is indeed a political book. But it seems to me that its overt address to ideology in which dynamics of empire are specified and sharply countered is not necessarily the only or most politically potent dimension of her book. In my own reading, I do not usually share Kahl's diagnostics of empire or her understanding of what living with or addressing empire constitutes. But I nonetheless find myself gripped and touched by Kahl's volume, moved by her subtexts (subtexts that only partially or fragmentarily overlap with my own), and moved to new sympathetic connection to people and felt

---

19. Vernon K. Robbins, review, Review of Biblical Literature, July 2010.
20. Eric Noffke, review, Review of Biblical Literature, January 2011.

engagements with the forces that shape social bodies in a way that can only be described as political.

Indeed, in many cases, by addressing a text, a reader, or reading through its apparent and presumably cogent political agenda, ideological criticism may actually produce a weak understanding of texts' surprisingly volatile political currency. In some tension and some overlap with Kahl is Wes Howard-Brook and Anthony Gwyther's book *Unveiling Empire: Reading Revelation Then and Now*. The pun in the title of the book of course gestures not only to the meaning of "apocalypse" (literally, to uncover: *apokalyptein*), but to their own work's heavy indebtedness to epistemologies of uncovering and sight. What Howard-Brook and Gwyther seek to reveal is a more accurate meaning for Revelation than the culture at large assumes through socio-historical and close literary work. But they also seek to remove some of the "blindness" to empire in the contemporary moment.[21] This is not to say that they aspire to objectivity on an overt level: Howard-Brook and Gwyther importantly embrace their work participating in contemporary meaning-making.[22] No less significantly, they describe the effects the text has had on them: "[o]ur reading of Revelation has left us with an awareness of how deeply we are mired in Babylon, but it has also left us more keenly seeking New Jerusalem."[23]

Howard-Brook and Gwyther's book additionally contains first-person accounts of experiences with empire, though in the somewhat subsidiary position of a dialogue in the last pages of the book. It is part of an encouragement to readers to reflect on their own lives. In this dialogue, for instance, they remark:

---

21. Howard-Brook and Gwyther, *Unveiling Empire: Reading Revelation Then and Now* (Maryknoll: Orbis, 1999), xv-xviii.
22. Ibid., xix.
23. Ibid., xxv.

[Howard-Brook:] Even as we sit here this moment, comfortably conversing before a nice computer, I recognize how the privileges of empire surround us: the peace and quiet on the street, the plentiful food in our refrigerators and at the local grocery a few blocks away, the Internet at our beck and call, the luxury of time to ponder these questions. Each day as I get out of bed, empire is part of the fabric of my daily life in which I am entangled without having made any conscious choices to be part of it.

[Gwyther:] For me that's how the seductiveness of Babylon really works: Babylon doesn't present me with difficult choices; it says to me, if I go with the flow, I can lead a happy and meaningful life.

[Howard-Brook]: That's exactly the problem. For people in our inner cities, or most folks around the world, empire arrives as a blunt instrument of oppression. For us, it's simply the air we breathe. To attempt to live in New Jerusalem is like trying to breathe different air![24]

With and through Revelation, the authors detail the entwinement of comfort and discomfort defining their lives within empire: empire's exhausting overpresence, eerie peacefulness, placating abundance, and the guilty knowledge of violence taking place elsewhere. They both evoke the mythological and affectively dense image of Babylon and lend it new visceral specificity, describing it as its own kind of consolation. The New Jerusalem, as an empire-less place, is as difficult to imagine as it is to enact, appearing as a strange or impossible bodily metaphor (what does it mean to breathe different air?).

The primary rhetorical sparring partner and counterpoint for Howard-Brook and Gwyther's reading is the relatively recent cadre of rapture theologies and (pre/post) millennial movements that they characterize as socially disengaged and unhistorical readings of Revelation.[25] "Revelation, contrary to the first impressions of many

---

24. Ibid., 268.
25. Ibid., xix-xxx.

mainstream Christians, did not arise from [sic] a vacuum," they write.²⁶ They then attempt to understand these more spiritualized interpretations by "taking seriously the modern anxieties that lead many people to seek 'wisdom on high' as a way of finding the 'truth' about our lives."²⁷ One of their social explanations for the success of such interpretations is that:

> America's own myths are unable to account for the situation in which people live, people will look elsewhere for answers. In other words, as long as politicians and advertisers continue to appeal to people's pursuit for the "American dream" of self-made, family-based, happy-faced prosperity, premillenialism and other forms of apocalyptic thinking will prosper.²⁸

I admire the way Gwyther and Howard-Brook pursue affect here through the attention paid to anxiety and loss in contemporary America. But their emphatic rhetorical differentiation from contemporary rapture theologies belies what might be understood as a set of robust affective *similarities* between their project and such theologies. I am reminded of the recent end-of-the-world predictions of Harold Camping in which Revelation was used as part of a mash-up of biblical texts, producing an interpretation that caused thousands of people across the nation to wait in anxious anticipation of a "rapture" that would save them from this earthly life. Interviews in newspapers charted the utopian hopes and desires of Camping's following. "I was hoping for it because I think heaven would be a lot better than this earth," shared Keith Bauer, a truck driver who followed the predictions that the world would end on May 21, 2011. He was expecting relief from mounting credit card debt and other bills.²⁹ Other people much like Bauer, in dire financial straits, were

---

26. Ibid., xxix.
27. Ibid., xxix.
28. Ibid., 17.

relieved to be able to stop worrying about money, and some others simply figured there had to be something better than this life.³⁰

While these people were often treated as foolish or naïve or as some kind of cultural curiosity by the larger public, what Camping's predictions surfaced were not just senses of heavenly entitlement or moral scolding. They also surfaced, as Howard-Brook and Gwyther suggest, the many and various gaping wounds of contemporary living; the pain of being bound to the world. Despite the different interpretational strategy for Revelation, the affective thrust of both millennialism and Howard-Brook and Gwyther's own reading of Revelation is based in a kind of pained disillusionment with American imperial promises. The Camping followers awaiting the rapture and

29. In a 2011 *Los Angeles Times* article, Christopher Goffard writes, "[b]ut to others who put stock in Camping's prophecy, disillusionment was already profound by late morning. To them, it was clear the world and its woes would make it through the weekend. Keith Bauer, a 38-year-old tractor-trailer driver from Westminster, Md., took last week off from work, packed his wife, young son and a relative in their SUV and crossed the country. If it was his last week on Earth, he wanted to see parts of it he'd always heard about but missed, such as the Grand Canyon. With maxed-out credit cards and a growing mountain of bills, he said, the rapture would have been a relief." Goffard, "In the End, Rapture Believers Weren't Going Anywhere," *Los Angeles Times*, May 22, 2011. Bauer's quote was reported by the Associated Press. Cf. Max Reed, "How True Believers Dealt with the Failed Apocalypse." Gawker, May 22, 2011, http://gawker.com/5804346/how-true-believers-dealt-with-the-failed-apocalypse.
30. It seemed to me that the thrust of many stories I read about the (failed) apocalyptic hopes inspired by Camping revolved around people's financial decisions—spending their life's savings, quitting jobs, and so on, as if to suggest that in light of the oncoming rapture, people could have a relationship to their lives that was not so bound by American expectations of financial success, or burdened by the pressures of not being a "winner" in the capitalist system. In one interview from NPR: "'[k]nowing the date of the end of the world changes all your future plans,' says 27-year-old Adrienne Martinez. She thought she'd go to medical school, until she began tuning in to Family Radio. She and her husband, Joel, lived and worked in New York City. But a year ago, they decided they wanted to spend their remaining time on Earth with their infant daughter. 'My mentality was, why are we going to work for more money? It just seemed kind of greedy to me. And unnecessary,' she says. And so, her husband adds, 'God just made it possible — he opened doors. He allowed us to quit our jobs, and we just moved, and here we are.' Now they are in Orlando, in a rented house, passing out tracts and reading the Bible. Their daughter is 2 years old, and their second child is due in June. Joel says they're spending the last of their savings. They don't see a need for one more dollar. 'You know, you think about retirement and stuff like that,' he says. 'What's the point of having some money just sitting there?' 'We budgeted everything so that, on May 21, we won't have anything left,' Adrienne adds." Barbara Bradley Hagerty, "Is the End Nigh? We'll Know Soon Enough," National Public Radio, May 7, 2011.

end of the world and liberal biblical scholars might be qualitatively distinct on several fronts—the latter a fanatic reader of the specificity of the text, the former a group who finds little need in verifying whether a rapture even occurs in Revelation and mostly finds context as a category unnecessary for reading the Bible. But that is exactly the point: both groups, however different their ideologies may be, have similar affects reflected in and amongst their constituencies. They both await a kind of triumph and both express loss and shame over the United States' economic situation.[31] Made helpless by empire, and helplessly knit into it, they want to transcend it, whether through heavenly rescue or analysis, and see some manner of true reality exposed.

Howard-Brook and Gwyther are not able adequately to account for how there might be readings with *different* politics without claiming that some readers read the text better than others. Such an approach, that sees in texts a bottom line or singular positioning with respect to empire (even if it is an ambivalent one), does not quite fully capture the dynamic corporealities of texts: their textural unevenness, their quirky circulations and impacts, or their particular proclivity to change in both shape and emphasis depending upon what or who makes contact with it.

Revelation itself is an interesting case in that it is one of the few texts of the New Testament canon that has been read for its affective force. Most famously, perhaps, Adela Yarbro Collins discusses the senses of powerlessness and aggression that haunt Revelation.[32] Greg

---

31. Catherine Keller has noted in the first chapter of her book *Apocalypse Now and Then: A Feminist Guide to the End of the World* (Minneapolis: Fortress Press, 1996), Revelation "scripts" all kinds of visions ranging in their politics from the fundamentalist conservative to the liberationist, and ranging in their apparent religiosity, as well (cf. especially 4-12). As I suggested at the beginning of this chapter, I am not so sure about the notion of being "scripted," but I am interested in how that apparent scripting happens across ideological lines.
32. Adela Yarbro Collins, *Crisis and Catharsis: The Power of the Apocalypse* (Philadelphia: Westminster Press, 1984), 141-164.

Carey similarly imagines disillusionment and alienation to be at the base of Revelation's violent revenge fantasies.[33] While Elisabeth Schüssler Fiorenza cues in on the "emotionally persuasive" character of Revelation,[34] and Christopher Frilingos likewise sees Revelation as trying to guide and/regulate the affective responses of its audiences,[35] neither of these readings spend much time speculating on the specificity of Revelation's affects. Most of these recognitions have also distilled Revelation and its persuasiveness down into its socio-political agenda—in other words, they suggest what precisely Revelation persuades its readers towards. But if we take readers as different as Gwyther and Howard-Brook and Camping's followers as examples, it seems that Revelation's ability to persuade its readers towards a single coherent cause is hardly convincing.

Revelation *does* possess however, at least in the present, a stunningly consistent capacity to attract and/or generate poignant and various permutations of melancholy victory—a mourning of the perils of belonging to the world right beside idealized hopes, even certainties, for somehow overcoming them. The affectivity of text and reader are indistinguishable, since this combination of senses of vulnerability and triumph are nothing if not embodied in the central symbol of Revelation, its lamb who conquers. As the oblique pun of Gwyther and Howard-Brook's title implicitly suggests, to "unveil" and expose imperialism and colonialism has its own aggressive fantasies of victory resonating, more specifically, with the sexually charged and spectacular exposure of Babylon in Revelation 17.

---

33. Greg Carey, "Symptoms of Resistence in the Book of Revelation," in *The Reality of Apocalypse: Rhetoric and Politics in the Book of Revelation*, ed. David L. Barr (Leiden: Brill, 2006), 169-180.
34. Elisabeth Schüssler Fiorenza, *The Book of Revelation: Justice and Judgment*, 2nd ed. (Minneapolis:Fortress Press, 1998), 181-205.
35. Christopher Frilingos, *Spectacles of Empire: Monsters, Martyrs and the Book of Revelation* (Philadelphia: University of Pennsylvania Press, 2004), 39-63.

If the politics of ideological approaches are not straightforward, neither are the politics of the project of "returning to Rome" itself. The advent of interest in the Roman Empire in the fields of New Testament and Early Christianity is part of a more extensive cultural pattern in which, as Vilashini Cooppan has observed, the Roman Empire serves as a trope for European and American cultural self-understanding. She considers Joseph Conrad's *Heart of Darkness* alongside Michael Hardt and Antonio Negri's *Empire*, conservative justifications for invasions of Iraq and Afghanistan, and Hollywood films such as *Gladiator* (which by itself links to the filmic tradition of *The Fall of the Roman Empire*, *Ben-Hur* and *Spartacus*). She writes:

> *Gladiator*'s American Rome, like that invoked in current discussions of US empire, is continuous with a broader tradition in which the nation returns to Rome in order to speak its own history: the founding, for example, with its republican language; or the cold war, with its global rhetoric of good and evil empires, its domestic concerns with new social movements of liberation. Not only did the epic spectacles of the 1950's and 1960's represent Hollywood's effort to woo back an audience increasingly defecting to television as its preferred leisure activity, but they also served what Leslie Felperin calls 'a more mass-psychological function,' working out anxieties about the west's imperial role in the new world order.[36]

This culture-wide return to Rome seems to have given biblical studies a new kind of cultural currency because of its contemporary political implications (cf. John Dominic Crossan's bestseller *God and Empire* or any number of History Channel specials on Rome and early Christianity). Biblical studies cashes in on this currency even while there are also varying levels of explicitness with which scholars are "speaking [their] own history" and "working out anxieties about

---

36. Vilashini Cooppan, "The Ruins of Empire: The National and Global Politics of America's Return to Rome," in *Postcolonial Studies and Beyond*, ed. Ania Loomba, et al. (Durham: Duke University Press, 2006),

217

the west's imperial role." Some scholars speak in the language of direct political engagement, others are more suggestively or even provocatively analogical, and plenty of scholars pursuing the Roman imperial context for Christianity make no mention of American or European imperialism at all. The issue Cooppan raises, however, is not about explicit political engagement. Whether explicitly political or not, scholarship on New Testament and the Roman Empire is participating in a psycho-social and affective dynamic in which relationships to empire are worked out on the "big screen" of the Roman imperial era.

Cooppan's larger point is primarily made in opposition to Hardt and Negri's conception of empire in an era of globalization as placeless, all-encompassing, and continuously morphing, in effect voiding the category of the nation.[37] Using the film *Gladiator* as an example, she shows that its own "global reach" as a film (its international casting and reception) accompanies profound "national meaning" for the United States, and ultimately "veils nationalism with globalism."[38] Embedded in this, however, is another grievance: she worries about the association of Rome and American imperialism creating "an unbroken return of a political form over a span of two thousand years," giving a sense of "empire's immortality," rather than approaching empire as a "historically specific, territorially based, nationally directed, discursively managed system of domination."[39] And so we find ourselves at a prickly impasse: while the analogizing of Rome with contemporary imperialism in biblical studies enables critique through its interpretation of texts as imperially steeped and/ or subversive of empire, it simultaneously preempts some of its own

---

37. Cooppan, "The Ruins of Empire," in Loomba et al., *Postcolonial Studies and Beyond*, 87-91.
38. Ibid., 92.
39. Ibid., 84.

political efficacy through a certain immortalizing of empire, implicit in the very "return to Rome."

Without diminishing Cooppan's historicizing and particularizing of empire, it seems that she imagines history as a one-way street. We "return" to Rome, project *onto* an unchanging past that is dead and over. One might respond to Cooppan, equally historically, that the United States (among other modern empires) does not simply return to Rome to understand itself; it has been actively styled in the image of Rome, consciously or otherwise, and has done so using biblical terms, texts, and conceptualities, long before the field of New Testament "rediscovered" the Roman empire. And even while Rome haunts us, the modern historical description of Rome is necessarily drawn up with the experiences and knowledge of modern empires.

So what do we do with Cooppan's objection that political intervention through historical work may actually be hampered by the temporal universalizing embedded in so many Rome-U.S. analogies, but on the other hand obsessive particularizing or ignoring the relationship altogether also has its fantasies?

The connected compatibility between readers and texts, such as the one between Revelation and its contemporary readers, is usually described as ideological reproduction. But thinking affectively about this relationship generates a less judgmental analysis that does not prioritize the text's meaning over readers' experiences, treat the text's meaning as obvious, or imagine the readers as only unconsciously duplicating dynamics of the text. Texts, as I have intimated, are affectively dynamic bodies, bodies that touch and move us, corporealities into which our own corporealities coalesce.

It may be in fact that this slippery referentiality of Rome, particularly its capacity to arouse interest and absorb attachments, and these various affective fusions/diffusions between text and reader intervene mercifully in the suspicious thrust of the field's treatment of empire. Rome or the contemporary United States, Revelation's pains or our own, empire or something else entirely: we do not always know what we are talking about, or where the past ends and the present begins.

*   *   *   *

While I do wish to highlight the personal and the anecdotal as important pieces of the contemporary scholarly reflection on empire, this should not be mistaken for a simple call to revive autobiographical criticism. Which is why, though I am not typically one for making claims about intentionality, I want to stress both the cultivated and the accidental vibrancy of Kahl's work as well as the way the clumsy poetics of the first-person phenomenological description of empire in Gwyther and Howard-Brook both illuminate and are handicapped by their moralizing and scientism. The brief forays into autobiography or first person self-narration, in these cases at least, bespeak an at least momentary "openness to being haunted," an availability to reader (if even only periodic), that can and should be appreciated.[40] But they also remind us that the poignant and efficacious dimensions of our work happen in uneasy and quirky relationship to us, our authoritative knowing, and our most cogent reading strategies.

Indeed, that unpredictable relationship between our knowing and our efficaciousness extends to autobiographical writing itself. Though across a number of disciplines autobiographical writing has been associated with terms like "self-disclosure" and "transparency" (which also denote ethics), autobiography is, after all, a genre, a style of storytelling, and one with certain ethical and epistemological

---

40. In fact Freccero's openness to being haunted is, by her description, a passive disposition, something that suggests cultivation and effort, but not control by any means. See Carla Freccero, *Queer/Early/Modern* (Durham: Duke University Press, 2006), 69-104.

predicaments, as the trend of autobiographical criticism ended up unearthing in its tenure.[41] In autobiography, the self that is "exposed" to the reader is already a fictional self or guise: it is, despite and because of its confessional form, rather *im*personal in that it engages social conventions of readability and truth production.[42] Most unfortunately (for me, at least), it implies a level of self-knowledge that becomes much less tenable after theories of the unconscious: what we tell about ourselves when we wax personal often has a masterful presumption about our own ability to know exactly what formed us and how it has done so. Judith Butler writes in *Giving An Account of Oneself* that autobiographical forms demand, or at least prefer, "the seamlessness of the story to something we might tentatively call the truth of the person, a truth that, to a certain degree . . . might well become more clear in moments of interruption, stoppage, open-endedness—in enigmatic articulations that cannot be easily translated into narrative form."[43] Interestingly, however, in this same volume, Butler describes autobiography in eminently historical terms:

---

41. The critiques are blistering: sustained autobiographical and personal interventions can feel "indulgent" —indulging, particularly, the usual speakers by putting themselves provocatively at the center of attention. See, for example, Susan Henking, "Who Better to Indulge? (Self) Indulgent Theorizing and the Stuff of Ambivalence," *Semeia* 72 (1995): 239-246. Other objections include that autobiographical criticism sometimes evacuates from its reading more substantial political and social concerns (though Kahl and Gwyther and Howard-Brook, among others, provide powerful counter-examples of this), or even mitigates questions of accountability. For a full list of objections to autobiographical or "confessional" critical gestures, see Aram H. Veeser's introduction to *Confessions of the Critics: North American Critics' Autobiographical Moves,* ed. Veeser (New York: Routledge, 1996), ix-xxvi.
42. As Erin Runions writes in her trenchant questioning of autobiographical criticism, "[i]n short, I wonder if autobiographical criticism is one more instance of the social control of simulacrum…I wonder if it is one more of these media projections of the internalized gaze, one in fact that both creates a market and demands self-regulation in one shot. Look at me looking at myself. Consume me, consume my scholarship" (Erin Runions, "The Panopticon Gone Mad?" in *The Recycled Bible: Autobiography, Culture, and the Space Between,* SBLSS, ed. Fiona Black [Atlanta: Society of Biblical Literature, 2006], 185-94 [187]).
43. Judith Butler, *Giving An Account of Oneself* (New York: Fordham University Press, 2005), 64. The subtext in this, much more explicit in her book, is that identity is one such coherent narrative of being.

> The 'I' can tell neither the story of its own emergence nor the conditions of its own possibility without bearing witness to a state of affairs to which one could not have been present, which are prior to one's own emergence as a subject who can know, and so constitute a set of origins that one can narrate only at the expense of an authoritative knowledge. Indeed, when the 'I' seeks to give an account of its own emergence, it must, as a matter of necessity, become a social theorist.[44]

Rather than think of this merger of history and autobiography as an obvious self-referentiality in which history is instrumentalized for our own self-description, or even a more sophisticated version of the feminist axiom "the personal is political," we might read Butler as suggesting that to give an account of oneself and to give an account of history share a similar gesturing towards self-understanding in a larger social picture. They thus also inhabit the same space of unknowing.[45]

In fact, if the practices of history and autobiography reflect each other or merge in certain ways, we might be able to theorize out of their parallel ambiguities, potencies, and shortcomings. Crafting a turn in the poststructuralist critique of biographical and authorial referentiality, literary critic Jane Gallop has recently reclaimed liveliness and authorial presence in writing, as well as contact (or the desire for it) between readers and writers. She does so through the apparently counterintuitive choice of the concept of the "death of the author." Taking the death of the author out of its vaunted place in the history of theory, Gallop foregrounds a startling conflictedness in

---

44. Ibid., 8.
45. I am, perhaps obviously at this point, attracted to autobiography, or more broadly to first person narrative writing. Maybe I am too beguiled by the sense autobiography gives of contact with the writer, but I am less pessimistic about the autobiographical form than some postmodern critics, in part because, in the wake of these critiques, I am not plotting explicit self-expression (whatever that is) as any kind of solution to biblical scholarship's larger ethical problems. I do think, however, that whatever its success or failures on other levels, autobiographical and personal gestures mitigate the discipline's historical tendencies towards frightened rigidity, even if such gestures also undo or outdo those who make them.

the "originary moment" of this current theoretical given. She notes that Michel Foucault's essay "What is an Author?", however often it is cited for killing off authorship, barely takes up the "death of the author" relative to its more emphatic interest in historicizing the "author-function." Likewise, while Roland Barthes's name is practically shorthand for the death of the author, his writing as a corpus is not so insouciant regarding the author's death: "As an institution, the author is dead: his person . . . has disappeared . . . but in the text, in a certain way, I desire the author," Barthes writes in *The Pleasure of the Text*.[46] Not only does Barthes confess to a desire for the author despite the author's passing, but he also, in an earlier publication, seems to invite a "friendly return of the author."[47]

Gallop resourcefully reconsiders the author's death within the more shaded reflections of Barthes on relationships between readers and writers. She reads Barthes's quote, above, as suggesting not a total evacuation of the writer from texts, but rather as the disappearance of the masterful god-Author, or author-as-monument. The Author, as a monument, is only an abstraction, and was never alive. The institution of Author has collapsed, died. But *authors*, plural and corporeal, live on with a kind of ghostly existence even after they have died. Barthes writes: "The author who returns...is a simple plural of 'charms' . . . a source of vivid novelistic glimmerings . . . in which we nonetheless read death more surely than in the epic of destiny; this is not a (civil, moral) person, this is a body."[48]

Gallop reads Barthes as theorizing a relationship with authors to be something like the autobiographical fiction of Proust and Genet,

---

46. Jane Gallop, *The Deaths of the Author: Reading and Writing in Time* (Durham: Duke University Press, 2011), 29-31.
47. Gallop comments on the "friendly return of the author" in Barthes' *Sade, Fourier, Loyola*, "Thus the author dies in an overexposed Barthes and returns in an underexposed Barthes; the imbalance in the reception of these texts tends to obscure the return and exaggerate the finality of the death" (Ibid., 30).
48. Ibid., 40.

in which one encounters and is touched by the writer in fragments and details ("vivid, novelistic glimmerings"), fragments that break off and live on in the life, the "dailiness," as Gallop puts it, of the reader, details that "come to touch . . . some future body."[49] This is the author as more mortal, both more dead and more alive. Authors live on in the body of the text, in incidental moments of its expansive and complex specificity. The Author as monument (or as God) is ostensibly behind the text, in control of the text. On the other hand, authors are lost, scattered in the middle of their texts.[50] As Barthes writes, "[i]f by a twisted dialectic there must be in the Text, destroyer of every subject, a subject to love, that subject is dispersed."[51]

Without explicitly taking up affect, Gallop's reading of Barthes offers an affective account of the contingencies and impacts of reading and writing. We are present in our work, but not self-present. Authors are lost to readers, but still touch them. This speaks equally to our own writing, autobiographical or otherwise, and to the ancient writing in which we are so invested. Subjectivities mingle and scatter, move through and touch each other via the affectivity of writing and history.[52]

In other words, *contact happens* between readers and writers, those supposedly separate domains of past and present, through such ghostly returns and the affective contagion and corporealities of texts.

---

49. Ibid., 45.
50. For a companionable set of reflections within biblical studies on ghostliness and fragmented presence in texts, see Fiona Black, "Writing Lies: Autobiography, Textuality and the Song of Songs," in *The Recycled Bible: Autobiography, Culture, and the Space Between*, SBLSS, ed. Fiona Black (Atlanta: Society of Biblical Literature, 2006), 161-184.
51. Quoted in Gallop, *Deaths of the Author*, 42.
52. This touching of a future body, this dispersion and living on in fragmentary ways through the text is resonant with Puar's reframing of all bodies as contagious, as well as Freccero's queer ethics of history and "penetrative reciprocity" of haunting. Carolyn Dinshaw has also written about Foucault, Barthes, and an im- or non-personal contact through texts/history, particularly in *Getting Medieval: Sexualities and Communities* (Durham: Duke University Press, 1999). She describes her works as "queerly historical" in that it "creates a relation across time that has an affective or erotic component" (50).

It is the disorienting force of that contact that we hope to allay or avoid by systematizing our own readings so intensely, or more particularly by excavating the dead as artifact, locating them ever more specifically in the past even while we remain affectively mixed up in them. We do not have to dig up the various people we describe as Christians: we are already touched, possessed, and affected by them in myriad ways for which we cannot fully account. Besides, no matter how systematized our readings, what we call historical work is inevitably a cobbling together of quirky and tangentially related fragments: pieces of texts found in trash piles, architectural detritus, the particles and slivers of more recent relationships, the fading marks and partial casings of events scattered across time, and the forces of our affectivity producing momentary coherences between all these things.

The confusions, diffusions, and helical movement between ourselves and the texts we read, between self-narration and history, between past and present, mean that to digress is not to lose sight of history or the texts we read as much as to follow the moments where we are welded to them, to admit to being lost in them. Whether we admit it or not, we will never be totally able to discern who or what we are talking about in our work. This disarms any self-righteous claims we might make about the politics or allegiances of our work, for sure. Embracing the oblique, circumlocutory, and inexact nature of our work, however, may have other virtues, if not other politics: more affectively textured readings for one, and a heightened sensitivity for the uncertain dimensions of our own captivations, imperial or otherwise, for another.

Conclusion

History is an expressive enterprise; it emerges as one kind of recourse for those forces that move and exceed us. Yet the fields of biblical studies and early Christian studies, in a distinct way, have built their prestige through an apparently unaffected self-presentation, prizing precision of categories and coherence of method above almost all else. The field has done so even as the rest of the world's readers of the Bible relate to it in an unequivocally emotional key. What does critical inclusion of our affectivity into reading look like? How might the affectivity of texts, forceful and uncertain as that affectivity is, be part of historical work?

In this book I have inquired about the historical, interpretive, and ethical implications (and limitations) of Christian identity as an optic, and offered constructive re-readings of ancient literature—re-readings that move Christian identity aside—suggesting that the emergence of Christianity or Christian identity might be rather understood as an affective history of diasporic trauma and its forgetting. I have suggested that what appears now as a phenomenon is, in part, an assemblage of colonial and diasporic affects: desires for transcendence (Hebrews and the Gospel of John), fantastic rhetorical turns (Ignatius), diasporic articulations of counter-belonging (Secret Revelation of John), and epic imaginations of significance (Acts), to name a few. These feelings and responses have been disconnected from their embeddedness in pain, social fracture, and violence. The term "Christian," then, crops up at the convergence of the imperial production of populations and the allure of even imperiled visibility when there is nothing left to lose.

But I have also suggested taking more seriously the grief and longings, hopes, and disappointments that surface in historical work; and I have named some of the ways we as readers are haunted by these ancient texts, and by pasts the vicissitudes of which we cannot be totally certain. One of the things that affect and diaspora theories do for the study of the Bible and "early Christian" history is to resource scholarship's own complicated, affective entanglements to provoke more textured descriptions of ancient belonging and life in the slipstream of empire. Our felt relationship to texts and our experience of the present are indices and temperatures out of which critical reflection can and should arise.

Some recent work in the fields of New Testament and Early Christianity has, in the wake of Foucaultian historiography, emphasized the discursive and power-inflected dimensions of history, and I have not rejected this trend by any means. Perhaps obviously, this project does not propose any kind of simple return to history as a self-evident set of events, nor does it abandon analyses of power interests in historical narration. But this project does engage recent work in cultural studies to inquire about what we presume such historiographical approaches to accomplish, and it likewise offers some alternative modes for thinking about the ongoing life of the past, as well as the motivations and effects of historical narration.

"Christian identity" as an optic, for instance, has produced some deeply sensitive reflections about the interpretive implications of texts and their rhetorics, as well as an almost radical new awareness about the tight social maneuvering and intimate social entanglements within the New Testament and associated ancient literature. At the same time, the very term "Christian identity" as an historical lens houses in it premises that contradict the impulses of this scholarship; primarily, it houses the premise that there was some sense of distinct or recognizable Christian belonging in the first two centuries, and that a given text is interested in it. While discursive approaches such as those talking about the construction of Christian identity would seem to avert the problem of historical referentiality, there is in the very term a curious attachment to Christian belonging as a historical given.

My particular elaboration of affect theory here is, as I see it, both an effect of the consciousnesses instilled by scholarship on Christian identity, and a way of putting those consciousnesses into hyperdrive, since so much work in affect theoretical circles *starts* from the fluidity, interconnectedness, and ambiguity constitutive of social life. My engagement with diaspora theory likewise extends and lends new language to postcolonial and empire-critical approaches, in that it more directly centralizes the strange productivity of violence and its multifarious and multiplying reverberations. What is more, so much theoretical work on diaspora sees creative and seemingly strange fusions to be central to collectivity itself.

The combined considerations of affect and diaspora provoke what I hope is a more or differently textured set of social readings for ancient literature. Acts is read not as a text always already implicated in imperial Christianity and colonial mission, but as a haunted chronicle of imperial enchantment, diasporic disappointment, and a kind of compensatorily grandiose self-imagination. Far from any kind of Gnostic anti-social world-denigration, Secret Revelation of John is instead a cosmic recapitulation of a desire for homeland, and a mode of preserving some vestige of hope and vulnerability despite feeling that the world has been overrun, even infected, by badness. I suggest Hebrews and the Gospel of John, rather than being thoroughly de-localized theological statements, borrow transcendent imaginations at the very moments when they are most embroiled in the stickiness of place. The Gospel of Truth, usually read for its erotic force and esoteric conceptualities, gets recast here as a traumatized affective re-association of pain with pleasure, one that also seeks relief from the immediacy of its social traumas through heightened, speculative language.

My readings do not produce a dramatic overturning of scholarship before me, nor do they necessarily bring any new historical information to light. My readings do, however, represent a substantial change in historical orientation to these texts and their relationships to each other by abandoning the term "Christian" as a central (or even in some cases a viable) category, and instead reading for diasporic negotiations, losses, and attempts at healing. Following scholarship that has emphasized the diversity of what we call "early Christianity," I propose no fundamental similarities or differences between these texts. But I do find productive historical connections between them: textural, affective, and thematic resonances and companionabilities that speak to the vicissitudes of colonial life. Many of these textural and thematic resonances are expressed in and across the chapters themselves, but I imagine—and hope the reader will find—more than I had the time or space to assemble.

My readings of ancient literature and my affective re-framing of scholarship also represent a change of orientation to our involvements with the texts we read, and to our assumptions about what constitutes political interpretation. While the affective inter-corporeality of text and reader is a resource for reading, rather than an obstacle, it is not a straightforward one: as I suggested in the last chapter, the inter-corporeality of text and reader complicates the valences of our political interventions. This aspect of the project points to the way

I have engaged affect both as substantive dimension of bodily and subjective life, and as an analytic of emotions. I do not strongly contrast affect and emotion, but view emotions as simply the named instantiation of the substantive, corporeal force of affect. But I do find these two separate ways of theorizing affect productive for different reasons. Affect, generalized, allows space for broader theorizing about intersubjective relations and the inherent contingency of materiality. Affect as emotion invites specified phenomenological description, and tighter scrutiny into the circuits of feeling that form and re-form collectives.

Bringing affect and diaspora as categories of experience to these texts has been fully a literary, historical, and epistemological undertaking. I am somewhat embarrassed to admit its scope, even while I take pleasure in the bluster of such expansive projects (regardless of whether they are mine or someone else's). However, the aspirations and impulses for the project fell much more along the lines of micro- than macro-conceptualizations. In particular, affect theory seemed to step in at moments, some of which are recounted either directly or obliquely in these chapters, in which my other critical vocabularies broke down or felt tired. For one, I had begun to grow weary of the subtle but distinct moralizing posture I was taking towards the literature I was studying, a posture that developed coincidentally alongside my increasing historical/analytical proficiency (and, it should be noted, a sharpening political progressivism), and ended up often overshadowing my no less distinct, and certainly more complicated, resonances with these same texts. (I will leave alone, for now, the relational conundrums such moralizing produced.) I mean *moralizing* and *resonance* not to signify the poles of "negative" and "positive" affectivity, but rather to indicate the quality of my engagement. Moralizing, in the form of either praise or denunciation, was very often a deflection of my more thorny and disconcerting affections, attachments, recognitions, revulsions, and hurts regarding not just the texts "themselves," but the personal and social subtexts they informed and evoked. The seemingly small question of how to give my affective resonances with this literature (and those of my students, colleagues, relatives, and friends) some critical consideration quickly took up more space, and veered in different directions, than I had anticipated. It turns out that the personal and social subtexts, however partial or indeterminate, were hardly beside the point.

There are other trajectories possible in the academic study of the Bible, obviously, (and I do not claim to have rid myself of all my moralizing impulses), but that this is my trajectory is perhaps telling. Such a trajectory is telling about the tools and conflicts of the discipline, of course, a theme I have amply addressed already. But that this is *my* trajectory is also telling in that it gives one context for my attraction to thinking about affect, and thus for many threads within this project. I offer it less as an explanatory note than as a part of this project's practice of collective critical self-reflection and reflexivity; I put it forth as a part of the ongoing conversation about the stakes of how, and why, we read.

Bibliography

Achtemeier, Paul. "Between Text and Sermon: 1 Peter 1:13-21." *Interpretation* 60, no. 3 (2006): 306-308.

Africa, Thomas. "Urban Violence in Imperial Rome." *The Journal of Interdisciplinary History* 2, no. 1 (1971): 3-21.

Ahmed, Sara. *The Cultural Politics of Emotion*. New York: Routledge, 2004.

Aitken, Ellen Bradshaw. "Portraying the Temple in Stone and Text: the Arch of Titus and the Epistle to the Hebrews." *Sewanee Theological Review* 45, no. 2 (2002): 131-51.

———. "Reading Hebrews in Flavian Rome." *USQR* 59, no. 3-4 (2005): 82-85.

Alexander, Loveday. *Acts in Its Ancient Literary Context: A Classicist Looks at the Acts of the Apostles*. New York: T & T Clark, 2005.

Althusser, Louis. *Lenin and Philosophy and Other Essays*. New York: Monthly Review Press, 1971.

Anderson, Benedict. *Imagined Communities*. New York: Verso Press, 1983.

Aristides. *Works*. Translated by C. A. Behr. Loeb Classical Library. Cambridge: Harvard University Press, 1973.

Ascough, Richard S. "The Thessalonian Christian Community as Professional Voluntary Association." *JBL* 119, no. 2 (2000): 311-28.

———. "Translocal Relationships Among Voluntary Associations and Early Christianity." *Journal of Early Christian Studies* 5:2 (1997): 223-241.

———. "Bringing Chaos to Order: Historical Memory and the Manipulation of History." *R&T* 15, no. 3-4 (2008): 280-303.

Ashbrook Harvey, Susan, and David Hunter, eds. *The Oxford Dictionary of Early Christian Studies*. Oxford: Oxford University Press, 2010.

Athanassiadi, Polymnia, and Michael Frede, eds. *Pagan Monotheism in Late Antiquity*. Oxford: Oxford University Press, 1999.

Attridge, Harold. *The Epistle to the Hebrews: A Commentary on the Epistle to the Hebrews*. Hermenia Commentary Series. Minneapolis: Fortress Press, 1989.

———. "The Gospel of Truth as an Exoteric Text." Pages 239-255 in *Nag Hammadi, Gnosticism and Early Christianity*. Edited by Charles W. Hedrick, and Robert Hodgson, Jr. Peabody, Mass: Hendrickson Publishers, 1986.

———. "Let Us Strive to Enter That Rest: The Logic of Hebrews 4:1-11." *HTR* 73, no. 1-2 (1980): 279-88.

Aune, David E. *The New Testament and Its Literary Environment*. Philadelphia: The Westminster Press, 1987.

Axel, Brian Keith. "The Diasporic Imaginary." *Public Culture* 14, no. 2 (2002): 411-28.

———. *The Nation's Tortured Body: Violence, Representation and the Formation of a Sikh "Diaspora."* Durham: Duke University Press, 2001.

Bailey, Randall, Tat-Siong Benny Liew, and Fernando Segovia, eds. *They Were All Together in One Place? Towards Minority Biblical Criticism*. SBLSS. Atlanta: Society of Biblical Literature, 2009.

Baker, Cynthia M. "'From Every Nation Under Heaven'": Jewish Ethnicities in the Greco-Roman World." Pages 79-100 in *Prejudice and Christian Beginnings: Investigating Race, Gender, and Ethnicity in Early Christian Studies*. Edited by Laura Nasrallah and Elisabeth Schüssler Fiorenza. Minneapolis: Fortress Press, 2009.

Balch, David. "Hellenization/Acculturation in 1 Peter." Pages 81-101 in *Perspectives on First Peter*. Edited by Charles H. Talbert. Macon, Ga.: Mercer University Press, 1986.

———. "The Genre of Luke-Acts: Individual Biography, Adventure Novel or Political History?" *SwJT* 33, no. 1 (1990): 5-19.

Barr, David L., ed. *The Reality of Apocalypse: Rhetoric and Politics in the Book of Revelation*. Leiden: Brill, 2006.

Barrett, C. K. "The Eschatology of the Epistle to the Hebrews." Pages 363-393 in *The Background of the New Testament and Its Eschatology: Essays in Honor of C. H. Dodd*. Edited by W. D. Davies and David Daube. Cambridge: Cambridge University Press, 1956.

Bates, Matthew W. "Justin Martyr's Logocentric Hermeutical Transformation of Isaiah's Vision of the Nations." *JTS* 60, no. 2 (2009): 538-55.

Batten, Alicia. "Neither Gold nor Braided Hair (1 Timothy 2:9; 1 Peter 3.3): Adornment, Gender and Honour in Antiquity." *NTS* 55, no. 4 (2009): 484-501.

Bauckham, Richard, and Daniel Driver, Trevor Hart and Nathan MacDonald, eds. *The Epistle to the Hebrews and Christian Theology*. Grand Rapids: Eerdmans, 2009.

Beare, Rhona. "Invidious Success: Some Thoughts on the Aeneid XII." *Proceedings of the Virgilian Society* 64 (1963-64): 18-30.

Benjamin, Jessica. *Like Subjects, Love Objects: Essays on Recognition and Sexual Difference*. New Haven: Yale University Press, 1995.

Bennett, Jane. *Vibrant Matter: A Political Ecology of Things*. Durham: Duke University Press, 2010.

Bersani, Leo. *Is the Rectum a Grave? And Other Essays*. Chicago: University of Chicago Press, 2010.

Bickerman, Elias J. "The Name of the Christians." *HTR* 42, no. 2 (1949): 109-24.

Black, Fiona, ed. *The Recycled Bible: Autobiography, Culture, and the Space Between*. SBLSS. Atlanta: Society of Biblical Literature, 2006.

Bockmuehl, Marcus. "Abraham's Faith in Hebrews 11." Pages 364-73 in *The Epistle to the Hebrews and Christian Theology*. Edited by Richard Bauckham, et al. Grand Rapids: Eerdmans, 2009.

Bonz, Marianne Palmer. *The Past as Legacy: Luke-Acts and Ancient Epic*. Minneapolis: Fortress Press, 2000.

Boring, M. Eugene. *1 Peter*. Abingdon New Testament Commentaries. Nashville, TN: Abingdon Press, 1999.

Boswell, John. *Christianity, Social Tolerance, and Homosexuality*. Chicago: University of Chicago Press, 1980.

Boyarin, Daniel. *Border Lines: The Partition of Judaeo-Christianity*. Divinations: Rereading Late Ancient Religion. Philadelphia: University of Pennsylvania Press, 2004.

_____. *Dying for God: Martyrdom and the Making of Christianity and Judaism*. Figurae: Reading Medieval Culture. Stanford: Stanford University Press, 1999.

_____. *A Radical Jew: Paul and the Politics of Identity*. Divinations: Re-reading Late Antique Religion. Berkeley: University of California Press, 1994.

Brakke, David. *The Gnostics: Myth, Ritual and Diversity in Early Christianity*. Cambridge: Harvard University Press, 2012.

Braziel, Jana Evans, and Anita Mannur, eds. *Theorizing Diaspora*. Malden, Mass.: Blackwell Publishing, 2003.

Brennan, Teresa. *The Transmission of Affect*. Ithaca: Cornell University Press, 2004.

Brent, Allen. "Ignatius of Antioch and the Imperial Cult." *VC* 52, no. 1 (1998): 30-58.

_____. *Ignatius of Antioch: A Martyr Bishop and the Origin of the Episcopacy*. New York: Continuum/T & T Clark, 2007.

Briggs, Sheila. "The Deceit of the Sublime: An Investigation into the Origins of Ideological Criticism in Early Nineteenth Century Biblical Criticism." *Semeia* 59 (1992): 1-23.

Brown, Peter. *The Body and Society: Men, Women and Sexual Renunciation in Early Christianity*. New York: Columbia University Press, 1988.

─────. *The Making of Late Antiquity (Carl Newell Jackson Lectures)*. Cambridge: Harvard University Press, 1978.

Brown, Wendy. *Politics Out of History*. Princeton: Princeton University Press, 2001.

Buell, Denise Kimber. "God's Own People: Specters of Race, Ethnicity, and Gender in Early Christian Studies." Pages 159-90 in *Prejudice and Christian Beginnings: Investigating Race, Gender, and Ethnicity in Early Christian Studies*. Edited by Laura Nasrallah and Elisabeth Schüssler Fiorenza. Minneapolis: Fortress Press, 2009.

─────. *Why This New Race?: Ethnic Reasoning in Early Christianity*. New York: Columbia University Press, 2005.

Burrus, Virginia. "Heretical Woman as Symbol in Alexander, Athanasius, Epiphanius, and Jerome." *HTR* 84, no. 3 (1993): 229-48.

─────. "The Gospel of Luke and the Acts of the Apostles." Pages 133-55 in *A Postcolonial Commentary on the New Testament Writings*. Edited by Fernando F. Segovia and Rasiah S. Sugirtharajah. London: T & T Clark, 2011.

─────. *Saving Shame: Martyrs, Saints and Other Abject Subjects*. Divinations: Re-reading Late Antique Religion. Philadelphia: University of Pennsylvania Press, 2008.

─────. *The Sex Lives of Saints: An Erotics of Ancient Hagiography*. Divinations: Re-reading Late Ancient Religion. Philadelphia: University of Pennsylvania Press, 2004.

Butler, Judith. *Bodies That Matter: On the Discursive Limits of "Sex."* New York: Routledge, 1993.

_____. *Giving an Account of Oneself*. New York: Fordham University Press, 2005.

_____. "Melancholy Gender-Refused Identification." *Psychoanalytic Dialogues* 5, no. 2 (1995): 165-80.

_____. *Precarious Life: The Powers of Mourning and Violence*. London: Verso Press, 2004.

_____. *Undoing Gender*. New York: Routledge, 2004.

Calaway, Jared. "Heavenly Sabbath, Heavenly Sanctuary: The Transformation of Priestly Sacred Space and Sacred Time in the 'Songs of the Sabbath Sacrifice' and the Epistle to the Hebrews." Ph.D. diss., Columbia University, 2010.

Campbell, William S. *Paul and the Creation of Christian Identity*. London: T & T Clark, 2008.

Caputo, John D., and Michael J. Scanlon, eds. *Transcendence and Beyond: A Postmodern Inquiry*. Indiana Series in the Philosophy of Religion. Bloomington: Indiana University Press, 2007.

Carey, Greg. "Symptoms of Resistance in the Book of Revelation." Pages 169-80 in *The Reality of the Apocalypse*. Edited by David L. Barr. Leiden: Brill, 2006.

Carter, Warren. *John: Storyteller, Interpreter, Evangelist*. Peabody, Mass.: Hendrickson, 2006.

Castelli, Elizabeth. *Martyrdom and Memory: Early Christian Culture Making*. Gender, Theory and Religion. New York: Columbia University Press, 2007.

_____, and Hal Taussig, eds. *Reimagining Christian Origins: A Colloquium Honoring Burton L. Mack*. Valley Forge, Pa: Trinity Press International, 1996.

de Certeau, Michel. *The Writing of History*. New York: Columbia University Press, 1992.

Cho, Grace. "Diaspora of Camptown: The Forgotten War's Monstrous Family." *Women's Studies Quarterly* 34, no. 1-2 (2006): 309-31.

_____. "Voices from the *Teum*: Synesthetic Trauma and the Ghosts of the Korean Diaspora." Pages 151-69 in *The Affective Turn: Theorizing the Social*. Edited by Patricia Ticineto Clough with Jean Halley. Durham: Duke University Press, 2007.

Chow, Rey. *The Age of the World Target: Self-Referentiality in War, Theory and Comparative Work*. Durham: Duke University Press, 2006.

_____. *Writing Diaspora: Tactics of Intervention in Contemporary Cultural Studies*. Arts and Politics of the Everyday. Bloomington: Indiana University Press, 1993.

Clausen, Wendell. "An Interpretation of the Aeneid." *Harvard Studies in Classical Philology* 68 (1964): 139-147.

Cohen, Shaye J. D. *The Beginnings of Jewishness: Boundaries, Varieties, Uncertainties*. Berkeley: University of California Press, 1999.

_____. "Crossing the Boundary and Becoming a Jew." *HTR* 82, no. 1 (1989): 13-33.

Collins, Adela Yarbro. *Crisis and Catharsis: The Power of the Apocalypse*. Philadelphia: The Westminster Press, 1984.

Collins, John J. *Between Athens and Jerusalem: Jewish Identity in the Hellenistic Diaspora*. Grand Rapids: Eerdmans, 2000.

Conzelmann, Hans. *The Theology of St. Luke*. Minneapolis: Fortress Press, 1982.

Cooppan, Vilashini. "The Ruins of Empire: The National and Global Politics of the Return to Rome." Pages 80-100 in *Postcolonial Studies and Beyond*. Edited by Ania Loomba, et al. Durham: Duke University Press, 2006.

Cotter, Wendy. "The Collegia and Roman Law: State Restrictions on Voluntary Associations, 64 BCE-200 CE." Pages 74-89 in *Voluntary Associations in the Graeco-Roman World*. Edited by John S. Kloppenborg and Stephen G. Wilson. London: Routledge, 1996.

Crimp, Douglas. *AIDS: Cultural Analysis/Cultural Activism*. Cambridge, MIT Press, 1987.

Crossan, John Dominic. *The Historical Jesus: The Life of a Mediterranean Jewish Peasant*. New York: HarperOne, 1993.

_____, and Jonathan L. Reed. *In Search of Paul: How Jesus' Apostle Opposed Rome's Empire with God's Kingdom*. New York: HarperCollins, 2004.

Culianu, Ioan. "The Angels of the Nations and the Origins of Gnostic Dualism." Pages 78-91 in *Studies in Gnosticism and Hellenistic Religions: Presented to Gilles Quispel on the Occasion of His 65th Birthday*. Edited by R. van den Broek and M. J. Vermaseren. Leiden: Brill, 1981.

Cvetkovich, Ann. *An Archive of Feelings: Trauma, Sexuality, and Lesbian Public Cultures*. Durham: Duke University Press, 2003.

Daniel-Hughes, Carly. "Bodies at Rest, Bodies in Motion: Status, Corporeality, Sexuality and Negotiations of Power at Ancient Meals." Paper presented at the annual meeting of the Society of Biblical Literature. Meals in the Greco-Roman World Seminar. New Orleans, La., November 2009.

_____. "The Sex Trade and Slavery at Meals." Paper presented at the annual meeting of the Society of Biblical Literature. Meals in the Greco-Roman World Seminar. Boston, Mass., November 2008.

Davies, W. D., and David Daube, eds. *The Background of the New Testament and Its Eschatology: Essays in Honor of C.H. Dodd*. Cambridge: Cambridge University Press, 1956.

Davies, W. G. *The Gospel and the Land: Early Christianity and Jewish Territorial Doctrine*. Berkeley: University of California Press, 1974.

Derrida, Jacques. *Specters of Marx: The State of the Debt, the Work of Mourning and the New International*. New York: Routledge, 2006.

Deleuze, Gilles, and Felix Guarttari. *A Thousand Plateaus: Capitalism and Schizophrenia*. Translation and foreword by Brian Massumi. Minneapolis: University of Minnesota Press, 1987.

Dibelius, Martin. *The Book of Acts: Form, Style, Theology*. Edited by K. C. Hanson. Minneapolis: Fortress Press, 2004.

Downing, Gerald. "Pliny's Prosecution of the Christians: Revelation and 1 Peter." *JSNT* 34 (1988): 105-23.

Dube, Musa W. *Postcolonial Feminist Interpretation of the Bible*. Atlanta: Chalice Press, 2000.

_____. "Reading for Decolonization (John 4:1-42)." *Semeia* 75 (1996): 37-59.

_____, and Jeffrey Staley, eds. *John and Postcolonialism: Travel, Space and Power*. New York: Sheffield Academic Press, 2002.

Dunning, Benjamin H. *Aliens and Sojourners: Self as Other in Early Christianity*. Divinations: Re-reading Late Antique Religion. Philadelphia: University of Pennsylvania Press, 2009.

_____. *Specters of Paul: Sexual Difference in Early Christian Thought*. Divinations: Re-reading Late Antique Religion. Philadelphia: University of Pennsylvania Press, 2011.

Elliott, John H. *1 Peter: A New Translation with Introduction and Commentary*. The Anchor Yale Bible Commentaries. New York: Random House, 2000.

Elliott, Neil. *Liberating Paul: The Justice of God and the Politics of the Apostle*. Minneapolis: Fortress Press, 1994.

Eng, David L. *The Feeling of Kinship: Queer Liberalism and the Racialization of Intimacy*. Durham: Duke University Press, 2010.

_____, and David Kazanjian, eds. *Loss: The Politics of Mourning*. Berkeley: University of California Press, 2003.

Epictetus. *Discourses, Books I and II*. Translated by W. A. Oldfather. Loeb Classical Library. Cambridge: Harvard University Press, 1925.

Esler, Philip. *Conflict and Identity in Romans*. Minneapolis: Fortress Press, 2009.

Eusebius, *Ecclesiastical History. Books I-V*. Translated by Kirsopp Lake. Loeb Classical Library. Cambridge: Harvard University Press, 1926-1965.

Evans, Craig. "Mark's Incipit and the Priene Calendar Inscription: From Jewish Gospel to Greco-Roman Gospel." *Journal of Greco-Roman Christianity and Judaism* 1 (2000): 67-81.

Fanon, Franz. *Black Skin, White Masks.* Translated by Richard Philcox. New York: Grove Press, 2008.

Fanthom, Elaine. "Dialogues of Displacement: Seneca's Consolations to Helvia and Polybius." Pages 173-92 in *Writing Exile: The Discourse of Displacement in Greco-Roman Antiquity and Beyond.* Edited by Jan Felix Gaertner. Leiden: Brill, 2007.

Fineman, Joel. "Gnosis and the Piety of Metaphor: The Gospel of Truth." Pages 327-38 in *The Rediscovery of Gnosticism: Proceedings of the International Conference on Gnosticism at Yale, New Haven, Connecticut, March 28-31, 1978, vol. 1.* SHR XLI. Edited by Bentley Layton. Leiden: Brill, 1980.

Foucault, Michel. *Language, Counter-Memory, Practice.* Ithaca: Cornell University Press, 1977.

Freccero, Carla. *Queer/Early/Modern.* Series Q. Durham: Duke University Press, 2006.

Fredricksen, Paula. "Mandatory Retirement: Ideas in the Study of Christian Origins Whose Time Has Come to Go." *SR* 35 (2006): 231-46.

Frilingos, Christopher. *Spectacles of Empire: Monsters, Martyrs, and the Book of Revelation.* Philadelphia: University of Pennsylvania Press, 2004.

Futrell, Allison. *Blood in the Arena: The Spectacle of Roman Power.* Austin: University of Texas Press, 1997.

Gaertner, Jan Felix. *Writing Exile: The Discourse of Displacement in Greco-Roman Antiquity and Beyond.* Leiden: Brill, 2007.

Gallagher, Catherine, and Stephen Greenblatt. *Practicing New Historicism.* Chicago: University of Chicago Press, 2000.

Gallop, Jane. *Anecdotal Theory.* Durham: Duke University Press, 2002.

_____. *The Deaths of the Author.* Durham: Duke University Press, 2011.

Gaventa, Beverly Roberts. "Witnessing to the Gospel in the Acts of the Apostles: Beyond the Conversion or Conversation Dilemma." *WW* 22, no. 3 (2002): 238-45.

Gelardini, Gabriele, ed. *Hebrews: Contemporary Methods—New Insights*. Leiden: Brill, 2005.

Gilhus, Ingvid. "Male and Female Symbolism in the Gnostic Apocryphon of John." *Temenos* 19 (1983): 33-43.

Gill, Christopher. *The Structured Self in Hellenistic and Roman Thought*. Oxford: Oxford University Press, 2006.

Glancy, Jennifer. "Notes on Early Christian Responses to Corporeality, Intimacy and Sexuality in Dining Culture." Paper presented at the annual meeting of the Society of Biblical Literature. Meals in the Greco-Roman World Seminar. New Orleans, La., 2009.

Goldberg, Greg, and Craig Willse. "Losses and Returns: The Soldier in Trauma." Pages 264-86 in *The Affective Turn: Theorizing the Social*. Edited by Patricia Ticineto Clough with Jean Halley. Durham: Duke University Press, 2007.

Gordon, Avery. *Ghostly Matters: Haunting and the Sociological Imagination*. Minneapolis: University of Minnesota Press, 1997.

Greenblatt, Stephen. *Shakespearean Negotiations: The Circulation of Social Energy in Renaissance England*. The New Historicism: Studies in Cultural Poetics. Berkeley: University of California Press, 1989.

Gregg, Melissa, and Gregory Seigworth. *The Affect Theory Reader*. Edited by Melissa Gregg and Gregory Seigworth. Durham: Duke University Press, 2010.

Guzmán, Patricio, director. *Nostalgia de la luz (Nostalgia for the Light)*. DVD. 2011.

Halberstam, Judith. *The Queer Art of Failure*. Durham: Duke University Press, 2011.

Hall, Stuart. "Cultural Identity and Diaspora." Pages 233-46 in *Theorizing Diaspora*. Edited by Jana Evans Braziel and Anita Mannur. Malden, Mass: Blackwell Publishing, 2003.

Halley, Janet, and Andrew Parker, eds. *After Sex?: On Writing Since Queer Theory*. Series Q. Durham: Duke University Press, 2011.

Hardt, Michael. "What Affects Are Good For." Foreword to *The Affective Turn: Theorizing the Social*. Edited by Patricia Ticineto Clough with Jean Halley. Durham: Duke University Press, 2007.

Harland, Philip. *Associations, Synagogues and Congregations: Claiming a Place in Ancient Mediterranean Society*. Minneapolis: Fortress Press, 2003.

_____. *Dynamics of Identity in the World of the Early Christians*. New York: Continuum, 2009.

Hays, Richard. "'We Have No Lasting City Here': New Covenentalism in Hebrews." Pages in 151-73 in *The Epistle to the Hebrews and Christian Theology*. Edited by Richard Bauckham, et al. Grand Rapids: Eerdmans, 2009.

Hedrick, Charles W., and Robert Hodgson Jr., eds. *Nag Hammadi, Gnosticism and Early Christianity*. Peabody, Mass.: Hendrickson Publishers, 1986.

Hennessy, Rosemary. *Profit and Pleasure: Sexual Identities in Late Capitalism*. New York: Routledge, 2000.

Holmberg, Bengt, ed. *Exploring Christian Identity*. Tübingen: Mohr Siebeck, 2008.

Hornsby, Theresa, and Ken Stone, eds. *Bible Trouble: Queer Reading at the Boundaries of Scholarship*. Atlanta: Society of Biblical Literature, 2011.

Horsley, Richard A., ed. *In the Shadow of Empire: Reclaiming the Bible as a History of Faithful Resistance*. Louisville: Westminster John Knox Press, 2008.

_____, ed. *Paul and Empire: Religion and Power in Roman Imperial Society*. Harrisburg: Trinity Press International, 1997.

Howard-Brook, Wes, and Anthony Gwyther. *Unveiling Empire: Reading Revelation Then and Now*. Maryknoll, N.Y.: Orbis, 1999.

Hübner, R. H. "Thesen zur Echtheit und Datierung der sieben Briefe des Ignatius von Antiochien." *ZAC* 1, no. 1 (1997): 44-72.

Hurtado, Larry. *One Lord, One God: Early Christian Devotion and Ancient Jewish Monotheism*. Minneapolis: Augsburg Fortress Press, 1988.

Hyatt, Philip T., ed. *The Bible in Modern Scholarship*. Nashville, Tenn.: Abingdon, 1965.

Janzten, Grace M. *Becoming Divine: Toward a Feminist Philosophy of Religion*. Bloomington: Indiana University Press, 1999.

Jervell, Jacob. *Luke and the People of God: A New Look at Luke-Acts*. Eugene, Ore.: Wipf and Stock, 2002.

Johnson-Debaufre, Melanie. "Inside Out and Upside Down: Acts 17:1-8 and the Outing of the Thessalonian Ekklesia." Paper presented at the annual meeting of the Society of Biblical Literature, New Orleans, La., 2009.

Johnsson, W. G. "The Pilgrimage Motif in the Book of Hebrews." *JBL* 97, no. 2 (1978): 239-51.

Jonas, Hans. "Response to G. Quispel's *Gnosticism and the New Testament*." Pages 279-93 in *The Bible in Modern Scholarship*. Edited by Philip J. Hyatt. Nashville, Tenn.: Abingdon Press, 1965.

Josephus. *Jewish Antiquities: Books 12-13*. Translated by Ralph Marcus. Loeb Classical Library. Cambridge: Harvard University Press, 1943.

Justin Martyr. *Dialogue with Trypho*. Translated by Thomas B. Falls. Revised with New Introduction by Thomas P. Halton. Edited by Michael Slusser. Washington, D.C.: Catholic University of America Press, 2003.

_____. *First and Second Apologies. Justin, Philosopher and Martyr: Apologies*. Translated by Dennis Minns and Paul Parvis. New York: Oxford University Press, 2009.

Kahl, Brigitte. "Acts of the Apostles: Pro(to)-Imperial Script and Hidden Transcript." Pages 137-56 in *In the Shadow of Empire: Reclaiming the Bible as a History of Faithful Resistance*. Edited by Richard A. Horsley. Louisville: Westminster John Knox Press, 2008.

_____. *Galatians Re-Imagined: Reading with the Eyes of the Vanquished*. Minneapolis: Fortress Press, 2010.

Käsemann, Ernst. *The Wandering People of God: An Investigation into the Letter to the Hebrews*. Translated by Roy A. Harrisville and Irving L. Sandberg. Minneapolis: Augsburg Fortress, 1984.

Keller, Catherine. *Apocalypse Now and Then: A Feminist Guide to the End of the World*. Minneapolis: Fortress Press, 1996.

King, Karen L. "Christianity without Canon" Paper presented at the fall meeting of the Jesus Seminar. New Orleans, 1996.

_____. "Factions, Variety, Diversity, Multiplicity: Representing Early Christian Differences for the 21st Century." *MTSR* 23 (2011): 216-37.

_____. *The Gospel of Mary of Magdala: Jesus and the First Woman Apostle*. Santa Rosa: Polebridge Press, 2003.

_____. *What is Gnosticism?* Cambridge: Harvard University Press, 2005.

_____. "The Problem of Jewish Christianity or How to Represent the Diversity of Early Christianity." Paper presented at the annual meeting of the Society of Biblical Literature Annual Conference. Early Jewish-Christian Relations Section. Washington, D. C., November 19, 2006.

_____. *The Secret Revelation of John*. Cambridge: Harvard University Press, 2006.

_____. "Toward a Discussion of the Category of 'Gnosis/Gnosticism': The Case of the *Epistle of Peter to Philip*." Pages 445-65 in *Jesus in apokryphen Evangelienüberlieferungen: Beiträge zu ausserkanonischen Jesusüberlieferungen aus verschiedenen Sprach- und Kulturtraditionen*. Edited by Jörg Frey, Jens Schröter, and Jakob Spaeth. Tübingen: Mohr Siebeck, 2010.

_____. "Which Early Christianity?" Pages 66-84 in *The Oxford Handbook of Early Christian Studies*. Edited by Susan Ashbrook Harvey and David Hunter. Oxford: Oxford University Press, 2010.

———. "Reading Sex and Gender in the Secret Revelation of John." *Journal of Early Christian Studies* 19:4 (2011): 519-538.

Klinghardt, Matthias. *Gemeinschaftsmahl and Mahlgemeinschaft*. Tubingen: Francke Verlag, 1996.

Kloppenborg, John S., and Stephen G. Wilson, eds. *Voluntary Associations in the Graeco-Roman World*. London: Routledge, 1996.

Koester, Craig. *Hebrews: A New Translation with Introduction and Commentary*. The Anchor Bible. New York: Random House 2001.

———. "Savior of the World." *JBL* 109, no. 4 (1990): 665-80.

Koester, Helmut. "Outside the Camp," *HTR* 55 (1962): 299-315.

Kotrosits, Maia. "Divinity as Excess." Paper presented at the annual meeting of the Society of Biblical Literature, San Francisco, Calif., November 2011.

———. "The Queer Life of Christian Exceptionalism." *Culture and Religion*. 15, no. 2 (2014): 158-65.

———. "The Rhetoric of Intimate Spaces: Affect and Performance in the Corinthian Correspondence." USQR 62, no. 3-4 (2011): 134-51.

———. "Romance and Danger at Nag Hammadi." *The Bible and Critical Theory* 8, no. 1 (2012): 29-52.

Kristeva, Julia. *Powers of Horror: An Essay on Abjection*. New York: Columbia University Press, 1982.

Lacan, Jacques. *Écrits: The First Complete Edition in English*. New York: W. W. Norton and Company, 2007.

Layton, Bentley, ed. *The Rediscovery of Gnosticism: Proceedings of the International Conference on Gnosticism at Yale, New Haven, Connecticut, March 28-31, 1978, vol. 1*. SHR XLI. Leiden: Brill, 1980.

———. *The Gnostic Scriptures: A New Translation with Annotations and Introductions*. Garden City, N.Y.: Doubleday and Company, 1987.

Lechner, Thomas. *Ignatius Adversus Valentinianos? Chronologische und Theologiegeschichtliche Studien zu den Briefen des Ignatius von Antiochien.* Leiden: Brill, 1999.

Levinskaya, Irina. *The Book of Acts in its Diaspora Setting.* The Book of Acts in its First Century Setting 5. Grand Rapids: Eerdmans, 1996.

Lieu, Judith. *Christian Identity in the Jewish and Graeco-Roman World.* Oxford: Oxford University Press, 2004.

_____. *Neither Jew Nor Greek? Constructing Early Christianity.* London: T & T Clark International, 2002.

Liew, Tat-Siong Benny. *What is Asian American Biblical Hermeneutics?: Reading the New Testament.* Intersections: Asian and Pacific American Transcultural Studies. Honolulu: University of Hawai'i Press, 2008.

Lim, Sung Uk. "Speak My Name: Anti-colonial Mimicry and the Samaritan Woman in John 4:1-42." *USQR* 62, no. 3-4 (2010): 35-51.

Lincoln, A. T. "Sabbath, Rest, and Eschatology in the New Testament." Pages 297-320 in *From Sabbath to Lord's Day: A Biblical, Historical, and Theological Investigation.* Edited by D.A. Carson. Eugene, Ore.: Wipf and Stock, 2000.

Long, A. A. *Epictetus: A Stoic and Socratic Guide to Life.* Oxford: Oxford University Press, 2002.

Loomba, Ania, et al. *Postcolonial Studies and Beyond.* Durham: Duke University Press, 2006.

Lopez, Davina. *Apostle to the Conquered: Re-Imagining Paul's Mission.* Minneapolis: Fortress Press, 2008.

Lotz, John-Paul. *Ignatius and Concord: The Background and Use of the Language of Concord in the Letters of Ignatius of Antioch.* New York: Peter Lang, 2007.

Luttikhuizen, Gerard. *Gnostic Revisions of Genesis Stories and Early Jesus Stories.* Leiden: Brill, 2006.

MacDonald, Dennis. *Does the New Testament Imitate Homer? Four Cases from the Acts of the Apostles.* New Haven: Yale University Press, 2003.

Mach, Michael. "Concepts of Jewish Monotheism during the Hellenistic Period." Pages 21-42 in *The Jewish Roots of Christological Monotheism: Papers from the St. Andrews Conference on the Historical Origins of the Worship of Jesus.* Leiden: Brill, 1999.

Mack, Burton. *A Myth of Innocence: Mark and Christian Origins.* Philadelphia: Fortress Press, 1988.

MacRae, George. W. "Heavenly Temple and Eschatology in the Letter to the Hebrews." *Semeia* 12 (1978): 179-99.

Marchal, Joseph. "Bio-Necro-*Biblio*-Politics?: Restaging Feminist Intersections and Queer Exceptions." Paper presented at the annual meeting of the Society of Biblical Literature, San Francisco, Calif., 2011.

Martin, Dale B. *The Corinthian Body.* New Haven: Yale University Press, 1995.

Mason, Steven. "Jews, Judeans, Judaizing, Judaism." *JSJ* 38 (2007): 457-512.

Massumi, Brian. *Parables for the Virtual: Movement, Affect, Sensation.* Durham: Duke University Press, 2002.

Matthews, Shelly. *Perfect Martyr: The Stoning of Stephen and the Construction of Christian Identity.* New York: Oxford University Press, 2010.

Metzger, James. *Consumption and Wealth in Luke's Travel Narrative.* Leiden: Brill, 2007.

Miller, Merrill, "The Problem of the Origins of a Messianic Conception of Jesus." Pages 301-36 in *Redescribing Christian Origins.* Edited by Ron Cameron and Merrill P. Miller. Atlanta: Society of Biblical Literature, 2004.

Miller, Patricia Cox. *The Corporeal Imagination: Signifying the Holy in Late Ancient Christianity.* Divinations: Rereading Late Antique Religion. University of Pennsylvania Press, 2009.

———. "Words with an Alien Voice: Gnostics, Scripture, Canon." *VC* 42, no. 4 (1988): 327-38.

Moore, Stephen D. *The Bible in Theory: Critical and Postcritical Perspectives.* Atlanta: The Society of Biblical Literature, 2010.

———. *Empire and Apocalypse: Postcolonialism in the New Testament.* The Bible in the Modern World Series. Sheffield, England: Sheffield Phoenix Press, 2006.

———. *God's Gym: Divine Male Bodies of the Bible.* New York: Routledge, 1996.

———. *Mark and Luke in Poststructuralist Perspectives: Jesus Begins to Write.* New Haven: Yale University Press, 1992.

———. and Yvonne Sherwood. *The Invention of the Biblical Scholar: A Critical Manifesto.* Minneapolis: Fortress Press, 2011.

Nasrallah, Laura. "The Acts of the Apostles, Greek Cities and Hadrian's Panhellion." *JBL* 127, no. 3 (2008): 533-66.

———, and Elisabeth Schüssler Fiorenza, eds. *Prejudice and Christian Beginnings: Investigating Race, Gender and Ethnicity in Early Christian Studies.* Minneapolis: Fortress Press, 2009.

Nguyen, V. Henry T. *Christian Identity in Corinth: A Comparative Study of 2 Corinthians, Epictetus and Valerius.* Tübingen: Mohr Siebeck, 2008.

Niang, Aliou C., and Carolyn Osiek, eds. *Text, Image and Christians in the Graeco-Roman World: A Festschrift in Honor of David Balch.* Eugene, Ore: Pickwick Publications, 2012.

O'Hara, James. *Death and the Optimistic Prophecy in Virgil's Aeneid.* Princeton: Princeton University Press, 1990.

Overman, J. Andrew, and Robert S. MacLennan, eds. *Diaspora Jews and Judaism: Essays in Honor of, and in Dialogue with A. Thomas Kraabel.* Atlanta: Scholars Press, 1992.

Pagels, Elaine. *Adam, Eve and the Serpent.* New York: Random House, 1988.

_____. "Christian Apologists and 'The Fall of the Angels': An Attack on Roman Imperial Power?" *Harvard Theological Review* 78 (1985): 301-325.

_____. "The Demiurge and His Archons—A Gnostic View of the Bishop and Presbyters?" *HTR* 69 (1976): 301-24.

_____, and Karen L. King. *Reading Judas: The Gospel of Judas and the Shaping of Christianity*. New York: Viking, 2007.

Paschke, Boris A. "The Roman *ad bestias* Execution as a Possible Historical Background for 1 Peter 5:8." *JSNT*. 28, no. 4 (2006): 489-500.

Pearson, Birger. *Gnosticism, Judaism and Egyptian Christianity*. Minneapolis: Fortress Press, 1990.

Penchansky, David. "Up for Grabs: A Tentative Proposal for Doing Ideological Criticism." *Semeia* 59 (1992): 35-41.

Penner, Todd, and Caroline Vander Stichele, eds. *Contextualizing Acts: Lukan Narrative and Greco-Roman Discourse*. SBLSymS; Atlanta: Society of Biblical Literature, 2003.

Penner, Todd, and Ruben Dupertuis, eds. *Reading Acts in the Second Century*. Durham, England: Acumen Publishing, 2012.

Peppard, Michael. *The Son of God in the Ancient World: Divine Sonship in its Social and Political Context*. New York: Oxford University Press, 2011.

Pervo, Richard. *Dating Acts: Between the Evangelists and the Apologists*. Santa Rosa: Polebridge Press, 2006.

_____. "The Gates Have Been Closed (Acts 21:30): The Jews in Acts." *JHC* 11 (2005): 128-49.

_____. *Profit with Delight: The Literary Genre of the Acts of the Apostles*. Minneapolis: Fortress Press, 1987.

Petterson, Christina. "The Land is Mine: Place and Dislocation in the Letter to the Hebrews." *Sino-Christian Studies* 4 (2007): 69-93.

Phillips, Adam. *Side Effects*. New York: Harper Perennial, 2006.

Phillips, Thomas E. "The Genre of Acts: Moving Towards Concensus?" *Currents in Biblical Research* 4, no. 3 (2006): 365-96.

Pippin, Tina. "Ideology, Ideological Criticism and the Bible." *Currents in Research: Biblical Studies* 4 (1996): 51-78.

Pliny. *Epistulae*. Translated by William Memoth. Revised by W. M. L. Hutchison. 2 Volumes. Loeb Classical Library. Cambridge: Harvard University Press, 1926-1965.

Polhill, John B. "The Relationship between Ephesians and Colossians." *RevExp* 70, no. 4 (Fall 1973): 439-50.

Puar, Jasbir K. *Terrorist Assemblages: Homonationalism in Queer Times*. Durham: Duke University Press, 2007.

Quispel, Gilles. "Valentinian Gnosis and the Apocryphon of John." Pages 118-127 in *The Rediscovery of Gnosticism: Proceedings of the International Conference on Gnosticism at Yale, New Haven, Connecticut, March 28-31, 1978, vol. 1*. SHR XLI. Edited by Bentley Layton. Leiden: Brill, 1980.

Reinhartz, Adele. *Befriending the Beloved Disciple: A Jewish Reading of the Gospel of John*. New York: Continuum, 2001.

_____. "Judaism in the Gospel of John." *Interpretation* 63, no. 4 (2009): 382-93.

Rensberger, David. *Johannine Faith and Liberating Community*. Philadelphia: Westminster Press, 1988.

Rhoads, David, David Esterline, and Jae Won Lee, eds. *Luke-Acts and Empire: Essays in Honor of Robert L. Brawley*. PTMS 151. Eugene, Ore.: Wipf and Stock, 2011.

Richey, Lance Byron. *Imperial Ideology and the Gospel of John*. CBQMS 43. Washington, D.C.: The Catholic Biblical Association of America, 2007.

Rivera, Mayra. *The Touch of Transcendence: A Postcolonial Theology of God*. Louisville: Westminster John Knox Press, 2007.

Rose, Jacqueline. *States of Fantasy*. Oxford: Clarendon Press, 1996.

Runions, Erin. "Empire's Allure: Babylon and the Exception to Law in Two Conservative Discourses." *JAAR* 77, no. 3 (2009): 680-711.

———. "The Panopticon Gone Mad?" Pages 185-94 in *The Recycled Bible: Autobiography, Culture, and the Space Between*. SBLSS. Edited by Fiona Black. Atlanta: Society of Biblical Literature, 2006.

Salevao, Iutisone. *Legitimation in the Letter to the Hebrews: The Construction and Maintenance of a Symbolic Universe*. JSNTSup 219. London: Sheffield Academic Press, 2002.

Sanders, Jack T. *The Jews in Luke-Acts*. Minneapolis: Fortress Press, 1987.

Schoedel, William. "Gnostic Monism and the Gospel of Truth." Pages 379-90 in *The Rediscovery of Gnosticism: Proceedings of the International Conference on Gnosticism at Yale, New Haven, Connecticut, March 28-31, 1978, vol. 1: The School of Valentinus*. SHR XLI. Edited by Bentley Layton. Leiden: Brill, 1981.

———. *Ignatius of Antioch: A Commentary*. Philadelphia: Fortress Press, 1985.

Schott, Jeremy. *Christianity, Empire and the Making of Religion in Late Antiquity*. Divinations: Rereading Late Ancient Religion. Philadelphia: University of Pennsylvania Press, 2008.

Schneider, Laurel. *Beyond Monotheism: A Theology of Multiplicity*. New York: Routledge, 2008.

Schwartz, Regina. *The Curse of Cain: The Violent Legacy of Monotheism*. Chicago: Chicago University Press, 1997.

Schüssler Fiorenza, Elisabeth. *The Book of Revelation: Justice and Judgment*. 2nd ed. Minneapolis: Fortress Press, 1998.

———. "The First Letter of Peter." Pages 380-403 in *A Postcolonial Commentary on the New Testament Writings*. Edited by Fernando F. Segovia and Rasiah S. Sugirtharajah. London: T & T Clark, 2009.

———. "The Followers of the Lamb: Visionary Rhetoric and Social-Political Situation." *Semeia* 36 (1986): 123-46.

———. *In Memory of Her: A Feminist Theological Reconstruction of Christian Origins*. New York: Crossroad, 1994.

_____. *Searching the Scriptures: A Feminist Commentary.* 2 Volumes. New York: Crossroad, 1994.

Sedgwick, Eve Kosofsky. *Epistemology of the Closet.* Second Edition. Updated with New Preface. Berkeley: University of California Press, 2008.

_____. *Tendencies.* Durham: Duke University Press, 1993.

_____. *Touching Feeling: Affect, Pedagogy, Performativity.* Durham: Duke University Press, 2003.

Segal, Alan. *Two Powers in Heaven: Early Rabbinic Reports about Christianity and Gnosticism.* Leiden: Brill, 2002.

Segovia, Fernando. *De-colonizing Biblical Studies: A View from the Margins.* Maryknoll, NY: Orbis, 2000.

_____, and Rasiah S. Sugirtharajah, eds. *A Postcolonial Commentary on the New Testament Writings.* Bloomsbury: T & T Clark, 2009.

Seland, Torrey. *Strangers in the Light: Philonic Perspectives on Christian Identity in 1 Peter.* Leiden: Brill, 2005.

Seneca the Younger. *Consolation to Helvia.* Translated by Moses Hadas. *The Stoic Philosophy of Seneca: Essays and Letters.* New York: W. W. Norton, 1958.

Shepherdson, Charles. *Lacan and the Limits of Language.* New York: Fordham University Press, 2008.

Smith, Mark S. *The Origins of Biblical Monotheism: Israel's Polytheistic Background and the Ugaritic Texts.* New York: Oxford University Press, 2001.

Staley, Jeffrey L. "Changing Women: Postcolonial Reflections on Acts 16:6-40." *JSNT* 73 (1999): 113-35.

_____. "'Dis Place, Man': A Postcolonial Critique of the Vine (the Mountain and the Temple) in the Gospel of John." Pages 32-50 in *John and Postcolonialism: Travel, Space and Power.* Edited by Jeffrey L. Staley and Musa M. Dube. London: Sheffield, 2002.

Stegeman, Wolfgang, and Luise Schottroff. *Jesus and the Hope of the Poor*. Translated by Matthew J. O'Connell. Eugene, Ore.: Wipf and Stock, 2009.

Stendahl, Krister. *Paul among Jews and Gentiles*. Philadelphia: Fortress Press, 1976.

Stewart, Kathleen. *Ordinary Affects*. Durham: Duke University Press, 2007.

Story, Cullen. *The Nature of Truth and the "Gospel of Truth" and the Writings of Justin Martyr: A Study of the Pattern of Orthodoxy in the Middle of the Second Christian Century*. NovTSup 25. Leiden: Brill, 1970.

Sugirtharajah, Rasiah S. *Exploring Postcolonial Biblical Criticism: History, Method, Practice*. Malden, Mass.: Wiley Blackwell, 2012.

———. *Postcolonial Criticism and Biblical Interpretation*. Oxford: Oxford University Press, 2002.

Talbert, Charles H., *Literary Patterns, Theological Themes, and the Genre of Luke-Acts*. Missoula, Mont.: Scholars Press, 1974.

———. "Once Again: The Plan of 1 Peter." Pages 41-51 in *Perspectives on First Peter*. Edited by Charles Talbert. Macon, Ga.: Mercer University Press, 1986.

———, ed. *Perspectives on First Peter*. Macon, Ga.: Mercer University Press, 1986.

———. *Reading Acts: A Literary and Theological Commentary on the Acts of the Apostles*. Macon, Ga.: Smith and Helwys, 2005.

Taussig, Hal. *In the Beginning Was the Meal: Social Experimentation and Early Christian Identity*. Minneapolis: Fortress Press, 2009.

———, ed. *A New New Testament: A Bible for the 21st century Combining Traditional and Newly Discovered Texts*. New York: Houghton Mifflin Harcourt, 2013.

———, Jared Calaway, Maia Kotrosits, Celene Lillie, and Justin Lasser. *The Thunder: Perfect Mind: A New Translation and Introduction*. New York: Palgrave Macmillan, 2010.

Tellbe, Mikael. *Christ Believers in Ephesus: A Textual Analysis of Early Christian Identity Formation in a Local Perspective*. Tübingen: Mohr Siebeck, 2009.

Terada, Rei. *Feeling in Theory: Emotion after the Death of the Subject*. Cambridge: Harvard University Press, 2001.

Tertullian. *Apology and De Spectaculis*. Translated by T. R. Glover. Loeb Classic Library. Cambridge: Harvard University Press, 1931.

Townsend, J. "Missionary Journeys in *Acts* and European Missionary Societies." *AThR* 86, no. 2 (1986): 99-104.

Trebilco, Paul. *The Early Christians in Ephesus from Paul to Ignatius*. Tübingen: Mohr Siebeck, 2004.

Tyson, Joseph B. *Images of Judaism in Luke-Acts*. Columbia: University of South Carolina Press, 2010.

———. *Luke, Judaism and the Scholars: A Critical Approach to Luke-Acts*. Columbia: University of South Carolina Press, 1999.

van Unnik, Willem Cornelis. "The 'Gospel of Truth' and the New Testament." Pages 79-129 in *The Jung Codex: A Newly Recovered Gnostic Papyrus*. Edited by Frank L. Cross. London: A. R. Mowbray, 1955.

Veeser, Aram H., ed. *Confessions of the Critics: North American Critics' Autobiographical Moves*. New York: Routledge, 1996.

de Vos, Craig S. "Finding a Charge that Fits: The Accusation Against Paul and Silas at Philippi." *JSNT* 74 (1999): 51-63.

Walsh, Joseph J. "On Christian Atheism." *VC* 45, no. 3 (1991): 255-77.

Wedderburn, A. J. M. "Sawing Off Branches: Theologizing Dangerously *Ad Hebraeos*." *JTS* 56, no. 2 (2005): 393-414.

West, M. L. "Towards Monotheism." Pages 21-40 in *Pagan Monotheism in Late Antiquity*. Edited by Polymnia Athanassiadi and Michael Frede. Oxford: Oxford University Press, 1999.

Whitlark, Jason. "'Here We Do Not Have a City That Remains': A Figured Critique of Roman Imperial Propoganda in Hebrews 13:14." *JBL* 131, no. 1 (2012): 161-71.

Williams, Michael. *The Immovable Race: Gnostic Designation and the Theme of Stability in Late Antiquity*. Leiden: Brill, 1985.

_____. *Rethinking "Gnosticism": An Argument for Dismantling a Dubious Category*. Princeton: Princeton University Press, 1996.

Wilson, Robert McLain. "Valentinianism and the Gospel of Truth." Pages 133-41 in *The Rediscovery of Gnosticism: Proceedings of the International Conference on Gnosticism at Yale, New Haven, Connecticut, March 28-31, 1978, vol. 1: The School of Valentinus*. SHR XLI. Edited by Bentley Layton. Leiden: Brill, 1981.

Wimbush, Vincent. "'Not of the World': Early Christianities as Rhetorical and Social Formation." Pages 23-36 in *Reimagining Christian Origins: A Colloquium Honoring Burton L. Mack*. Edited by Elizabeth Castelli and Hal Taussig. Valley Forge, Pa.: Trinity Press International, 1996.

_____. *African Americans and the Bible: Sacred Texts and Social Textures*. New York: Continuum, 2001.

Wynn, Jonathan R. "Haunting Orpheus: Problems of Space and Time in the Desert." Pages 209-30 in *The Affective Turn: Theorizing the Social*. Edited by Patricia Ticineto Clough with Jean Halley. Durham: Duke University Press, 2007.

Wolfson, Elliot R. "Inscribed in the Book of the Living: Gospel of Truth and Jewish Christology." *JSJ* 38, no. 2 (2007): 234-71.

Yamazaki-Ransom, Kazuhiko. "Paul, Agrippa I, and Antiochus IV: Two Persecutors in Acts in Light of 2 Maccabees 9." Pages 107-21 in *Luke-Acts and Empire: Essays in Honor of Robert L. Brawley*. Edited by David Rhoads, David Esterline, and Jae Won Lee. PTMS 151. Eugene, Ore.: Wipf and Stock, 2011.

_____. *The Roman Empire in Luke's Narrative*. New York: T & T Clark, 2010.

Yeo, Khiok-khng. *What Does Jerusalem Have to Do with Beijing? Biblical Interpretation from a Chinese Perspective*. Harrisburg: Trinity International, 1998.

Index

1 Thessalonians, 35
2 Maccabees, 92–93
1 Peter, 49n5, 61–66, 68, 77, 79, 85–86, 89, 105, 138, 144–45, 150, 187
2 Baruch, 187n27

Achtemeier, Paul, 61–62, 86
Aeneid, 109–11, 113
Aeropagus, 100–101
affect: and Christ, 68; and diaspora, 10–15, 45, 61, 82–83, 85, 228; theories of, 4–14, 19–20, 24–25, 41, 229, 245
aggression, 9, 38, 134, 141, 210, 215–16
Agrippa, King, 49n5, 89–90, 104, 107
Ahmed, Sara, 4, 17n24, 19n30, 30n20, 40n52, 106nn40–41, 191–92

alienation and belonging, 12, 42, 145, 167, 179n12, 189, 195, 216
aliens and foreigner rhetoric, 63–64, 130
Allison, Dorothy, 181–82
Althusser, Louis, 39–41
Amazons, 60
anti-Judaism, 29, 38, 87n3, 112
Antioch and the term Christian, 89–90
Antiochus IV, 92–93, 97
Arch of Titus, 74, 149n5
Ascough, Richard, 34–36, 56, 58, 69n60, 86n1, 88n4
assemblage, 54–55, 57, 60n31, 81, 227
associations, Greco-Roman, 10, 28n13, 34–35, 56–59, 80n83, 180n13

259

authenticity: as diasporic discourse, 96, 198; and the "true Israel," 94–96, 102
autobiography/autobiographical criticism, 7n15, 20, 209, 220–24
Axel, Brian Keith, 10n18, 11, 73n68, 81n84, 135–36, 138

Babel, tower of, 102
Babylon, 64, 133, 211–12, 216
Babylonian exile, 131
Barthes, Roland, 223–24
belief, 1, 9, 29n15, 73, 128, 150
Boyarin, Daniel, 2n1, 30n18, 36, 40n48, 41–43, 49n4, 53n14, 57n25, 72n65, 196, 197, 198n51
butch-femme discourses, 142, 178, 190–91
Butler, Judith, 30n21, 31–32, 32n26, 39–41, 48, 221–22

Camping, Harold, 213–14, 216
Carey, Greg, 216
Cho, Grace, 165–67, 194n41
Chow, Rey, 11, 27n12, 44n60, 96, 102–3, 103n34
Christian: first ancient uses, 57–60, 104–5; anachronism of, 32–33; as slander, 104–5

Collins, Adela Yarbro, 215
colonization, 10–11, 67, 91n8, 138, 162n34, 204n5
Colossians, 188–89, 192, 199
convert/conversion, 68n54, 90–92, 95, 97, 101, 179n12
Cooppan, Vilashini, 15n22, 217–19
Corinth/Corinthians, 34, 35n34, 56n21, 180n13
cosmic rhetoric/aspirations, 79, 111, 120, 130, 132, 137, 143, 147, 159, 167, 172, 187, 189
cosmopolitanism, 101, 129, 130–31, 145, 157, 189n30
creation motifs: 120, 126, 154, 208; and social critique, 120, 143; in Isaiah, 133
Cvetkovich, Ann, 10n18, 18, 141–44, 173, 178–84, 190–91, 193, 196

Derrida, Jacques, 26, 32n26
diaspora: and affect theory, 10–15, 45, 61, 82–83, 85, 165–68, 228, 231; and Christianity, 37–38; and postcolonial theory, 10–16; and Israel, 34, 64–68, 73–74, 94–96, 102–3, 131, 144–45, 154–55, 188; Sikh, 73n68, 135–37

disillusionment, 43, 107, 140, 157, 214, 216
Dube, Musa, 159–60, 204n6
Dunning, Benjamin, 63, 204n62

ekklesia, 49n5, 50n7, 57, 70n62
empire, 1, 14, 15n22, 16–17, 53, 69, 85, 89, 91, 112, 203, 209–12, 215, 217–20, 228; and Christian identity, 1, 51, 62–63, 70n60; and national belonging, 16–17, 217–18; Roman Empire, 62–63, 68–69, 70, 86–87, 113n59, 120, 130n31, 204, 217–20
empire criticism, 12–13, 15, 203–5, 229
empiricism, 21, 25
Ephesians, 188–89, 192–93, 199
Ephesus, 98
ethics: and autobiography, 220; and grief, 30–32; in history and biblical interpretation, 7, 13, 114, 222n45, 224n52, 227; and paranoia, 38
ethnos/ethnē, 16, 102–3
exceptionalism: Christian and the U.S., 39, 51–54, 60; Israelite, 52, 66
Exodus, 124, 151, 154

faith (*pistis*), 150–52, 155, 193, 209n19; and identity, 103; and Ignatius, 72n63, 72n65
family and belonging, 39, 108, 109n47, 113, 184, 186, 187n27, 189–90
Foucault, Michel, 9, 13n21, 30, 31n22, 39, 40n49, 52n12, 63, 223, 224n52
Freud, Sigmund, 31, 40, 166, 178n8, 191, 193

Galatians, 48–49, 90, 109n48, 187n24, 207–8
Gallop, Jane, 83n86, 222–24
Gauls, 60, 208
Genesis, 14, 120–22, 124, 126–27, 133n38, 134
gentiles, 62, 65–66, 68, 89–90, 91–93, 97–99, 188–89, 196–97; mission to the, 89–90
Gnostic/Gnosticism, 2n1, 13, 28, 33n30, 115, 119–22, 127, 143, 149, 175, 176, 229; redeemer myth, 119n3
Gordon, Avery, 17–18
Gospel of John, 1, 115, 131, 147–49, 159–70, 180n13, 227, 230

Gospel of Luke, 92n10, 105n37, 106nn38–39, 107, 110–14, 161n31
Gospel of Mary, 36n41
Gospel of Thomas, 36n41
Gospel of Truth 18, 115, 142–43, 173–200, 230
grief, 26, 29–32, 38, 42, 228; diasporic, 118, 121, 130, 140, 168
Gwyther, Anthony, and Wes Howard-Brook, 113n59, 211–16, 220–21

Halberstam, Judith, 194
Hall, Stuart, 11, 66–67
Harland, Philip, 34–36, 56–58, 64n46, 75n71
haunting: and history 17, 26, 32, 45, 203, 207n12, 219–20, 224n52, 228; and Ignatius, 75–76, 79; and the nation, 1, 8, 16, 45, 76, 79, 85, 89, 160, 177, 193, 199; and trauma/violence, 38n45, 39, 103, 114n61, 115, 160, 164, 176, 194–95, 199, 229
heresy/heresiology, 2n1, 28, 57n25, 94n15, 175n4, 179, 196–99

historiography, 32n26, 37, 47–48, 50–51, 86n1, 87–88, 228; feminist, 30n17; poststructuralist, 28, 44
homeland, 34–35, 73, 102n32, 103, 121, 135, 138, 155, 164, 166–67, 229
Hosea, 187n27
hybridity, 14, 99n29, 101n31, 114

identity: as an analytic, 10, 53–55, 57, 60, 69, 82, 145; Christian 1, 2n1, 3, 14, 17, 27–45, 47–50, 52–55, 57, 59, 61–63, 68, 75n71, 78, 85, 86–89, 100, 105, 114, 144, 168n46, 172, 189, 197–98, 227–29; and diaspora 66–67, 73, 131–32, 145n43, 160n29, 166; Paul's, 90–91, 93–97
ideology/ideological criticism, 15, 27n11, 38, 40n49, 55n19, 80, 148, 209–10
idols/idol worship, 98–100, 132–34, 187n24
Ignatius of Antioch, 61, 69–72, 74–81, 89, 105, 144, 227
immovability, 122, 130
immovable generation/race 122, 126, 139, 140
interpellation, 39–41, 57

INDEX

intersectionality, 54
Irenaeus, 121n5
Isaiah, 121, 131–34, 145, 198
Israel, 8, 11n19, 14–15, 34–35, 39n46, 41–42, 65–66, 68–69, 71, 73–77, 79–81, 86–87, 91, 93–97, 100, 102, 105–8, 111–13, 118–19, 122–23, 131–33, 144–46, 150–52, 155–58, 161–62, 164, 177, 187–90, 195, 198

Jerusalem temple, 14, 35, 74–75, 91, 93, 99, 117–18, 132, 144, 148, 152n9, 153–54, 156–57, 160–62, 165, 169, 187n27, 188
Jews (*hoi ioudaioi*), 72, 164–65
Judaism, 15, 28, 41–43, 57n25, 62, 64n45, 71–73, 76, 90, 94–95, 119, 127–28, 148, 196–98; *ioudaismos* 72–77, 80–81
Justin Martyr, 120 n. 4, 196–99

Kahl, Brigitte, 49n4, 80n83, 91n8, 106nn38–39, 206–11, 220–21
Khalistan, 135–38, 155
King, Karen, 2n1, 29, 33n30, 36, 57n5, 82n85, 119–21, 122n6, 123, 167n45

Lacan, Jacques, 40–41, 44n59, 136n47, 138n51, 174n2, 185–86
Letter of James, 37n42
Letter to the Hebrews, 1, 115, 131, 146–58, 165, 167, 169–70, 177, 180n13, 187–89, 227–30
liberation/liberation rhetoric, 13n21, 53, 143, 159, 160n29, 162n34, 166, 215n31, 217
Logos, 128, 196–97

Maccabees, 72
martyrs/martyrdom, 49, 57n25, 69, 70n60, 70n62, 71–73, 78–80, 92, 93n13, 104, 136–37
Massumi, Brian, 5n6, 17n24, 21, 24–25, 44n59, 54n16, 55n19, 88n4, 114n62
"master narrative" of Christianity, 30
Matthews, Shelly, 30n17, 92–97, 112n57
monotheism, 127–29, 133, 109n30, 208
Moore, Stephen, 6–7, 20, 31, 27n11, 48n2, 204n5, 205
Moreland, Milton, 74, 99n29, 100, 105n37
Moses, 128
mourning, 26, 31, 113, 216

263

nation/national belonging, 11,
 14–16, 18, 45, 51–54, 61, 64,
 80, 81n84, 85, 101, 102, 106,
 108–11, 130n31, 131–33,
 135–36, 145–46, 160–61, 177,
 188, 189–90, 195, 199, 209,
 213, 217–18. *See also ethnos*
nostalgia, 143
Nostalgia for the Light, 21–22, 27,
 195

objectivity, 14, 25, 27, 29, 82, 158,
 205n8, 211
orthodoxy, 7, 28, 29n15, 33,
 57n25, 72, 179, 197–98
origins: Christian, 29, 15, 30n18,
 50, 86, 204n6; diasporic claims
 to, 11, 35, 67, 73, 81n84, 96,
 118, 138n51, 149, 155, 166;
 and self-narration, 222

paranoia, 5–6, 38, 205n8
patriotism, 106, 109
Paul, 9, 35, 49n4, 89–95, 97–101,
 103–9, 111, 180n13, 189,
 204n5, 207–9
penetration, 60n33, 178, 191
Pentecost, 34n31, 101–3, 108,
 115n64, 145
Peter, 94, 103n35

Pharisees, 90, 94, 95n19, 99, 117,
 160n29, 163
Philo of Alexandria, 102n32, 126,
 156n17
place (and diaspora), 11, 67, 73,
 74, 103, 130–31, 138n51, 145,
 147–50, 153n11, 154–55, 160,
 162, 164–66, 170–71, 177, 230
Plato/Platonism, 120, 123n10, 126,
 130, 134, 154
Pliny, 58–59, 69–71, 90
postcolonial theory/criticism,
 11–13, 15, 69n60, 101n31,
 203–5, 229
Priene inscription, 137
Providence (*Pronoia*), 122n6,
 123n9, 125, 137, 140
Puar, Jasbir, 41n52, 51–55, 81n84,
 224n52

queerness; and affect, 10, 17n24,
 38, 41, 82; as assemblage, 54;
 and historiography, 32n26,
 47–55, 60, 61–62, 65; and
 identity, 43, 52–55; as
 transgression 49–53, 62, 65

racialization, 60, 77
Reinhartz, Adele, 163–64
rest (*katapausis*), 151, 153–56, 167,
 179n12, 184n20, 185–86

Revelation, 9, 37n42, 51n10, 204n5, 211–16, 219–20
Roman-Jewish War, 2n1, 75–76, 144–45, 156–57, 161–62, 157–58, 160–61, 187n27
Rome, symbolic value of, 113, 217–19

Samaritans/Samaritan woman, 159–64
Sammael, 134
Schenck, Kenneth, 156–57
Schneider, Laurel, 132
Schüssler Fiorenza, Elisabeth, 216
Sedgwick, Eve, 5–6, 13n21, 20n30, 38, 48, 202–5
Sherwood, Yvonne, 6–7, 20n31, 27n11, 205
Smith, Mark, 131–32
solidarity, 103, 107
Spillers, Hortense, 166
Stephen, 89, 91–94, 97
Stewart, Kathleen, 19n30, 201–3, 205
Stoic philosophy, 100, 120n4, 18, 139–40, 189n30
supersessionism, 13, 71–72, 95, 148, 157, 189

Taussig, Hal, 30n18, 34–36, 56–57
Tertullian, 60n32
Thessalonica, 50n7, 98, 100
torture, 12, 51, 69, 135–37, 152, 177
Trajan, 58–59, 69–71, 90
trauma, 1, 11–13, 17–18, 23–24, 30n19, 38n45, 76, 121, 141–42, 165, 173, 176–79, 181–84, 188, 191, 194–95, 198–99, 227, 233

universalism, 28, 34n31, 37, 55n19, 96n21, 102, 128–29, 130n30, 131, 145, 219
utopian, 87, 89, 107, 120–21, 17, 135–37, 147, 153, 213

vulnerability, 30, 141–43, 166, 178, 193, 216, 229

Way, the, 91, 95–99, 108–9

Yaldabaoth, 124–27, 132, 134, 136–39, 141, 168
Yamazaki-Ransom, Kazuhiko, 91n8, 92

www.ingramcontent.com/pod-product-compliance
Lightning Source LLC
Chambersburg PA
CBHW071152070526
44584CB00019B/2760